LOUISIANA STATE UNIVERSITY STUDIES

NUMBER THIRTY-NINE

CHAUCER'S *TROILUS*
A STUDY IN COURTLY LOVE

CHAUCER'S
TROILUS

A STUDY IN
COURTLY LOVE

THOMAS A. KIRBY

GLOUCESTER, MASS.

PETER SMITH

1958

TO

KEMP MALONE

"MYN OWENE MAISTER DEERE"

PREFACE

G EOFFREY CHAUCER was perfectly well aware of the fact that his *Troilus and Criseyde* is a poem of courtly love. In one of the numerous passages in which he refers to his source, he states that he has in general followed the "auctour" but confesses to having made certain additions to the love material in his poem (III, 1405–7):

> And if that I at loves reverence,
> Have any thing in eched for the beste,
> Doth therewithal right as youre selven leste.

I regard this as sufficient justification for the present book. My purpose has been to make a study of the courtly love tradition and of Chaucer's *Troilus* in the light of that tradition, especially to investigate its relation to the *Filostrato* of Boccaccio and to determine the nature and the effect of the changes which the English poet saw fit to make.

A word is perhaps desirable about the procedure I have adopted in the comparison of the *Troilus* with the *Filostrato*. There were two possibilities open: to go through the poems line by line from beginning to end or to take each of the characters and follow it through the events of the narrative. Both methods have obvious disadvantages, but I finally decided that the latter was the lesser of two evils. I have tried to avoid as much repetition as possible by referring to scenes

already discussed and, in certain instances, have been obliged
to anticipate observations to be made in a later paragraph
or chapter. This, together with a possibly too great literal-
ness in paraphrasing and translating, has resulted in a certain
stylistic awkwardness which I regret but consider unavoid-
able; had I been less literal, I would have been in most cases
less accurate. The observations on the various characters
might well have been brought together in a separate chapter
at the end, but it seemed preferable to add them to the appropriate chapters and I have therefore done this.

The questions which Boccaccio asked about the ancients
might be said to apply, *mutatis mutandis*, to any study of
courtly love: "Who in one day can penetrate the hearts of
the Ancients? Who can bring to light and life again minds
long since removed in death? Who can elicit their meaning?
A divine task that—not human! The Ancients departed in
the way of all flesh, leaving behind them their literature and
their famous names for posterity to interpret according to
their own judgment. But as many minds, so many opinions.
What wonder?" The field is vast, the literature of the subject
is great, and the problems are often difficult. I am fully aware
of the deficiencies of this study and yet, now that it is completed, I am happy in the thought that what I may not have
performed well, may inspire a wiser man to do better.

My thanks are due to all who in any way have aided me
in the present work. I am especially indebted to Dean Charles
W. Pipkin, editor of the *Louisiana State University Studies*,
for having made possible the publication of this volume in
that series, to Professor Marcus Wilkerson, Director of the
Louisiana State University Press, and to the members of
his staff. I am also under obligation to the officials of various libraries, especially to those of the Johns Hopkins University, the British Museum, and the Louisiana State University. David S. Blondheim and Gustav Gruenbaum, late of
the Johns Hopkins University, aided me materially; the
former read the text and translations for chapters II and III,

while the latter performed the same service for chapters v and vi; much of what is good in these portions of the book is due to the guidance of these men. Professor Nathaniel M. Caffee has read the volume both in manuscript and in proof and has made many helpful suggestions. I would particularly thank my wife, Josie Dyson Kirby, for continuing to live with me during the final stages of the production of this work. The dedication is a very inadequate acknowledgment of the encouragement and inspiration I have gained from one who is both a scholar and a friend.

And now, in the words of Pandarus, "Adieu! be glad! god spede us bothe two!"

T. A. K.

BATON ROUGE
SEPTEMBER, 1938

CONTENTS

PART ONE

AN OUTLINE OF THE COURTLY LOVE SYSTEM

I

OVID

THE STUDY of medieval love poetry demands the consideration of many diverse elements. Though the subject of the present investigation is a late Middle English poem, it is nevertheless for obvious reasons necessary, in studying the courtly love system, to give somewhat detailed consideration to French and Italian works of considerably earlier date. Only by such study can we fully grasp the real significance of that system which was so frequently employed in the literature of the time. What are the essential elements in the Provençal love poetry? How are the poets of the *dolce stil nuovo* related to the troubadours? What did Dante contribute to the system? Did Chrétien de Troyes play a part in developing the code? These and similar questions immediately come to mind when one thinks of medieval love poetry, and they must be adequately answered before attempting to analyze any particular poem. Though the *Troilus* is of somewhat later date than most of the writing in this genre, in its treatment of the conventions of love it is closely akin to the amorous poetry of the twelfth and thirteenth centuries and hence does not vary appreciably from this earlier courtly love poetry. The following pages contain, therefore, not a history of courtly love but, rather, a concise survey of the system as reflected in some of the literature of the period. Consequently, no attempt will be made to present more than the main tenets and bare essentials of the code, a proper understanding of which is necessary for the detailed study of the *Troilus* here attempted.

The supreme position of Ovid as the *fons et origo* of all succeeding love poetry is a commonplace of literary history. I do not mean to say that every subsequent writer of a love poem was immediately indebted to the author of the *Ars Amatoria*, but I need hardly insist on the fact that the great body of medieval love poetry is, in many respects, essentially Ovidian. Referring to the Provençal element in the later romances of northern France, W. P. Ker remarks of the Provençal lyric that "among the definite influences that can be proved and explained, one of the strongest is that of Latin poetry, particularly of the *Art of Love*. About this there can be no doubt, however great may seem to be the interval between the ideas of Ovid and those of the Provençal lyrists, not to speak of their greater scholars in Italy, Dante and Petrarch." [1] And again, this time with regard to the *Aeneid*, the *Heroides*, and the *Metamorphoses*, the same authority notes: "If anything literary can be said to have taken effect upon the temper of the Middle Ages, so as to produce the manners and sentiments of chivalry, this is the literature to which the largest share of influence must be ascribed." [2]

The perplexing problem of origins is one which cannot be dealt with here. The studies by Gaselee and Allen on this aspect of the Latin and vernacular love lyric are most stimulating and informative. Gaselee declares that the medieval Latin lyric is the result of three influences: the Song of Songs, the vernacular poems describing nature, and Ovid. He states in part:

. . . we are here no longer at the period of the early medieval Latin love-lyric, but nearly at its end; by the thirteenth century it is all but dead—lovers and minstrels wrote in the vernacular, Latin poetry is religious or didactic. The love poems had perhaps little influence upon any modern literary form: their extinction was too sudden and complete, and the remains that have come down to us are rather accidental —the contents of a few minstrels' song-books, and some scraps preserved because they were written out in collections of hymns and tropes: but in the short period of their efflorescence they were able to express deep feeling in terms of high and unfamiliar art. I hope I have been able to indicate their probable line of descent: they derive their *form* from the Christian hymn (itself founded on the late Latin lyric, touched by eastern influence), especially the hymns written in stanzas of iambic dimeters and dactylic tetrameters, and their *substance* from the Song of Songs and the nature-lyrics of the vernaculars, Ovid supervening later on. A curious descent—Ovid and the Shulamite, St. Ambrose and Erato: but this I think is their surprising genesis.[3]

Allen's studies bring him to a somewhat different conclusion, for he favors the vernacular origin almost to the exclusion of other possibilities: "... we find the native provincial popular element in the very beginnings of Western European Latin poetry." [4] Whichever of these positions is correct, they in no way affect the purpose of this chapter, which attempts to present Ovid as the most significant literary predecessor of the later, medieval love poets.[5] Whether or not a certain continuity of theme exists, the fact that Ovid supplies the natural background for a study of this sort remains incontrovertible.[6] There is no denying that the influence of the Latin poet was far-reaching, a fact which Professor Rand has emphasized as follows:

In the vernacular poetry of France and Germany, the Troubadours and the *Minnesänger*, who continue the tradition of the Goliards, turn back, like them, to Ovid for imagery, themes and part, at least, of his "art" and "remedies" of love. Whatever the poets may have thought of Corinna, a certain generalizing or symbolistic spirit in their poetry suggests the *Amores*, and one of their most delightful inventions comes, it would seem, direct from Ovid. This is the *alba* or *tageliet*, the song at dawn, in which the lover, like Ovid's gallant, upbraids the day for tearing him all too soon from the arms of his lady.[7]

The object of the next few pages is to present, largely by direct quotations from the Latin writings, certain features of Ovid's work that will lead to a better understanding of the courtly love system.[8] Love, as a science or art, is, as everyone knows, the subject matter of the *Ars Amatoria*. It is in this work that Ovid refers to himself as a "professor of love," a title amply justified by the attitude of succeeding centuries;[9] but he has presented his ideas elsewhere as well, notably in the *Amores*, the *Heroides*, and the *Metamorphoses*. The following quotations are taken from all these works.[10]

The following passage sets forth the notion of the God of Love as an irresistible power; it is from the *Heroides*, IX, 25–26:

> Quem non mille ferae, quem non Sthenelius hostis,
> Non potuit Iuno vincere, vincit amor.

The idea is repeated in greater detail in *Metamorphoses*, V, 363–70:

> videt hunc Erycina vagantem
> monte suo residens natumque amplexa volucrem
> "arma manusque meae, mea, nate, potentia," dixit,
> "illa, quibus superas omnes, cape tela, Cupido,
> inque dei pectus celeres molire sagittas,
> cui triplicis cessit fortuna novissima regni.
> tu superos ipsumque Iovem, tu numina ponti
> victa domas ipsumque, regit qui numina ponti . . ."

and again in *Amores*, I, i, 3–5:

> risisse Cupido
> dicitur atque unum surripuisse pedem.
> "Quis tibi, saeve puer, dedit hoc in carmina iuris?"

Love as the great tormentor is found in *Amores*, I, i, 25–26.

> Me miserum! certas habuit puer ille sagittas.
> uror, et in vacuo pectore regnat Amor.

Other passages in the same work reiterate this thought; cf. I, ii, 9:

> Cedimus, an subitum luctando accendimus ignem?

> acrius invitos multoque ferocius urget
> quam qui servitum ferre fatentur Amor.
> —I, ii, 17–18.

> O numquam pro me satis indignate Cupido,
> o in corde meo desidiose puer—

quid me, qui miles numquam tua signa reliqui,
laedis, et in castris vulneror ipse meis?
cur tua fax urit, figit tuus arcus amicos?
gloria pugnantes vincere maior erat.
—II, ix, 1–6.

ossa mihi nuda relinquit amor.
—II, ix, 14.

The lover is represented as the prey of Love in *Amores*, I, ii, 19–20:

En ego confiteor! tua sum nova praeda, Cupido;
porrigimus victas ad tua iura manus.

The ninth section of the first book of the *Amores* is entirely (46 lines) given over to the elaboration of the idea of the lover as a soldier (I, ix, 1–2):

Militat omnis amans, et habet sua castra Cupido;
Attice, crede mihi, militat omnis amans.

The poet goes on to say that just as it is unseemly for an old man to soldier, so likewise is it for him to love; the spirit the captain seeks in a valiant soldier is the same as that which the maid seeks in her lover; duty forces both the soldier and the lover to take a long road, endure all sorts of weather, and undergo difficulties of all kinds; each must make way through guards and sentinels. Love has made the poet "full of action and waging the wars of night" (45: inde vides agilem nocturnaque bella gorentem).

Love is the source of physical strength; cf. *Metamorphoses*, VIII, 142–44:

Vix dixerat, insilit undis
consequitur rates faciente cupidine vires
Gnosciacaeque haeret comes invidiosa carinae.

Of perhaps greater interest and significance for the present study is Ovid's treatment of love as a sickness or disease. This concept of love was a commonplace of medieval poetry and is found in its most elaborate form in the romances of Chrétien

de Troyes; consequently a somewhat detailed examination of
the Ovidian prototypes is in order at this point.

1. Love is both pleasant and painful:

> inpia sub dulci melle venena latent.
> —*Amores*, I, viii, 104.

> Haec sunt iucundi causa cibusque mali.
> —*Remedia Amoris*, 138.

2. Every lover is pale:

> Palleat omnis amans: hic est color aptus amanti;
> Hoc decet, hoc vultu non valuisse putent.
> —*Ars Amatoria*, I, 729–30.

> fugerat ore color.
> —*Heroides*, XI, 27.

> Esse quidem laesi poterat tibi pectoris index
> et color et macies et vultus et umida saepe
> lumina. . . .
> —*Metamorphoses*, IX, 535–37.

> . . . palles audita, Bybli, repulsa,
> et pavet obsessum glaciali frigore corpus.
> —*Ibid.*, 581–82.

> . . . fugitque
> et color et sanguis, animusque relinquit euntem.
> —*Ibid.*, X, 458–59.

3. The lover is wont to tremble:

> Vidit ut oppressa vestigia corporis herba,
> Pulsantur trepidi corde micante sinus.
> —*Ars Amatoria*, III, 721–22.

> hic mihi vae! miserae concutit ossa metus.
> —*Heroides*, III, 82.

> et meditata manu componit verba trementi.
> —*Metamorphoses*, IX, 521.

> . . . at illi
> poplite succiduo genua intremuere. . . .
> —*Ibid.*, X, 457–58.

4. Love induces fear:

Conloquii iam tempus adest; fuge rustica longe
Hinc pudor; audentem Forsque Venusque iuvat.
—*Ars Amatoria*, I, 607–8.

. . . quid tuta times?
—*Metamorphoses*, VII, 47.

Nerei, te vereor, tua fulmine saevior ira est.
—*Ibid.*, XIII, 858.

5. Loss of appetite marks the true lover:

sumebant minimos ora coacta cibos.
—*Heroides*, XI, 28.

Non illum Cereris, non illum cura quietis
abstrahere inde potest. . . .
—*Metamorphoses*, III, 437–38.

sex illam noctes, totidem redeuntia solis
lumina viderunt inopem somnique cibique
per iuga, per valles, qua fors ducebat, euntem.
—*Ibid.*, XIV, 423–25.

6. Sighing is characteristic:

spectet amabilius iuvenem, suspiret ab imo
Femina, tam sero cur veniatque roget.
—*Ars Amatoria*, III, 675–76.

Myrrha patre audito suspiria duxit ab imo
pectore.
—*Metamorphoses*, X, 402–3.

cui dum pectendos praebet Galatea capillos,
talibus adloquitur repetens suspiria dictis.
—*Ibid.*, XIII, 738–39.

7. Love makes sleep impossible:

Attenuant iuvenum vigilatae corpora noctes.
—*Ars Amatoria*, I, 735.

nec somni faciles et nox erat annua nobis
et gemitum nullo laesa dolore dabam.
—*Heroides*, XI, 29–30.

et tenuant vigiles corpus miserabile curae
adducitque cutem macies et in aera sucus
corporis omnis abit.
—*Metamorphoses*, III, 396–98.

at rex Odrysius, quamvis secessit, in illa
aestuat et repetens faciem motusque manusque
qualia vult fingit quae nondum vidit et ignes
ipse suos nutrit cura removente soporem.
—*Ibid.*, VI, 490–93.

8. Lovers usually weep:

nox ubi me thalamis ululantem et acerba gementem
condidit in maesto procubuique toro,
pro somno lacrimis oculi funguntur obortis,
quaque licet, fugio sicut ab hoste viro.
—*Heroides*, VIII, 107–10.

Dixit et ad faciem rediit male sanus eandem
et lacrimis turbavit aquas, obscuraque motu
reddita forma lacu est.
—*Metamorphoses*, III, 474–76.

ut vero coepitque loqui dextramque prehendit
hospes et auxilium submissa voce rogavit
promisitque torum, lacrimis ait illa profusis.
•—*Ibid.*, VII, 89–91.

Esse quidem laesi poterat tibi pectoris index
et color et macies et vultus et umida saepe
lumina. . . .
—*Ibid.*, IX, 535–37.

muta iacet, viridesque suis tenet unguibus herbas
Byblis, et umectat lacrimarum gramina rivus.
—*Ibid.*, IX, 655–56.

9. Lovers frequently yell or groan:

utque tuo motae, proles Semeleia, thyrso
Ismariae celebrant repetita triennia bacchae,
Byblida non aliter latos ululasse per agros
Bubasides videre nurus.
—*Metamorphoses*, IX, 641–44.

. . . 'o' dixit 'felicem coniuge matrem!'
hactenus, et gemuit.
—Ibid., X, 422–23.

10. Love causes fainting:

> linquor et ancillis excipienda cado.
> <div align="right">—<i>Heroides</i>, II, 130.</div>

Quod scelus ut pavidas miserae mihi contigit aures,
sanguinis atque animi pectus inane fuit.
—Ibid., III, 59–60.

11. The lover loses his wits:

> ipse secuturo similis stetit arduus arce
> 'qua' que 'via est vobis, erit et mihi' dixit 'eadem'
> seque iacit vecors e summae culmine turris.
> <div align="right">—<i>Metamorphoses</i>, V, 289–91.</div>

si mihi currenti fueris conspecta, morabor,
deque meis manibus lora remissa fluent.
—Amores, III, ii, 13–14.

12. Madness is common among lovers:

> Quid tibi mentis erat, cum sic male sana lateres,
> Procri? quis adtoniti pectoris ardor erat?
> <div align="right">—<i>Ars Amatoria</i>, III, 713–14.</div>

Tum vero maestam tota Miletida mente
defecisse ferunt, tum vero a pectore vestem
diripuit planxitque suos furibunda lacertos;
iamque palam est demens. . . .
—Metamorphoses, IX, 635–38.

nec satis est nymphae flere et lacerare capillos
et dare plangorem (facit haec tamen omnia) seque
proripit ac Latios errat vesana per agros.
—Ibid., XIV, 420–22.

13. Leanness is symptomatic of love:

> Arguat et macies animum: nec turpe putaris
> Palliolum nitidis inposuisse comis.
> Attenuant iuvenum vigilatae corpora noctes
> Curaque et e magno qui fit amore, dolor.
> <div align="right">—<i>Ars Amatoria</i>, I, 733–36.</div>

macies adduxerat artus;
sumebant minimos ora coacta cibos.
—*Heroides*, XI, 27–28.

14. Love can cause death:

luctibus extremum tenues liquefacta medullas
tabuit inque leves paulatim evanuit auras.
—*Metamorphoses*, XIV, 431–32.

Though consideration of Ovid might be much further extended, the above pages probably set forth some of his more important ideas in sufficient detail to form a concisely molded background for the study of the courtly love poetry. To characterize Ovid's theory of love is a well-nigh impossible task, but there are certain points which should be borne in mind; a complete discussion of this concept, it need hardly be stated, is quite beyond the scope of the present survey. The reader who turns from Ovid to, let us say, the troubadours is struck at once by the very manifest difference in the tone and spirit of the poetry; all of the nobility and exaltation of womanhood characteristic of Provence is entirely lacking. As Neilson puts it,

In Ovid the whole matter of winning the lady's good-will, of which the giving of presents is a detail, is simply a basely conceived means to an immoral end. . . . But in the Middle Ages, in that part of the literature inspired by the finer side of courtly love, the spending of thought, pains, or money to please one's lady is part of the quasi-religious worship offered her; and, to whatever extent this had a sensual basis, it was still one side of knightliness.[11]

A little further on we read: "Recommendations to concealment are frequent in Ovid; but here again the lower ethical level is apparent, for while in the chivalrous codes consideration for the lady is the motive insisted on, in Ovid it is fear of the husband or desire to carry on more intrigues than one without exciting the suspicions of the different mistresses." And again, "The paleness and sleeplessness of lovers, instead of being the genuine symptoms of the passion-struck youth, appear in Ovid as shams assumed for the purpose of working on the feelings of the intended victim." [12] In treating such an intangible thing as we are dealing with here, there is great danger of becoming almost purely subjective; yet in what way can we even attempt to explain the Ovidian concept other than by setting forth our own personal reaction to it? Briefly stated, it seems to be the outpouring of an artful and crafty writer, not at all inspired or in the least affected by the nobility of womanhood, but rather subordinated to a base and sensual end. This is more readily understandable when we remember that the position of woman in society at the beginning of the Christian era was quite different from that accorded her in medieval times. The Roman concept of love contained no suggestion of the Platonic, spiritual, or romantic but was regarded as something essentially physical. It could hardly be otherwise for, to the Romans, marriage was little more than a business agreement arranged by the parents:

Its basis, in fact, was not "*amor*," but "*fides*," that sense of moral integrity and commercial rectitude which forbids an honest man or woman to break an agreement, so long as the other party abides by its stipulations. In this conception of marriage there is no room for sentiment or sensuality, no opportunity for chivalry or romance: it is a pure matter of business and it will be a success or a failure according to the ease or difficulty with which the two partners work together. . . . It is true that the respect which a woman enjoyed was perhaps given to her rather as a child-bearer than as a wife. Certainly, "*matrimonium*" means, "the making a woman a mother," and the most honourable title that could be given her was not "*uxor*" or "*conjunx*" but "*matrona*" or "*materfamilias*." If, however, she was a mother, her position was unassailable; in the household she took a place only second to her husband, and over her children she exercised a very real control. Yet all this had little to do with the softer emotion of love, and the feeling which Horace's Sabine matron inspired in her husband would be more correctly described by the word "*reverentia*" than by the word "*amor*." [13]

Love, as conceived by Ovid, stands far removed from the impersonal Platonic concept on the one side and is equally distant from the individualized and spiritual medieval love on the other.

II

THE TROUBADOURS

ONE of the interesting developments in the history of human culture is the growth of the spiritual love of man for woman, something far loftier than the Platonic relationship of antiquity or the disparaging attitude of the first centuries of the Christian era. To describe this metamorphosis is not easy; Emil Lucka puts it this way:

The position of woman had changed; she was no longer the medium for the satisfaction of the male impulse, or the rearing of children, as in antiquity; no longer the silent drudge or devout sister of the first Christian millenary; no longer the she-devil of monkish conception; transcending humanity, she had been exalted to the heavens and had become a goddess. She was loved and adored with a devotion not of this earth, a devotion which was the sole source of all things lofty and good; she had become the saviour of humanity and queen of the universe.[1]

The idea is elaborated somewhat a little further on:

Infinite tenderness pervaded the nascent cult of woman. It seemed as if man were eager to compensate her for the indignity which he had heaped upon her for a thousand years. His instinctive need to worship had found an incomparable being on earth before whom he prostrated himself. She was the climax of earthly perfection; no word, no metaphor was sufficiently ecstatic to express the full fervour of his adoration; a new religion was created and she was the presiding divinity.[2]

It was in Provence that the new theory of love first took form, developed into the lofty expression of the love of man for woman, and then, after nearly two centuries, vanished into the silence whence it had sprung. But the spirit of the poetry inspired by that new love still persists. "The great historical fact belonging to the close of the eleventh century, besides the crusade," writes W. P. Ker, "is the appearance of French and Provençal poetry, which is the beginning of modern literature. With hardly a warning came the rhymes of William, Count of Poitou, the first of a school that includes every modern poet." [3] The marked difference in the attitude of man towards woman, strikingly revealed in the Provençal love lyric, was due, in large part at least, to the growth of the spirit of chivalry, the appearance of which may be said to inaugurate the Middle Ages. On this phase of the subject the words of Thomas Frederick Crane, who has given us such an admirable study of Italian social conditions, are illuminating:

This spirit was the result of the old German veneration for woman modified by Christianity, and applied to Feudal society. It is also probable that the relations of lord and vassal with the accompanying duties of loyalty and protection were influential in forming the new ideal of the relation of the sexes and the elaborate codes of gallantry. . . . The lover regarded his mistress partly with the adoration lavished upon the Virgin, and partly with feelings similar to those evoked by his complicated duties to his lord. It must also be borne in mind that marriage was generally a matter of arrangement between the two families, in which the bride had no voice. This fact is of the greatest importance, and explains some of the singular notions in regard to love which prevailed throughout the Middle Ages. Before marriage the life of a maiden was largely spent in the retirement of home, and it was only after marriage that she enjoyed greater liberty.[4]

The spread of the chivalric spirit resulted in a transformation of far-reaching importance. Under the formative influence of various institutions, notably the Church, the knights of the early Middle Ages, heroes in the Germanic tradition, underwent a gradual change until the chivalric warrior of the twelfth century was not only a brave and worthy knight but a polished gentleman and lover par excellence as well. It is only natural to expect that this institution of chivalry had some effect on the literature of the time, and, consequently, it is not surprising to find the troubadours laying the foundations for a new theory of love. The Provençal poets really formulated very little that was new but rather gave form and expression, in an original way, to a set of old ideas and endowed them with a new spirit. Vossler explains this fact as follows:

So it was in Provence that the new spirit took on the definite outline of a moral code. There first, partly from pleasure and love of beauty, partly from loftiness of soul and magnanimity, manly strength took up the defense of the weaker sex. Or, to look at it from the other side, woman's arts succeeded in securing a hold on man through his ambition and vanity, and in dictating to his warlike nature the laws of courtesy. Woman, whose mouth the medieval Church had closed, became the aristocratic lady who set her claims against the commands of the Church. The service of woman took its place beside religious worship; woman's code of morals rivaled that of the Church.

The most vital article of this code taught that love of woman and love-service lead man to moral dignity and to true chivalry. In the repetition, accentuation, and glorification of this dangerous maxim the minstrels of knighthood, the troubadours, found their chief delight.[5]

To comprehend more fully just what this new spirit was, we may now turn to the body of Provençal poetry and devote some attention to the love lyrics of the troubadours.[6] A favorite notion among the Provençal poets was that of love as the source of joy. _Joi_ (or the nearly as frequent feminine form _joia_) [7] occurs perhaps even more frequently than does _amor_ in the love lyrics. The troubadours looked upon their poetry as a source of exaltation and inspiration; one of the earliest and perhaps the greatest of them, Bernart de Ventadorn, gave expression to this feeling as follows (**XXXIX**, 1–8):

> Can l'erba fresch' e·lh folha par
> e la flors boton' el verjan,
> e·l rossinhols autet e clar
> leva sa votz e mou so chan,
> joi ai de lui, e joi ai de la flor
> e joi de me e de midons major;

> dans totas partz sui de joi claus e sens,
> mas sel es jois que totz autres jois vens.

With more particular reference to his poetry, he repeats the idea (**XV**, 5–7):

> per so es mos chantars cabaus
> qu'en joi d'amor ai et enten
> la boch' e·ls olhs e·l cor e·l sen.

And yet a third time (**XIII**, 20–21):

> del joi qu'eu ai, no vei ni au
> ni no sai que·m dic ni que·m fau.

Bernart might well be called the supreme poet of *joi*, for he is constantly giving vent to the feeling.[8]

Many other troubadours expressed themselves in much the same way as Bernart; among them may be noted Jaufre Rudel (Appel, **XV**, 22–23):

> Iratz e gauzens me·n partrai,
> quan veirai cest'amor de lonh;

and again in the same poem (43–46):

> Ver ditz qui m'apella lechai
> ni desiran d'amor de lonh,
> car nulhs autres iois tant no·m plai
> cum iauzimens d'amor de lonh.

Pons de Capdeuil (MW, **I**, 338–39):

> Et es razos e dregz, al mieu semblan,
> Qu'om la melhor am mais per bona fe,
> Sitot no 'l val; fols es qui s'en recre,
> Mas sierv' ades e ja re no 'l deman.
> Qu' assatz quier hom a senhor conoissen
> Qui l'am e 'l sierf; doncs s'ien am finamen
> Mi dons cui sui, be m degra joys venir,
> au'el genser es qu'om puesc el mon chauzir. . . .

Guillem de Cabestaing (MW, **I**, 110):

> Be m ten en son coman
> Amors, qu'en mi comensa

> Mans dolz plazers, e cre
> C'ad ops de leis me fe
> Deus, e per sa valensa.

Girault de Bornelh (MW, I, 184):

> Ar ai gran joy quant remembri l'amor
> Que ten mon cor ferm en sa fezeutat;
> Que l'autr' ier vinc en un vergier de flor
> Tot gent cubert ab chan d'auzels mesclat,
> E quant estei en aquels bels jardis,
> Lai m'aparec la bella flors de lis,
> E pres mos huels e sazic mon coratge,
> Si que anc pueis remembransa ni sen
> Non aic mas quant de lieys en cui m'enten.

Peirol (Bartsch, 152, 21–28; 153, 1–2):

> Nuls hom be non ama
> ni gen,
> que d'amor si clama,
> sitot mal l'en pren;
> cum plus m'enliama
> greumen,
> e m'art e m'aflama
> n'ai melhor talen.

Little need be said about the externalities of love as revealed in the poetry. The usual things are emphasized: beauty as the cause of love; the restlessness of the lover; his sighing, fainting, and sleeplessness; his joy at the sight of the lady and his sorrow when they are separated. Special prominence is given to the necessity for secrecy; Bernart de Ventadorn, for example, goes so far as to say that love which becomes known is not love at all (XXII, 21–24):

> c'amors, pois om per tot s'en vana,
> non es amors, mas es ufana,
> et es enois, vilani' e fondatz,
> qui no gara cui deu esser privatz;

and (VIII, 47–48):

> ja per me non er saubuda
> l'amors; ben siatz segura!

Practically all the troubadour love poems are addressed to married women. Realization of this fact is essential when reading the poetry and especially when discussing the emphasis on secrecy. Since the lady addressed in almost every case was another man's wife, it was by the very nature of things most important to be extremely discreet. Those who were not fared badly; Peire Vidal, we may note, lost his tongue, while Guillem de Cabestaing was deprived of something still more vital, his life!

Love as the source of all virtues and benefits, a point of view quite opposed to the Ovidian idea that love is a debasing experience, is a favorite theme with the troubadours. Bernart de Ventadorn frequently expresses this thought; the following is a characteristic example (XV, 1–4):

> Chantars no pot gaire valer,
> si d'ins dal cor no mou lo chans;
> ni chans no pot dal cor mover,
> si no i es fin' amors coraus.

See also **XXIV**, 17–24:

> Ben a mauvais cor e mendic
> qui ama e no·s melhura;
> qu'eu sui d'aitan melhuratz
> c'ome de me no vei plus ric,
> car sai c'am e sui amatz
> per la gensor qued anc Deus fei
> ni que sia el mon, so crei,
> tan can te terra ni dura.

The idea is widespread in the lyrics of the other troubadours as well: Pons de Capdeuil (MW, I, 348):

> Astrucx es selh cui amors ten joyos,
> Qu'amors es caps de trastotz autres bes,
> E per amor es hom guays e cortes,
> Francs e gentils, humils et orgulhos;
> Aqui on tanh, en fai hom mielhs mil tans
> Guerras e cortz don naisson faitz prezans:
> Per qu'ieu ai mes tot mon cor en amor;

E quar ai bon respieit que m fassa ric,
No planc l'afan qu'ieu trac ni la dolor.

Peire Raimon (MW, I, 147):

Mas fis amans non tanh que lev grans brutz,
Ans deu son cor celar et escondir
E'l ben e 'l mal qu'el vei d'amor grazir;
Qu'ab cortes ayps es hom per pro tengutz,
E que s guart be de faire falhimen
Ab escien;
Que de bon luec aven bos guazardos;
Que si domneys e cortejars no fos,
No fora pretz ni servirs ni honransa.

Arnaut de Marueil (MW, I, 161):

Tant es valens que, quan ben m'o cossir,
M'en nays erguelhs e'n creys humilitatz;

ibid. (183–84):

Dona, pros e valens
Corteza et avinens,
S'en ren ai conoissensa,
La vostra sovinensa,
Que m'es cor et escrima
La m dona e la m'aprima;
Per qu'ieu de totz mos bes
Vos ren laus e merces.

Peire Vidal (MW, I, 224):

E s'ieu sai ren dir ni faire,
Ilh n'aya 'l grat, que sciensa
M'a donat e conoissensa,
Per qu'ieu sui guays e chantaire,
E tot quant fauc d'avinen
Ai del sieu belh cors plazen,
Neis quan de bon cor cossire.

Raimon de Miraval (MW, II, 121):

Lo plus nescis hom del renh
Que la veya ni remir
Deuria esser al partir
Savis e de belh captenh.

The troubadour love lyric is often characterized as a purely intellectual product written according to an approved style rather than a free outpouring or personal effusion on the part of the poet.[9] Yet this is hardly so, for when we come to examine the singers' attitudes on various topics we often find widely differing views expressed. This is especially true in the case of chastity. The earliest of them certainly were much less nobly minded than those who came later. We have these lines from Jaufre Rudel (Appel, XV, 36–42):

> Dieus, que fetz tot quant ve ni vai,
> e formet cest'amor de lonh,
> mi don poder, que·l cor eu n'ai,
> qu'en breu veia l'amor de lonh
> veraiamen en locs aizis,
> si que la cambra e·l jardis
> mi resembles totz temps palatz.

And the same idea is suggested in Guillem de Cabestaing (Bartsch 80, 12–15):

> Qu'una no porta benda
> Qu'eu prezes per esmenda
> jazer, ni fos sos drutz,
> per las votras salutz.

That even the universally praised Bernart de Ventadorn shared this sentiment may be assumed from the following lines (XXVIII, 49–54):

> Be for' oimais sazos,
> bela domna e pros,
> que·m fos datz a rescos
> en baizan guizardos,
> si ja per als no fos,
> mas car sui enveyos,
> c'us bes val d'autres dos,
> can per fors' es faihz dos.

Another example is (XXVII, 41–45):

> res de be no·n es a dire,
> ab sol c'aya tan d'ardit

c'una noih lai o·s despolha,
me mezes, en loc aizit,
e·m fezes del bratz latz al col.

On the other hand, the references to chaste love are frequent and often have a note of sincerity which is sometimes lacking in the bolder expressions. Bernart's lyrics, like those of most troubadours, furnish abundant and annoyingly contradictory evidence on this score. In sharp contrast to the passages just quoted are the following (XXV, 49–50):

> Ja per drudaria
> no m'am, que no·s cove;

and again (VII, 39–40):

> car aitan rich' amor envei,
> pro n'ai de sola l'enveya!

That every genuine love lyric has its basis in reality, at least to a certain extent, is an observation which I suppose none will deny. Troubadour love poetry is rarely spiritual to a very lofty degree, just as it is only occasionally of the earth. Vernon Lee's characterization of medieval love poetry describes the Provençal attitude equally well: "Medieval love poetry, compared with the love poetry of Antiquity and the love poetry of the revival of letters, is, in its lyric form, decidedly chaste; but it is perfectly explicit; and, for all its metaphysical tendencies and its absence of clearly painted pictures, the furthest possible removed from being Platonic." [10]

Unwavering devotion characterizes most of the troubadours; for them love was the dominant force in life and, if we are to believe the evidence of the poetry, nothing else was accounted worth while. Love dominated their every thought and action; [11] only one of the Provençal poets was sufficiently heretical to disagree with this point of view; Marcabrun felt that love was false and empty and denounced it many times; a characteristic condemnation follows (Berry, p. 78, 19–21):

Amors es mout de mal avi;
Mil homes a mortz ses glavi,
Dieus non fetz tant fort gramavi.

But Marcabrun was certainly an exception, for, as has just been stated, love was the ruling passion with practically all of the troubadours, and unwavering devotion was certainly the most customary way of giving expression to the feeling. Bernart de Ventadorn, for example, confessed complete submission (XXXIII, 29–35):

Domna, vostre sui e serai,
del vostre servizi garnitz.
vostr' om sui juratz e plevitz
e vostra m'era des abans.
e vos etz lo meus jois primers
e si seretz vos lo derrers,
tan com la vida m'er durans.

Peire Vidal admitted that he was the complete property of his mistress; she might do with him as she pleased (Bartsch, 117, 27–28):

que ses tota retenensa
sui seus per vendr'e per dar.

Guillem de Cabestaing said that he was his lady's to command (MW, I, 115):

Qu' ieu fui noyritz enfans
Per far vostres comans.

The Provençal poet was not a slave to his mistress, but he was most assuredly her vassal. Bernart de Ventadorn is a highly representative illustration of this frequently expressed attitude (XXXI, 49–54):

Bona domna, re no·us deman
mas que·m prendatz per servidor,
qu'e·us servirai com bo senhor,
cossi que del gazardo m'an.
ve·us m'al vostre comandamen,
francs cors umils, gais e cortes!

This conception need not seem strange to us if we will but remember that much of the Provençal poetry was profoundly affected by the social conditions of the period in which it flourished.[12] In an earlier age Christianity had done much to improve the lot of womankind. Now, with the growth of chivalry, womanhood is once more exalted; not merely is woman raised to a position of dignity and respect, but soon becomes an object of adoration complete and entire. Accordingly it is not surprising to find the transition of the secular love song to the religious lyric anything but abrupt; indeed, it has been pointed out more than once that the distinction between the two is sometimes scarcely perceptible.[13] Unfortunately, however, this change did not begin to take place until the poetry had entered upon that final period of decadence after which it disappeared completely. The result is that, though the genuine secular love lyrics are among the world's greatest, the intentionally religious songs are few and inferior.

Patient and humble in the extreme, the troubadour devoted himself completely to his mistress, begged and implored her for permission to be considered in her service, and professed ecstatic joy on those rare occasions when the bestowal of a solitary kiss indicated approval. This idea of love-service was perhaps the most important contribution which the troubadours made to the theory of courtly love. Love rapidly came to be regarded as a religious cult with its own code of laws to which the lover must submit himself completely; infractions of these laws were theoretically fraught with serious consequences. One or two additional quotations may serve to illustrate in greater detail this idea of love-service and complete devotion.

Bernart de Ventadorn (IV, 1–8):

> Amors, e que·us es vejaire?
> trobatz mais fol mas can me?
> cuidatz vos qu'eu si' amaire
> e que ja no trop merce?

que que·m comandetz a faire,
farai o, c'aissi·s cove ;
mas vos non estai ges be
que·m fassatz tostems mal traire.

Ibid. (**XXV**, 59–60) :

si·lh platz, que m'aucia,
qu'eu no m'en clam de re !

Guillem de Cabestaing (MW, I, 109) :

Lo jorn qu'ie us vi, domna,. primieramen,
Quant a vos plac que us mi laissetz vezer,
Parti mon cor tot d'autre pessamen,
E foron ferm en vos tug mey voler :
Qu' aissi m pauzetz, domna, el cor l'enveia
Ab un dous ris et ab un simpl' esguar,
Que tot quant es mi fezes oblidar.

Arnaut de Marueil (MW, I, 161) :

Vas lo pays, pros domna issernida,
Vire mos huelhs on vostre cors estai,
E quan de vos plus pres no m puesc aizir,
Ten vos el cor ades, e cossir sai
Vostre gen cors cortes que m fai languir,
Lo bel semblant e 'l deport e 'l solatz,
Lo pretz e 'l sen e las beutatz de vos
Don, pois que us vi, no fui anc oblidos.

Peirol (MW, II, 28) :

Quant en premer la vi, me plac aitan,
Que de mon cor retener non puec ges :
Totz fo ab leis et ancaras i es.

In keeping with this attitude is the general tendency to deify one's *domna*. Whatever the cause of this constantly growing tendency—the growth of Mariolatry possibly contributed much—the effect was widespread, for it finally resulted in the *Vita Nuova* and the *Divina Commedia*. This feature of Provençal poetry is, in a way, particularly characteristic of the genre, for by far the greater number of the lyrics impress one as a reaching out for something unattainable, a constant striving toward the infinite. The deification of woman is certainly a significant manifestation of this tendency.

Pons de Capdeuil (MW, I, 350):

> Tant m'a donat e fin e ferm voler
> Leyals amors, que ja no m partrai mais
> De vos, dona, on ai mon bon esper;
> Tant etz valens, cortez' ab digz verais,
> Franch' e gentils, guay' ab humil semblan,
> Belh' e plazens, si que non es a dire
> Negus bos ayps qu'om puesc' en domn' eslire,
> E pus tant es vostre ricx pretz puiatz,
> Suffretz qu'ie us am, qu'ieu vuelh tot quan vos platz.

Peire Raimon (MW, I, 146):

> Per qu'ieu li m suy autreyatz e rendutz
> A fin amor, et a lieys cuy dezir;
> Que finamen m'an fait mei huelh chauzir
> La belha, qu'es flors e miralhs e lutz
> E caps e guitz de tot ensenhamen:
>   E pus tan gen
> Nafret mon cor d'un esgart amoros,
> D'als no m sove, ni no m fo saboros
> Nulhs autres bes, ni d'als non ai membransa.

Arnaut Daniel (MW, II, 75):

> D'autras vezer sui secs e d'auzir sors
> Qu'en sola lieis vei et aug et esgar. . . .

Peire Vidal (MW, I, 241):

> Ar m'er mon chant a virar
> Vas ma dona qui tenc car
> Plus que mos huelhs ni mas dens.

Finally, and in connection with this last point, we may note the troubadour belief in love as the source of all things sublime. Instances of this point of view are particularly frequent in the work of one of the noblest Provençals, Bernart de Ventadorn (XXXI, 9–12):

> Ben es mortz qui d'amor no sen
> al cor cal que dousa sabor;
> e que val viure ses valor
> mas per enoi far a la gen?

Ibid. (29–32):

> ben es mos mals de bel semblan,
> que mais val mos mals qu'autre bes;
> e pois mos mals aitan bos m'es,
> bos er lo bes apres l'afan.

The famous William (Guilhem) **IX**, the earliest and perhaps least representative of the troubadours, did not entirely share this point of view (Appel, **XI**, 25–30):

> Per son ioy pot malautz sanar
> e per sa ira sas morir
> e savis hom enfolezir
> e belhs hom sa beutat mudar
> e·l plus cortes vilaneiar
> e·l totz vilas encortezir.

Most of the poets, however, are more positive and do not hesitate to declare that love possesses distinct ennobling power:

Cercamon (Appel, **XIII**, 57–58):

> Cercamons ditz; treu er cortes
> hom qui d'amor se desesper.

Gaucelm Faidit (MW, II, 91):

> Tug cilh que amon valor
> Devon saber que d'amor
> Mov larguez' e guais solatz,
> Franchez' et humilitatz,
> Pretz d'amar, servirs d'onor,
> Gen teners, jois, cortezia.

Aimeric de Pegulhan (MW, II, 165):

> Enquera truep mais de be en amor,
> Qu'el vil fai pros, e'l nesci gen parlan,
> E l'escars larc e leyal lo truan,

E'l folh savi, e'l pec conoissedor,
E l'orgulhos domesg' e humilia. . . . .

E moutas vetz mi gart de vilania,
Que ses amor gardar no m'en sabria;
E manhs bos motz mi fai pessar e dir,
Que ses amor no i sabria venir.

One more problem remains to be solved before this brief and inadequate examination of the Provençal love lyric may be concluded; that is its relation to the work of Ovid. This aspect of the subject has been handled perhaps overconfidently, as far as results are concerned, in a dissertation by W. Schrötter, *Ovid und die Troubadours*.[14] While disagreeing with many of the details of this work, I find myself in accord with Vossler, who, in his review of Schrötter's work,[15] condemns the "reiche, aber im Grunde willkürliche, mechanische und langweilige Aufreihung von Parallelstellen aus Ovid und aus den Liedern der Trobadors, äusserliche Vergleiche, zweifelhafte, stückweise, zufällige Aehnlichkeiten. . . ." Vossler's statement of the desiderata in work of this type is so eminently sensible and so much to the point that I shall paraphrase it: The question of what influence a particular poet has exercised on this or that troubadour leads both the tyro and the experienced critic again and again to the fundamentally false fiction of influence as an active factor. Actually, the influencing factors are neither Ovid nor his books but solely and entirely the artistic individualities of the troubadours. Ovid occupies a singularly passive position. The correct formulation of the question, then, would be: why and to what extent and in what spirit have the Marcabruns, the Bernarts, the Raimbauts and Arnauts studied Ovid? How have they adapted, transformed, and appropriated him? These are, after all, fundamental problems whose completely successful solution demands deep knowledge, keen critical acumen, and a facile pen. Though I am in general agreement with what Vossler says about the mode of treatment which Schrötter adopts, yet I feel that the latter's conclusions on the particular point with which we are now concerned are informative, and they therefore furnish the basis of the following remarks.

First of all, as to the general resemblances between Ovid and the troubadour: 1. Both wrote for a cultivated public. 2. The lyrics of both have a courtly air; none of them seems intended for the common people. 3. Both were aware of their stations as poets and wrote to become famous. 4. Both were concerned with the artistic expression of love and were careful to devote attention to the theory of love, though the troubadours never systematized their views in anything like the works of Ovid before them or that of their north French contemporary, Andreas, in his treatise, the *De Amore*. 5. Both the Latin and the troubadour were concerned with the love of married women; the courtly attitude that love between married couples was impossible was paramount with the troubadours. And how can we tell that this was the case? The deduction is fairly simple; the *joc-parti* decisions tend to confirm this extra-conjugal point of view; the *alba* reflects an anguish one hardly expects from a man in the company of his wife at the break of dawn; and the *sirventes* are largely devoted to the celebration of secret meetings and rendezvous, the sort of thing one would not celebrate in lyric effusion if the poet's partner were his wife!

The contrasts are perhaps more numerous and more striking than the general resemblances: 1. The Ovidian poetry is written in a lightsome mood, probably more for the delectation of Ovid and his friends than anything else. The troubadour love lyric, on the other hand, is often a personal expression of the poet's feeling and as such is to be regarded as a sincere manifestation of emotion. 2. Ovid confuses the love of married women and of courtesans. The troubadour is concerned only with someone else's wife. 3. Ovid's work is learned; it is filled with mythological references, abounds in irony and flights of rhetoric, and doubtless reflects the author's experience in Roman society. However the troubadour

poetry be described, it can never be called learned. Despite
its elaborateness and perfection, it has much of the spontaneity and inspiration one usually associates with the lyric.
4. Ovid rarely praises woman; the troubadour love poetry is,
one feels justified in saying, an almost continuous panegyric,
one that is constantly being rewritten and reëxpressed for
nearly two centuries. The reader is always conscious of the
personal relation of the poet to his mistress. 5. Ovid treats
woman as his equal, except, perforce, the courtesan, whom
he considers beneath him. The troubadour lady, on the contrary, is always accorded a position far above that of the poet
by whom she is praised. 6. Ovid is filled with irony. The
troubadours are serious and wish to be understood in that
sense. 7. Perhaps the most important difference, certainly one
of great significance for the development of the Italian love
lyric, was that which concerned the power of love.' Ovid
taught that it had a debasing effect, while the troubadour
viewed it as something which exalted and ennobled all concerned. Schrötter's conclusion in this respect bears literal quotation:

Ovid sagt: Liebe erniedrigt. Die Troubadours sagen: Liebe veredelt.
    Ovid besingt selten andere als grob sinnliche Neigung. . . . Das
Grundthema Ovid's bleibt allerdings die sinnliche Liebe.
    Dagegen hat die Liebe der Troubadours aus dem Christentum einen
teilweise spirituellen Charakter angenommen. Dass der letzte und
höchste Wunsch des Liebenden auf zärtlichen Kuss und Umarmung
gerichtet ist, wird allerdings oft ausgesprochen und nie in Abrede
gestellt, nicht einmal von Jaufre Rudel. Aber was überwiegt und
das wertvollste Resultat des Minnesangs auch für die weitere Ent-
wicklung ausmacht (Dante's Vita Nuova und Commedia), das ist der
mystische Aufschwung und die Aufopferung, die entsagende Liebe
des dienenden Sängers. . . .[16]

Such was the troubadour love lyric. It came into being with
startling suddenness, flourished for but a short time, then vanished almost as quickly as it had appeared.[17] And yet it has
had an enduring quality which literary historians have too
frequently been inclined to neglect. To the poetry of other

lands and earlier times it owed little or nothing; to the poetry of medieval Europe it bequeathed much both directly and indirectly, in form as well as in content. As the immediately preceding pages have indicated, the troubadours were most original in their conception of love. They were the first modern poets to celebrate the sentiments induced by love, the joys and sorrows that are so ancient and yet so modern. Not only did they succeed in impressing their ideas on the aristocratic society of their time (the troubadour poetry reached its height in the last half of the twelfth century and the opening years of the thirteenth), but they also, from their Elysian fields, have had the satisfaction of seeing them spread to other lands and climes as well.[18] A knowledge of Provençal poetry is essential to a full understanding of the poetry, both secular and religious, of the later Middle Ages.

III

CHRÉTIEN DE TROYES

THE Provençal love lyric marks, as has been pointed out, the first stage in the development of a system of courtly love. Vague and contradictory though the poems often are, they nevertheless contain the elements of that code which found its fullest expression in the romances of Chrétien de Troyes—especially in what has been termed his courtly love trilogy, the *Cligés*, the *Lancelot*, and the *Yvain*—and in that priceless compendium of medieval love lore, the *De Amore* of Andreas Capellanus. After a few preliminary observations these works will be considered in the order named.

A remarkable characteristic of the literature of northern France before the mid-twelfth century is the almost wholly inferior position accorded the female figures. Women play a decidedly subordinate rôle; when present at all, they take but a minor part, far removed from the charming tyrant and all-inspiring goddess of later days. When one stops to think of Alde and Bramimonde of the *Chanson de Roland*, Guibourc of the *Guillaume d'Orange*, Belyssant of *Amis et Amile*, one realizes how strikingly true this is. And when present, the woman is far from being the all-inciting force that she is, for example, in the work of Chrétien. In his study of Chrétien, Cohen expresses the thought in this fashion:

C'est pour *France la douce*, c'est pour le suzerain *à la barbe fleurie*, c'est pour Dieu, le suzerain suprême, que le chevalier, au coeur, au corps, au corselet de fer, accomplit ses sublimes exploits. Il ne lui vient que rarement à la pensée de réserver, pour une part au moins, la dédicace de sa bravoure à quelque fine et douce figure, lointaine et hautaine, qui, un jour peut-être, l'en recompensera. On dira que cela est plus fort et plus mâle ainsi. Sans doute, comme le patriotisme d'Horace, mais combien aussi moins séduisant et moins français. De l'épopée ainsi que de la croisade, la femme est la grande sacrifiée.[1]

With the continuance of the Crusades and the growth of Mariolatry the status of woman rapidly changed, and it is not long before we find her being accorded a respectful and usually superior position. Without going into a detailed examination of the Crusades, we may note that women were prohibited from taking part in these expeditions. Cohen, quite justly I think, posits this question: "Est-ce que cet abandon conjugal ne serait pas pour beaucoup dans le développement du culte de la femme et de l'amour dans la seconde moitié du XIIe siècle? Le seigneur parti, la femme est reine; le mari absent, l'amant est roi." [2] The Crusades were not *the* reason for the change under discussion, but they certainly were an important contributing factor; for, though it is perhaps not entirely correct to say that the lover has become *roi*, after the Second Crusade at least woman is certainly fast assuming all the qualities of a queen; "la femme est reine" is no exaggeration.

Eleanor of Aquitaine occupies a position of unusual importance in the literary development of northern France. Granddaughter of William IX, Count of Poitiers, first of the troubadours, she thus assumes a unique position in the dissemination of Provençal thought; for, a month after her marriage to Prince Louis he became Louis VII, and she was thus raised to a position of far-reaching importance as Queen of France. Though this marriage was annulled in 1152, and despite the fact that through her union with Henry of Anjou she became Queen of England on his accession to the throne in 1154, she nevertheless probably remains best known by her earliest title, Eleanor of Aquitaine. In an illuminating article on the influence of the troubadours in northern France the distinguished Romance scholar, Paul Meyer, evaluates Eleanor's position in these words: "Les quinze ans pendant lesquels Eléonore fut reine de France (1137–52) sont probablement l'époque ôu la poésie courtoise du Midi commença à exercer une influence sensible sur celle du Nord." [3] There can be but little doubt that Eleanor was in large part responsible for those ideals of courtly conduct and unwavering devotion soon to become the idols of European society and about to appear in literature as the *amour courtois* of Chrétien's romances. Important though Eleanor is as the instigator and promoter of these ideals, she deserves most to be remembered as the mother of Marie, Countess of Champagne; for, as patroness of Chrétien de Troyes, Marie undoubtedly did more than any other single figure to advance the cause of literature in twelfth-century France. It may also be noted that the author of the *De Amore*, Andreas Capellanus, was resident for a time at Marie's court. The most important evidence of Marie's influence on Chrétien is of course the statement at the beginning of the *Lancelot* (l. 26) that the Countess of Champagne provided him with the subject matter and spirit (*matiere et san*) of the poem. Gaston Paris concludes that "Marie de Champagne et les siens a été le principal foyer de la propagation en France de l'idéal social, sentimental et poétique dont j'ai indiqué les origines." [4] He notes her relationship to Eleanor and remarks on the latter:

Elle appela à elle plusieurs troubadours, et on peut croire que ce fut elle qui fit connaître et imiter leur art compliqué aux poetes qui voulaient lui plaire. La galanterie à laquelle se livrait avec passion ne dut pas exercer autour d'elle une moindre influence, et les brillantes assemblées qu'elle présidait furent bientôt imitées ailleurs. Sa fille Marie avait hérité et de son amour pour le monde et les plaisirs et de ses goûts littéraires. [5]

The extent of their influence becomes more significant when one stops to consider that Eleanor became queen in 1137 and that Marie was Countess of Champagne from 1164 to 1198; thus these two ladies very nearly controlled the literary fortunes of France for the better part of a century. Consequently it is only natural to find reflections of this influence in the work of Chrétien. "Entraîné par le courant des idées senti-

mentales qui s'épanouissent autour de lui, le poète champen-
ois compose sa trilogie admirable de l'amour courtois: *Cligès,
Lancelot, Yvain*." [6]

Before proceeding to a consideration of these romances, we
may briefly note Chrétien's position as an exponent of courtly
love. Of late years there has been a tendency on the part of
some scholars to cast doubts on Chrétien's reliability as an
exponent of the courtly system. Among others, for example,
Charles Grimm makes these statements: "A certain irony,
however, which I think can be seen throughout the works of
Chrestien (in varying degrees, to be sure) and a certain
matter-of-factness which appears time and again in his treatment of women, lead me to the opinion that he was not perhaps as firm a believer in the theories which he was expound-
ing as has been thought and said"; he "did not take very seriously the science of courtly love, and even considered it as
foolish"; and he "had too much common sense . . . to accept
and fully believe in genuine courtly love. I should even go
further and say that he had a real distaste for the art or science
of love. . . ." [7] Though there may be some elements of truth
in this attitude, yet I prefer to adopt the traditional and still
most widely spread view of Chrétien's work: ". . . the sentiments of courtly love attain their full growth in the epics of
Chrétien de Troies. He is the preëminent poetic representative
of chivalry. Love and adventure are his themes, and his imagination adorned the court of Arthur with the brilliance of
achievement and refinement of manners which made the cav-
aliers of the Round Table the ideal models of mediaeval
knighthood." [8] Considerable study of Chrétien has convinced
me that this point of view is still the correct one. Poets, we
may be thankful, are not usually as consistent as their critics
would have them. I feel that a writer should not seize upon a
half dozen isolated passages scattered through *Erec, Cligés,
Lancelot,* and *Yvain* and then proceed to draw conclusions
without considering the spirit, the design, and the literary
convention which inspired most of Chrétien's poetry.

It is particularly appropriate that discussion of Chrétien's work should open with the consideration of the *Cligés*, for this is the first of his romances in which love is treated as an art or science.[9] The nurse, Thessala, is described (3095–96) as

> Thessala qui mout estoit sage
> D'amors et de tot son usage;

and another, much more definite mention of the same thing, together with reference to a court of love, is found in 3865–68:

> Vos qui d'amors vos feites sage,
> Qui les costumes et l'usage
> De sa cort maintenez a foi,
> N'onques ne faussastes sa loi. . . .

The poem has been described as one in which are to be found

nearly all the subtleties with which mediaeval poets decked out their theories of love. Such a sudden change of tone [i. e., from the *Erec* to the *Cligés*] must be largely ascribed to external influences. Doubtless Chrétien had in the interval become acquainted with the love-songs of the troubadours, or at least with those of Bernart de Ventadorn and Peire Rogier. But he does not merely reproduce their thoughts. With an originality which left its trace on all succeeding amourists, he develops tenuous ideas with amazing delicacy and subtlety, theorizes over causes, as one trained in the Scholastic Logic, and studies profoundly the impulses and movements of the human heart.[10]

The *Cligés* is divided into two parts, of which the first, about a third of the whole, relates the love story of Alexander, son of the Emperor of Greece and Constantinople, and Soredamors, sister of Gawain and niece of Arthur. The fruit of their union is the hero of the story, Cligés, whose amorous adventures make up the second part of the tale, the romance proper.

The Emperor and Empress, Alexander and Tantalis, have two sons, Alexander and Alis. Alexander, the elder son and heir to the throne, is the central figure in the first part of the romance. He is so bold that he refuses to become a knight in Greece and sets out for Arthur's court, where he is well re-

ceived. He becomes one of Gawain's friends and falls in love
with his sister, Soredamors, who heretofore has been scornful
of love. Messengers now arrive telling of the revolt in England as the result of the King's absence from the country. A
huge army is prepared; Alexander is made a knight, conducts
himself valiantly in the ensuing campaign, vanquishes the
traitorous villain, Count Angrés, and is rewarded with the
hand of Soredamors. The wedding takes place that same day,
and in due time Cligés, the real hero of the romance, is born
(2382).

In the meantime the aged Emperor of Greece, Alexander's
father, who realizes that his end is near, summons his nobles
and asks them to search for his son and heir. Messengers start
out, but they are shipwrecked and only one survives. This
dastardly scoundrel returns to Greece and relates that all the
others have been lost in a storm at sea while they were escorting Alexander back and that he is the sole survivor. As a result
of this fabrication Alis is of course made emperor. When news
of this reaches Alexander, he immediately decides to assert
his rights and sets out for Athens. Alis is obdurate, however,
and will not surrender the throne. They finally reach a compromise: Alis agrees never to marry and thus assures the ascent of Cligés to the throne. The deaths of Alexander and
Soredamors conclude the first part of the narrative (2623).

Shortly after this, Alis, unmindful of his promise to his
brother and urged on by wicked counselors, decides to seek
the hand of the daughter of the Emperor of Germany. Cligés,
as a member of his uncle's entourage, visits the court of the
German emperor and sees his daughter, Fenice; they immediately become enamored of each other. The wedding of
Alis and Fenice, however, takes place as planned, but through
the skill of her nurse, Thessala, who brews a magic potion
which the King drinks, the marriage is never consummated
and Fenice remains a virgin (3363).

Following this the Duke, to whom Fenice was espoused,
attacks Alis and a fierce struggle ensues; Cligés is wounded

and Fenice carried off. Cligés rescues her and they return to Germany, where both emperors joyfully receive them. The Duke, however, is angry with Cligés and challenges him to battle; they fight; the Duke is subdued and humiliated (4574).

Having obtained leave from both uncle and sweetheart, Cligés now embarks for Britain, there to achieve glory at Arthur's court. Longing for Fenice finally causes his return, and a Romeo-and-Juliet ruse is employed to bring them together. Thessala brews another potion, which makes Fenice appear dead; Cligés is to rescue her from the grave and their happiness will be supreme. In the meantime, however, there arrive three aged physicians from Salerno who promise to restore the lady to life. When all their cures fail, they resort to violence only to be discovered by a thousand ladies peeking through a small crack in the door! These enraged females break in, rescue Fenice, and kill the doctors (6050).

That evening Cligés rescues her from her grave in the church and carries her off to the elaborately equipped tower, made ready by his slave, Jehan. Fully recovered, she remains there very happy with Cligés for over a year until they are discovered by Bertrand, one of the Emperor's knights, who accidentally comes upon them in the garden while he is in pursuit of his hawk. Cligés and Fenice, with Thessala as well, make their escape, but the faithful Jehan is brought before the enraged emperor. Events are soon brought to a happy end, however; for Alis dies, the two lovers return, are married, crowned at once, and live happily (6751–58):

> De s'amie a feite sa fame,
> Meis il l'apele amie et dame,
> Que por ce ne pert ele mie,
> Que il ne l'aint come s'amie,
> Et ele lui tot autresi,
> Con l'an doit feire son ami.

In *Le Chevalier de la Charrete* or the *Lancelot*, to give it its shorter title, Chrétien carries his treatment of love to extremes. This poem, above all others, certainly deserves to be known as the epic of courtly love; for here through constant repetition and elaboration the poet has so developed his theme that it passes beyond all reasonable bounds. It has already been remarked that Marie, Countess of Champagne, supplied both the *matière* and *sens* of the romances; [11] and Professor Nitze has indicated that in his treatment of the *sens* Chrétien made full use of a favorite medieval rhetorical device, *interpretatio* or *expolitio*, which consisted, in general, in saying the same thing in as many different ways as possible. [12] This fact accounts in part for the length of the poem and should help the reader to understand that all the repetition, far from being mere idle multiplication of words, is a definitely established and highly approved procedure from the point of view of medieval rhetoric.

As the *Lancelot* opens, we find Arthur and his court at Camelot on Ascension Day. A strange knight bursts in on them and makes this challenge: that the King entrust his Queen, Guenevere, to a champion, both of whom should follow him to the woods; if he is able to defend the Queen and bring her back safely, the challenger will free all the knights that he holds imprisoned. Hearing this, the seneschal, Kay, announces he will leave the King's service; Arthur is perturbed at this and sends the Queen to interview Kay; the latter agrees to remain in the King's service if Arthur will grant whatever favor he requests. The King readily assents—the so-called rash boon—and Kay accordingly demands that he be entrusted with the Queen and that they be allowed to follow the challenger. The King cannot go back on his word, and consequently he is obliged to yield. Kay and the Queen ride off. Gawain, having obtained the royal permission, rides after them to see what happens; the rest of the court follows (246).

Riding far ahead and alone, Gawain meets a knight (Lancelot, though he is not named until much later) who begs the loan of one of his horses; Gawain agreeing, the knight jumps on the nearest one and rides off. Gawain overtakes him, finds the horse slain and the knight afoot. A cart (*charrete*) driven by a dwarf approaches; Lancelot is told that if he will get into the cart—a most disgraceful thing to do, for the cart was the equivalent of a pillory—he will learn tidings of the Queen. Common sense and reason urge him not to do so, but love drives him to the opposite conclusion and, after a moment's hesitation, he climbs in. Gawain declines the dwarf's invitation to do likewise but follows them on his horse (398).

Arrived at a castle, they are hospitably welcomed and feasted. When it comes time to retire, their hostess shows the two knights three beds, one of which they are forbidden to use. The knight of the cart, however, disobeys this injunction; in the course of the night a flaming lance descends from the ceiling and comes so close as to wound him slightly. The bed is set on fire but he extinguishes it, swings the lance into the middle of the hall, and returns to his sleep. The next morning, as they sit at the window after Mass, they see a bier passing by and being followed by a crowd which is led by a tall knight and the Queen. When she disappears from sight, the knight tries to hurl himself from the window and is only prevented from doing so by Gawain's interference. After this they leave the castle but are unable to overtake the Queen. They meet a damsel who tells them that Guenevere has been abducted by Meleaganz, son of Bademaguz, King of Gorre. There are two dangerous approaches to this land, one the Water Bridge, the second and more perilous the Bridge of the Sword. Gawain chooses the former and Lancelot the latter. Lancelot performs many brave and notable feats and undergoes various strange adventures before his arrival in the land of Gorre: arrival at the second castle and rescue of the damsel; the chastity test; finding of the golden comb with some strands of Guenevere's hair; his ecstasy; the visit to the church where tombs are reserved for some of Arthur's knights (Lancelot raises the top of one bearing the inscription that whoever accomplishes that feat will liberate all those imprisoned in that land); the passage of stones; the falling portcullis; the proud challenger and the loathsome damsel. During all these exploits Lancelot is urged on by one force alone: his love for the Queen. It is his unwavering devotion that enables him to come through all these perils victorious (2978).

The sword bridge consists of a polished, gleaming sword, two lances long, at either end firmly fixed to a tree trunk. This extends over a very swift and terrible stream; the combination of the water and the sword dismays his two companions, but the knight of the cart remains undaunted; he removes his armor and proceeds to cross; though badly cut, he does not care, for love assuages his wounds. On reaching the other side he sees a strong tower before him. In one of the windows sits King Bademaguz, upright and loyal, with his son, Meleaganz, who delights in treachery and villainy. Recognizing Lancelot's worth, Bademaguz urges his son to surrender the Queen to Lancelot, but he refuses to yield and finally agrees to meet him in battle. The next day the two engage in combat before a tower wherein the Queen sits. It is only now, when one of the damsels asks Guenevere the name of this knight, that we are told definitely that he is "Lanceloz del Lac" (3676). Though Meleaganz wins at first, Lancelot, encouraged by a glance from the Queen, soon has him in his power, and it is only when Bademaguz intercedes, and Guenevere likewise, that the fighting ceases. The combat is postponed for one year; the people rejoice at this and Lancelot presents himself to the Queen. She, however, greets him in a cold and haughty fashion and refuses to welcome him. Lancelot is amazed at this but as an obedient lover he does not ask for any explanation; he takes his leave, his heart remaining with her while the eyes, weeping, go with his body. Neither Bademaguz nor Kay can explain the Queen's conduct (4030).

As Lancelot goes toward the Water Bridge to seek Gawain, followers of Bademaguz capture him and Guenevere hears that he is dead; in turn, he hears that the Queen is dead and tries to destroy himself. It turns out of course that both rumors are false; Lancelot returns to Bademaguz' court and has a rendezvous with Guenevere. He wounds his hands removing the bars from her window but gets in safely and spends the night unobserved with the Queen, this in spite of Kay's sleeping in the same room. Next morning, however, Meleaganz visits Guenevere and finds the bed stained with blood from Lancelot's fingers; but naturally he suspects Kay and accuses the Queen of having lain with him during the night. Lancelot appears as the Queen's defender, swears Kay is innocent, and proceeds to fight Meleaganz; the struggle is halted as before by the interference of Bademaguz. Lancelot goes off to see Gawain but is taken prisoner by a dwarf. His companions meet Gawain crossing the Water Bridge, and the latter agrees to search for Lancelot (5198).

In the meantime a letter comes to Bademaguz saying that Lancelot is safe at Arthur's court. The Queen, therefore, together with Kay and Gawain, sets out, only to learn on her arrival that the letter was a forgery and that Lancelot is not at that court. Lancelot, imprisoned, hears of the tournament instigated by the Lady of Nouaz and the Lady of Pomelegloi to provide them with suitors, learns that the Queen will be present at it, and ardently desires to attend. The lady of the house where he is held says she will release him provided only that he swears to return and give her his love. Lancelot swears this, receives a horse and armor from her, and rides off. At the tournament he is at first victorious; but on receipt of a message from the Queen, who alone recognizes him, he allows himself to be defeated. On the second day she commands him to win, and he emerges victorious; all the ladies are wildly enthusiastic about him, but he rides off as he has promised, and thus ends the "wooing" tournament (6104).

Meleaganz is very angry at Lancelot's absence and on his return causes him to be walled up in a stone tower on an island in the sea near Gorre; the only opening in it is the small window through which he receives food. Meleaganz goes to Arthur and presents himself as ready to battle with Lancelot, in accordance with the agreement made the year before. Gawain says he will take Lancelot's place if he is not found before the year is up. Meleaganz rejoins his father on the latter's birthday and finds him holding a joyous court at Bude. He relates what he has done but is roundly reproved by Bademaguz. Meleaganz' sister, in the meantime, finds Lancelot, releases him, restores him to health, and provides him with a horse so that he is enabled to return to court. He arrives just as Meleaganz and Gawain are about to clash. All rejoice; the Queen grants him her heart, and Arthur proposes to preside over the combat. Lancelot easily conquers Meleaganz and decapitates him. No one feels any pity for the rascal, the King and all others exult, and Lancelot is led off triumphantly. At this point Godefroiz de Leigni concludes the narrative rather abruptly by telling us that he has continued the story from the point at which Lancelot was imprisoned in the tower (6150).

> Tant an a fet: n'i vost plus metre
> Ne mains, por le conte mal metre.
> —7133-34.

The first part of the *Yvain*, or *Le Chevalier au Lion*, is taken up with Calogrenanz' story of the marvelous spring. Seven years ago while traveling through the forest of Broceliande in search of adventure, he was warmly received at a castle by the vavasor, whose beautiful daughter helped him to disarm and entertained him with her company. Calogrenanz willingly assents to the vavasor's request that he stop by on his return from his adventures and rides off the next morning (268).

Coming to a clearing where wild bulls are fighting, he sees a rustic lout of hideous appearance who, in reply to Calogrenanz' questioning, states that he is the man who tends the cattle; in return Calogrenanz lets him know that he is a knight in search of adventure to test his prowess. On learning this the churl tells of the fountain that boils though the water is cold as marble; it is overshadowed by a tree with evergreen foliage, on which hangs an iron basin with a chain long enough to reach the spring; beside it is a massive stone. If water is poured on the stone with the basin, such thunder, lightning, and torrential rain will result that all the wild creatures will issue forth from the wood, the trees will crash, and so on. If he survive all these things, he will be more fortunate than any knight heretofore. Calogrenanz immediately embarks on this adventure, and all turns out as predicted; there is lightning from fourteen directions, snow, rain, hail; a hundred times he is nearly killed by lightning bolts and falling trees, but God comforts and preserves him. When it is all over, multitudes of birds flock to the pine tree so that they completely fill it; their beautiful and joyous song impregnates him too with happiness. Hearing riders approach he mounts, only to find that all the commotion was caused by a single knight, who looks fierce as a lion and is angry at the destruction of his woods and house. They fight, he is unhorsed, and the knight leads away his steed. Then remembering his host's request, Calogrenanz, though much ashamed, walks back and as before is graciously received by the vavasor (580).

Arthur is so impressed by this tale that he decides to visit the spring and witness its wonders. Grieved since he wanted this adventure for himself and anxious to avenge Calogrenanz' shame, Yvain rides off alone ahead of the court and arrives at the spring. All happens as before except that the knight is fatally wounded and rides off pursued by Yvain. The knight rides into the castle, but Yvain is caught between two portcullises and finds himself virtually imprisoned there. A damsel, Lunete, approaches, warns him of his plight, and promises assistance; for once, on an errand to Arthur's court, Yvain had been the only knight to honor her. She gives him a ring which he is to return later, provides food, and warns him that as long as he remains seated on the couch, he will be in-

visible and consequently safe from searchers. Knights of the
castle now enter, eager to avenge their lord's death. Yvain is
secure, however, and they depart without finding him; yet
something equally serious happens, for he sees the widow and
falls deeply in love with her (1360–63):

> Son cuer an mainne s'anemie
> S'aimme la rien qui plus le het.
> Bien a vangiee et si nel set
> La dame la mort son seignor.

Love and shame hold Yvain there: love for the widow, shame
that he has no token to prove his exploit. Lunete promises to
make possible his escape. She also urges the lady to seek another husband, for all her knights are not worth a straw, and
there must be someone to defend the country against Arthur's
projected visit; but the lady, much incensed, bids her begone
and never to mention the subject again. Yet in a little while
she has a change of heart, reasons the matter out, and finds
herself in love with Yvain. The next time Lunete visits her,
the lady is very gracious, wishes to know all about Yvain, and
expresses a desire to see him at once. Lunete explains that it
will take several days for him to make the trip from Arthur's
court; in the meantime she bathes and grooms Yvain in preparation for his visit. She equips him richly and when she tells
him that he must yield to the lady's complete possession of his
body, even of his heart, he readily agrees (1942).

In the presence of the lady (who we soon learn is named
Laudine) he is at first speechless but finally confesses his
complete submission to her will. The knights are fully agreed
that she should take another husband and, much pleased with
Yvain's appearance, urge her to marry him at once; thus their
consent serves merely to strengthen her desire. The wedding
takes place and there is great rejoicing (2162).

As lord of the castle, Yvain receives Arthur and his men
and entertains them for a week. Gawain urges Yvain not to
adopt a life of indolence now that he is married and urges him

to accompany the King to the tournaments. Laudine rashly gives her consent but stipulates that if he does not return within a year of that day, he will forfeit her love. She gives him a protecting ring, and the company departs. Yvain is much distressed at leaving his lady, so much so that, though his body leaves her, his heart remains behind. He has great success in the tournaments and overstays his leave. A damsel comes bearing a greeting to Arthur and all of his knights except Yvain, who is denounced as a faithless and deceitful lover; she demands the return of the ring and, taking it from him, departs. Yvain now leaves the knights and is so distressed that he loses his senses and goes mad. He wanders into the forest and is cared for by a hermit. He is finally cured of his madness by the use of some of Morgan's salve, applied by one of three damsels who found him in the forest. They ride back together, Yvain is nursed and cared for at the castle and, when Count Aliers and his men come up to plunder, Yvain gains the praise of all for repelling them single-handed. He refuses to stay longer with them and rides off. In the next adventure he rescues a lion from a serpent; so grateful is the lion that he chooses Yvain as his life companion, and they prove inseparable (3484).

Returning to the spring, Yvain learns of Lunete's sad plight. She has been accused of treachery, and the only two men who will defend her are Gawain and Yvain, neither of whom is to be found. Laudine considered that Lunete had deceived her, and she is denounced to the court. She, however, is undaunted and says that she will provide a champion within forty days; but though she has visited many courts, no defender is to be found, and she is doomed to die on the morrow. Yvain sets out with the lion; he fights the giant, Harpin of the Mountain, thus rescues the King's four sons from death, and saves the daughter from being surrendered to the giant. The only reward he requests is that the four sons, the daughter, and the dwarf go to Gawain and inform him of his conduct; he gives his name as the Knight of the Lion (4291).

When Yvain comes to the chapel and spring, he finds the damsel has been dragged out and is now on the pyre ready to be burned. The treacherous seneschal and his two brothers try to urge him to desist, but Yvain refuses; they fight, the seneschal is killed, and the other two surrender. Laudine and Lunete are reconciled, and Yvain is urged to linger until both he and the lion are fully recovered from their wounds. He replies that he will not do this until his lady removes her displeasure and anger, names himself the Knight of the Lion, and rides off. Lunete recognizes him and promises help when the opportunity presents itself (4634).

Yvain now experiences several other adventures. He adopts the cause of a younger sister who is being cheated out of her inheritance and in the course of this undertaking visits the town of Pesme Aventure and frees three hundred maidens who are being held prisoner and cruelly treated by two sons of the devil. When he finally reaches Arthur's court, he finds himself obliged to engage in combat with Gawain, for he is the elder sister's champion. They fight all day but, at darkness, draw, each enraged at the other's prowess. Then they make themselves known to one another, and both are very happy again. The King awards the younger sister her rights. When the lion, who took no part in the struggle, comes up and joins Yvain, they recognize him as the killer of the giant, and he stays with Arthur until his wounds are cured (6526).

In the meantime Laudine is very uneasy on account of the ease and speed with which anyone can upset the peace of her domain by means of the magic fountain. Under oath she promises to do everything to help the Knight of the Lion to recover his lady's love and restore him to favor. Lunete rides out, discovers Yvain beneath the pine at the spring, and tells him of her mistress's oath. They ride back, and Laudine and Yvain are happily united (6803–5):

Mout an est a buen chief venuz ;
Qu'il est amez et chier tenuz
De sa dame et ele de lui.

As in the case of the troubadour poets, no space will be devoted to recounting and examining the commonplaces of courtly love as found in the works of Chrétien ; such studies as those of Neilson or Mott (see bibliography) quote and examine in detail passages of this type. The courtly love conceits are as ancient as the Chinese language and as modern as the latest movie ; the symptoms of love as mentioned in the chapter on Ovid are very much the same in the literature with which we are now concerned.[13]

With these three romances [14] of Chrétien firmly in mind, we may well stop and examine them individually for a moment before trying to synthesize Chrétien's work. Madame Lot-Borodine outlines the evolution of Chrétien's work in this fashion :

I. *L'idéal chevaleresque plus fort que l'amour.*
EREC
L'inégalité des deux sexes avec la domination du mari sur sa femme.
L'amour est un désir chez tous les deux.
L'épouse dévouée et fidèle.

II. *L'amour considéré comme la puissance souveraine.*
a) CLIGÉS
L'égalité parfaite des deux sexes.
L'amour est un désir raffiné : l'art d'aimer.
La grande amoureuse.
b) LANCELOT
L'harmonie rompue : la prédominance de la dame sur l'ami.
L'amour est un culte chez lui et l'amour est un caprice chez elle.
L'amante hautaine et tyrannique : l'adultère mondain.
c) YVAIN
La révolte vaine de l'homme au nom de la chevalerie contre le toute-puissance de l'amour.
Lui aime, elle se laisse aimer.
La dame impitoyable et cruelle.

III. *L'idéal religieux plus fort que l'amour.*

PERCEVAL

L'inégalité des deux sexes avec la femme sacrifiée au devoir
  abstrait ; la Quête du Graal.
L'amour redevenu désir instinctif.
L'amie tendre et soumise.

Ainsi tout se résume en ces trois mots qui ont hanté le rêve du moyen
âge : la Gloire, l'Amour, Dieu.[15]

Considering the lucidity and exactness with which the
above table traces Chrétien's development, one may feel that
further consideration of Chrétien's work is scarcely necessary.
Yet a good deal remains to be pointed out, particularly with
regard to the *Lancelot*, the spirit of which represents so fully
the courtly love code: "*La Charrette* . . . est donc le code
mis en action de l'amour absolu et avec beaucoup moins de
pédantisme que dans Cligés, où Chrétien est peut-être encore
trop près de ses études ovidiennes. Nous sommes plus loin du
petit Éros armé des flèches et du carquois et plus près d'une
psychologie un peu plus physiologique." [16]

There is one verse in the poem which fully characterizes the
ideal courtly lover and serves equally well as an epigram-
matic summary of the poem (3816–19):

> Mout est qui aimme obëissanz
> Et mout fet tost et volantiers,
> La ou il est amis antiers,
> Ce que s'amie doie pleire.

At the great tournament in which Lancelot fought, one of
Guenevere's ladies noticed Lancelot's remarkable devotion
and spoke to the Queen in this fashion (5928–34):

> Dame, onques ne vi
> Nul chevalier tant deboneire,
> Qu'il viaut si outreemant feire
> Trestot quanque vos li mandez ;
> Que se le voir m'an demandez,
> Autel chiere tot par igal
> Fet il del bien comme del mal.

From the beginning to the end of the poem Lancelot is absolutely devoted to Guenevere and always subject to her authority; there is not the slightest indication that he ever thought about anyone or anything else, for even in the course of his adventures all his movements are motivated solely by his love for the Queen. He is always ready to satisfy her slightest whim; he will risk everything to avenge her upon her ravisher. "L'amour règne dans son âme avec une tyrannie sans nul contre-poids; il y est le principe des actions les plus hardies et les plus nobles, comme il le fait passer par-dessus toutes les considérations, même de gloire et de conscience. C'est le type absolu de l'amoureux tel qu'il a longtemps été conçu dans la poésie, et rêvé, sinon réalisé, dans la vie." [17] He is then the *amis antiers* and, as such, Chrétien's supreme triumph in character portrayal and psychological analysis. In this respect Chrétien is definitely linked with the troubadours; for as was pointed out in the preceding chapter, the idea of submission and devotion to one's lady is one of the distinguishing characteristics of the Provençal love lyric.[18] Especially important at the moment are Cross and Nitze's conclusions on this point:

Thus, there can be no doubt that *l'amour courtois* as it is presented to us in Chrétien's story of Lancelot owes its distinctive mark to the influence of the troubadours. There, and not in Ovid, nor in Geoffrey, nor in Wace, nor in the *Eneas*, is the idea developed of the *amis antiers:* the lover who loves even when his passion appears unrequited and who is willing to sacrifice all for Love. On the other hand, all evidence is lacking to show that the early troubadours organized this idea into the compact system that we find in the *Charrete* and in Andreas' *De Amore*. That was the achievement of Mary of Champagne, of her chaplain, Andreas, and of Chrétien de Troyes.[19]

What the characteristics of this system were has been admirably stated by Gaston Paris in his famous *Lancelot* article already referred to.[20] Frequent quotation has made it almost a classic utterance, and hence it deserves to be quoted in full at this point:

1. Il est illégitime, furtif. On ne conçoit pas de rapports pareils entre mari et femme ; la crainte perpétuelle de l'amant de perdre sa maîtresse, de ne plus être digne d'elle, de lui déplaire en quoi que ce soit, ne peut se concilier avec la possession calme et publique ; c'est au don sans cesse révocable d'elle-même, au sacrifice énorme qu'elle a fait, au risque qu'elle court constamment, que la femme doit la supériorité que l'amant lui reconnaît.

2. A cause de cela, l'amant est toujours devant la femme dans une position inférieure, dans une timidité que rien ne rassure, dans une perpétuel tremblement, bien qu'il soit d'ailleurs en toutes rencontres le plus hardi des guerriers. Elle au contraire, tout en l'aimant sincèrement, se montre avec lui capricieuse, souvent injuste, hautaine, dédaigneuse ; elle lui fait sentir à chaque moment qu'il peut la perdre et qu'à la moindre faute contre le code de l'amour il la perdra.

3. Pour être digne de la tendresse qu'il souhaite ou qu'il a déjà obtenue, il accomplit toutes les prouesses imaginable, et elle de son côté songe toujours à le rendre meilleur, à le faire plus 'valoir' ; ses caprices apparents, ses rigueurs passagères, ont même d'ordinaire ce but, et ne sont que des moyens ou de raffiner son amour ou d'exalter son courage.

4. Enfin, et c'est ce qui résume tout le reste, l'amour est un art, une science, une vertu, qui a ses règles tout comme la chevalerie ou la courtoisie, règles qu'on possède et qu'on applique mieux à mesure qu'on a fait plus de progrès, et auxquelles on ne doit pas manquer sous peine d'être jugé indigne.[21]

That this is precisely the type of love elaborated in the *Lancelot* is of course self-evident ; that the summary does not apply equally to all of Chrétien's romances is likewise clear.[22] The *Cligés*, in its portrayal of the feelings of both the lovers, as well as on account of their marriage, does not come up to this standard, while the later *Yvain* surpasses it ; for here the lover and his lady are finally married. Yet save in this one respect the whole poem is developed fully in accord with the most approved courtly love teaching. It is this fact which caused Mme Lot-Borodine to characterize it as the work of Chrétien "la plus conforme à l'idéal de l'art courtois." [23]

In an article on Ovid and Chrétien de Troyes, F. E. Guyer, referring to this analysis, states that it "could be applied to Ovidian love with very little modification." [24] This statement certainly needs qualification, for though Chrétien and Ovid have many points in common, there is scant justification for so sweeping a statement as that just quoted. As to Paris' first point, both Chrétien and Ovid are in accord; love is something that must be kept secret and carried on in a clandestine manner if it is to be successful. That the lover always occupies an inferior position is quite true, as we have seen in Chrétien's work; but it is not at all correct to apply the remark to Ovid; as a general thing he treats the lover and lady as equals and, furthermore, the fact that he does not distinguish between the love of married women and of courtesans proves that he has no such clear-cut distinction in mind. The third point is only in part correct. In the case of both writers the lover accomplishes wonderful exploits solely to please his lady and win her favor, but the Ovidian lady is not at all concerned with the moral or spiritual improvement of her lover; "à le faire plus 'valoir' " is probably furthest from her thoughts. It must be insisted that there is a distinct difference between Ovid's view of love as an art and that of Chrétien and the courtly school; it is, to be sure, largely a matter of degree rather than of any essential difference, just as we are accustomed to speak of nineteenth-century Germany; yet what a difference there is between the loose-knit Germany of the post-Napoleonic era and the federated empire under Bismarck! In similar fashion Ovid's work may be regarded as an art of love, but it is quite different from the medieval conception of love as an art. This was no doubt due to the love of authority, so characteristic of the Middle Ages; it is for that reason we find love duly codified and systematized in approved philosophical fashion in the *De Amore*. "Le moyen âge, avec sa tendance logicienne et généralisatrice, devait transformer en rigides maximes les frivoles préceptes de cette théorie mondaine." [25] The "frivoles préceptes" of Ovid on the one hand and the "rigides maximes" of Andreas on the other clearly indicate what I meant when I stated above that Ovid's view of love as an art and that of Chrétien and the courtly school are distinctly different.

There is one more point which may be mentioned in speaking of Ovid and Chrétien and that is the ennobling power of love. The Latin poet regarded love as a debasing force, equally fatal to both the lover and his mistress. The French romancer, however, as we have seen, takes the opposite point of view and portrays the lover as strengthened and ennobled by love, while the lady is presented in varying degrees of idealization. This treatment of the lovers was probably due as much to the all-pervasive influence of the twelfth-century Church as to that of the troubadour lyrics; where the influence of the latter stops and the former begins is well-nigh impossible to establish.

This study of the northern French concept of courtly love as exemplified in the work of Chrétien de Troyes may be brought to an appropriate close by quoting Cross and Nitze's conclusions on Chrétien's treatment of love:

. . . There are three phases in the evolution—if that be the right word—of Chrétien's concept of the lover. The first may be termed "chivalric." It is based on the social equality of the sexes, as illustrated by Geoffrey of Monmouth's description of the Arthurian court. Here the lover is the social counterpart of his beloved; she stimulates him to bravery, he her to loyalty. To quote once more the words of the "exemplar" of chivalry:

> Por la noblesce de s'amie
> Fait juvenes hum chevalerie.

While the Ovidian *oisdive* (*otium*) belongs to this phase, chivalry steps in to correct it.

The second phase, due more particularly to the direct influence of the Latin poet and of the *Eneas*, may be called Ovidian. This aspect is illustrated by the *Cligés*, but also by the *Charrete*, and, in a diminishing degree, by the *Ivain*. To it are due the *plets d'amor*, or love-soliloquies; the *signa* of the lover afflicted as if by a disease; to some degree, the love-madness (familiar also to the Celts); and a great deal of the imagery the poet employs.

The third phase is Provençal. Its essence consists in the conception of Love as an end in herself. Not merely as an art, for that is clearly Ovidian, but as an art with the triumph of Love as its supreme aim. This phase is worked out as a social "system" in the *Tractatus de amore* of Andreas Capellanus, and illustrated in the *Roman de la Charrete*. It was, so Dante tells us, from the prose *Lancelot*, which incorporates Chrétien's romance, that Paolo and Francesca drew the fire of their passion, with the result that

Quel giorno più non vi leggemmo avante.[26]

IV

ANDREAS CAPELLANUS

T
HE *De Amore*, that unique treatise on medieval love which has received frequent mention in these pages, deserves particularly to be considered in connection with Chrétien's work, for the ideas of both Andreas and Chrétien are much the same.[1] Details of the author's life, scanty though they are, and discussions of the probable date of composition of the book need not detain us here.[2] It is sufficient to know that he was sometime chaplain to Marie, Countess of Champagne; hence he must have been living during her lifetime and apparently wrote his book within the years 1174 and 1190.

Probably the best summary of the *De Amore* is the concise account which serves as an introduction to the volume, the *accessus ad amoris tractatum* as it is termed: "First, therefore, we are to see what love is and why it is called love, and what is the effect of love, and among whom love may exist, how love is acquired, retained, augmented, diminished, brought to an end and of the idea of mutual love, and what one of the lovers should do if the other breaks his promise."[3] Two of the three books are devoted to the exposition of love along these lines while the third, strangely enough, is practically a renunciation of the advice detailed in the first two;[4] this is of passing interest since it parallels Ovid's treatment of love and foreshadows Chaucer's famous passage, the epilogue to the *Troilus*. This book is a scathing denunciation of women and an analysis of the grounds on which love is to be avoided or rejected. The two concluding paragraphs graphically reflect the spirit which pervades Book III:

Sumas ergo, Gualteri, salubrem tibi a nobis propinatam doctrinam et mundi penitus vanitates omittas, ut, quum venerit sponsus nuptias celebrare maiores, et clamor surrexerit in nocte, sis praeparatus cum lampadibus occurrere sibi ornatis secumque ad nuptias intreire divinas, nec te oporteat tempore opportunitatis instantis tuae lampadis serotina ornamenta disquirere et ad sponsi domum ianua clausa venire ac verecundam vocem audire.

Studeas ergo, Gualteri, lampades semper ornatas habere, id est caritatis et bonorum operum ornamenta tenere. Memento etiam vigilare semper, ne in peccatis dormiendo te inveniat sponsi repentinus adventus. Cave igitur, Gualteri, amoris exercere mandata et continua vigilatione labora, ut, quum venerit sponsus, inveniat te vigilantem, nec de corporis iuventute confisum mundana delectatio te faciat in peccati dormitione iacere ac de sponsi tarditate securum, quia, eiusdem sponsi voce testante, nescimus diem neque horam.[5]

Far different from this sort of thing, however, is the tone which characterizes the elaborate analyses of Books I and II. With all the minuteness of a scholastic treatise and the orderly arrangement of a philosophical disquisition the author discusses love in all its aspects. Since this section comprises by far the greater part of the work—312 of the 361 pages in Trojel's edition—the following paragraphs will attempt, not a running summary of the contents, but rather a detailed exposition of certain portions which are of particular value in setting forth the essence of the courtly love system as understood and interpreted by a contemporary. For this purpose the sixth chapter of Book I is most significant in both importance and extent (filling 205 of the 361 pages); it is entitled: "In what manner love may be acquired and in how many ways." [6] These are five: "bodily beauty, uprightness of character, fluent eloquence of conversation, abundance of riches, and the easy granting of anything desired," [7] i. e., great generosity. The author adds, however, that the last two means should not be accredited and ought to be expelled from the court of love, "ab aula propulsandos amoris."

Andreas now proceeds to explain the part of conversation in love-making. Howsoever eloquent one may be, that alone and unaided will not necessarily awaken love in the heart of the beloved; but really worth-while conversation will add to the stings of love and thereby prove the worth of the suitor.[8] How this is to be accomplished is brought out by means of a series of eight conversations carried on by lovers of the same or varying social rank: a plebeian man to a plebeian woman, a plebeian man to a noble woman, a plebeian man to a more noble woman, a noble man to a plebeian woman, a noble man to a noble woman, a more noble man to a plebeian woman, a more noble man to a noble woman, and finally a more noble man to a more noble woman. These conversations as a whole form an interesting body of evidence of great cultural value in estimating this particular phase of medieval social life. Any one of them could be considered representative, but I have chosen for analysis the fifth one, that of the noble man with a noble woman (*loquitur nobilis nobili*), chiefly because it contains the shorter code of rules formulated by Andreas; the longer will be discussed in its proper place later on.[9]

In this conversation the man begins almost immediately to express his great admiration for and devotion to the lady; she, however, is quite obdurate and, though agreeing to let the suitor see her frequently, nevertheless remains firm in her determination never to become subject to Venus.[10] Undaunted the lover continues his praise, though he makes it a bit less flattering now, for he tells her of the pains and torments she will bring upon herself by not being generous with her love; but she remains unmoved: the whole world will not cause her to change her opinion.[11] However, she asks him to tell her something about all these torments, and the suitor then relates in great detail his dream about the palace of Love. As reported, it is a handsome structure, quadrangular in shape, situated at the very center of the world. Here dwells Love with three groups of ladies. The door facing the east belongs to Love, while the remaining doors are for the others; the ladies at the south keep their door always open and linger about its threshold, but those at the west door not only keep it open but wander around outside. Entirely different from these are the ladies at the north door who keep it shut and never know what is going on outside the palace.

The lady does not understand this account and is quite mystified. At her request the man explains that those at the south door are those who are generous with their love, yet hesitate and consider well before bestowing it; those at the west gate are ordinary women (*mulieres communes*) who accept all, reject none, and hence are freely accessible to the physical passion of all.[12] The ladies at the north door accept no suitors and deny entry to everyone. These three groups are respectively those who love and do not refuse worthy lovers; those who do not really love but accept all, i. e., the prostitutes (*meretrices*); and, thirdly, those who refuse to love.

The lady admits that she belongs at the north door and confesses that she feels secure rather than abused or reviled on that account.[13] As a final effort the suitor commands her to listen while he describes the endless punishments prepared for her. One day while he was riding with Robert the Esquire (*armiger*) and many other knights through the royal forest of "Francia," he came upon a most delightful and luxuriant meadow where they stopped and rested. When they were ready to proceed, the others had no difficulty in finding their horses, but his had wandered some distance away; consequently by the time he had recovered it the others had ridden out of sight. Yet, looking around, he rejoiced to see at the other end of the meadow people who he supposed were his former companions; on riding nearer, however, he found them to be complete strangers. They were all beautifully attired and one of them, wearing a golden crown, was particularly handsome and distinguished. Following him was a group of beautiful women, after whom came a band of knights to keep away the wrangling mob close behind; this was composed of both men and women making so much noise that their good intentions as suitors were turned into helplessness and distress. A third and last group of ladies, very beautiful to be sure but dressed in a garb both distasteful and outmoded, completed this motley crowd. They were wearing garments made of fox skin, though it was midsummer, and riding ugly, lean nags without either bridle or saddle. No one assisted them or gave them any attention.

On an ugly, limping horse behind all these people rode a beautiful lady who called the lover to her and told him he would not find his master there, that he had already ridden far in another direction. He begs her to show him the right way, but she is unable to do this until the crowd arrives at the place where it belongs. At his request, however, she explains the full significance of all this crew: the knight with the golden crown is the God of Love; the first group of ladies are those who loved wisely and truly and are now enjoying their reward; the second are those unclean women who continually and promiscuously indulged their sensual appetites; the last group is made up of those women who during their lives refused to love. The lady who has been acting as his informer belongs to this unhappy class. He realizes how great are the rewards and how terrible the punishments of love and begs her to allow him to ride away immediately so that he may inform all women. She responds that he must wait until he has become familiar with not only their torments but also their joy and bliss.

During this conversation they have been riding all the time and are now arrived at a meadow of such beauty and charm that no mortal man might ever see the like. This space was divided into three circles. In the center of the first one, the innermost, was an ancient tree from whose roots gushed forth a wonderful nectar-like spring; this spring flowed in several directions and refreshed everything within the circle. Near the tree sat the Goddess of Love on a richly decorated throne. This first circle was called *amoenitas* because everything charming and delightful was to be found there. The second circle completely surrounding the first was called *humiditas*, for several of the streams from *amoenitas* overflowed and quite submerged it. Though the water was so cold here that it would not support life, yet the heat was terrific and no trees provided shade. *Siccitas* was the name of the third and outermost circle; here everything had dried up, the sun shone incessantly, and the earth was as hot as a fiery furnace.

A beautiful path led through these two circles to *amoenitatem;* no one traveling along it was aware of these torments. The King of Love crossed by means of this road and took his place beside the Queen; the first group of women followed, each one taking her place on a handsomely decorated chair; the knights sat where they wished. Here was joy and bliss indescribable.[14] The second group of women followed but could come up only to the edge of the first circle. *Humiditas* was their allotted territory and there, complaining loudly, they were obliged to remain. So likewise was the third group confined to *siccitatem;* these women who had refused to love suffered most of all, for the ground was so hot that they could not stand and the only place where they could sit was on the bundles of thorns which were lying about but were being moved constantly.

Much impressed, the lover now begs once more for permission to leave, but his companion says that she cannot allow that; he must first dismount and then, when the King approaches, seek the favor from him; and whatever he commands, the lover must not fail to do.[15] Brought to the King, he thanks him for having allowed him to see all these wonders, asks him to accept him as his servant, begs to know the rules of love, and requests that he release from her torments the woman who has acted as his guide. The monarch replies that the lover has been allowed to see all these things in order to spread the fame of the King of Love, and he commands him to relate all that he has seen to any woman who seems to be straying from the path of love, in order that her reward will be bliss and not torment. He then informs him that the twelve chief rules of love are:

Duodecim autem scias esse principalia quae sequuntur amoris praecepta:

I. Avaritiam sicut nocivam pestem effugias et eius contrarium amplectaris.

II. Castitatem servare debes amanti.

III. Alterius idonee copulatam amori scienter subvertere non coneris.

IV. Eius non cures amorem eligere, cum qua naturalis nuptias contrahere prohibet tibi pudor.

V. Mendacia omnino vitare memento.

VI. Amoris tui secretarios noli plures habere.

VII. Dominarum praeceptis in omnibus obediens semper studeas amoris aggregari militiae.

VIII. In amoris praestando et recipiendo solatia omnis debet verecundiae pudor adesse.

IX. Maledicus esse non debes.

X. Amantium noli existere propalator.

XI. In omnibus urbanum te constituas et curialem.

XII. In amoris exercendo solatia voluntatem non excedas amantis.[16]

It need hardly be added that after this the *nobilis-nobili* conversation came to a speedy and happy conclusion: the lady chose the south door!

The seventh dialogue, that between the more noble man and the noble woman, is of interest because of the spirited discussion as to whether true love can exist between married couples. The man maintains that it cannot while the woman as stoutly asserts the opposite. They finally agree to submit the case to a third party and by mutual agreement write to the Countess of Champagne. She replies under date of May 7, 1174, and upholds the man, i. e., agrees that love cannot exist between married couples;[17] for "real jealousy cannot be found among them; without it true love cannot exist as its own rule states: 'who is not jealous cannot love.' "[18] The Countess adds that she had rendered this decision after mature reflection and that it has been approved with the advice of many ladies.[19]

Four of the six remaining chapters of Book I deal with the love of clergymen, nuns, peasants, and harlots respectively; two others treat of love obtained by money and of love too quickly granted.[20] Book II bears the title: *Qualiter amor retineatur*. The first chapter describes how love once acquired

may be preserved; chapters II, III, and IV relate how it may
be increased, diminished, and finally brought to an end. The
fifth chapter reveals how love for another may be recognized,
while the sixth deals with unfaithfulness. Chapter VII contains the twenty-one decisions rendered in as many different
love disputes. Chapter VIII contains the all-important *regulae amoris*, the second or longer code referred to above.[21]
The following paragraph gives a brief account of the discovery of these laws.

A British knight was riding through the royal wood on his
way to visit King Arthur when suddenly a beautiful maiden
on a handsomely equipped horse rode up and informed him
that without her help he could accomplish nothing. She added
further, just as his beloved at home had told him, that he
would not succeed in his love affair until he brought her the
victorious falcon which is said to sit on a golden perch at Arthur's court. The knight was greatly astonished at her knowing all this and begged her assistance in overcoming all the
difficulties he must meet before his lady will accept him.
Obligingly, she furnished him with her horse, which she said
would carry him wherever he wished to go, and furthermore
she urged him to keep on undaunted until he accomplished
his purpose. This he did, undergoing several strange adventures but finally arriving at Arthur's palace. There after
proving his worth in combat before the assembled court, he
was allowed to take the falcon; as he did so, he saw a small
sheet of paper (*chartulam*) with writing on it; this was fas-
tened with a golden chain to the pole on which the falcon
perched. Reading the note he found that "this is the letter in
which are written the rules of love that the King of Love himself has proclaimed with his own mouth. You must take this
with you and make the rules known to lovers, if you wish to
carry the falcon away peacefully." [22] He took the letter,
sought and obtained permission to leave, and rode forth.
After going a short distance, he met the same damsel who
had been of assistance to him. She rejoiced over his victory and

allowed him to return to Britain, not without reminding him, however, that if he should ever yearn for her, she might be found here in this same place. After receiving thirteen kisses he rode off, read the love rules, and made them known to all the world. They are thirty-one in number and may be referred to as the "longer code":

Sunt autem regulae tales:
    I. Causa coniugii ab amore non est excusatio recta.
    II. Qui non zelat, amare non potest.
    III. Nemo duplici potest amore ligari.
    IV. Semper amorem crescere vel minui constat.
    V. Non est sapidum, quod amans ab invito sumit coamante.
    VI. Masculus non solet nisi plena pubertate amare.
    VII. Biennalis viduitas pro amante defuncto superstiti prae-scribitur amanti.
    VIII. Nemo sine rationis excessu suo debet amore privari.
    IX. Amare nemo potest, nisi qui amoris svasione compellitur.
    X. Amor semper consvevit ab avaritiae domiciliis exsulare.
    XI. Non decet amare, quarum pudor est nuptias affectare.
    XII. Verus amans alterius nisi sui coamantis ex affectu non cupit amplexus.
    XIII. Amor raro consvevit durare vulgatus.
    XIV. Facilis perceptio contemptibilem reddit amorem, difficilis eum carum facit haberi.
    XV. Omnis consvevit amans in coamantis aspectu pallescere.
    XVI. In repentina coamantis visione cor contremescit amantis.
    XVII. Novus amor veterem compellit abire.
    XVIII. Probitas sola quemque dignum facit amore.
    XIX. Si amor minuatur, cito deficit et raro convalescit.
    XX. Amorosus semper est timorosus.
    XXI. Ex vera zelotypia affectus semper crescit amandi.
    XXII. De coamante suspicione percepta zelus et affectus crescit amandi.
    XXIII. Minus dormit et edit, quem amoris cogitatio vexat.
    XXIV. Quilibet amantis actus in coamantis cogitatione finitur.
    XXV. Verus amans nil bonum credit nisi, quod cogitat coamanti placere.
    XXVI. Amor nil posset amori denegare.
    XXVII. Amans coamantis solatiis satiari non potest.
    XXVIII. Modica praesumptio cogit amantem de coamante suspicari sinistra.

XXIX. Non solet amare, quem nimia voluptatis abundantia vexat.
XXX. Verus amans assidua sine intermissione coamantis imaginatione detinetur.
XXXI. Unam feminam nil prohibet a duobus amari et a duabus mulieribus unum.[23]

This second part of the tract is brought quickly to an end. We are told how the lover returned and made the rules of love known to the lady for whose sake he undertook all these adventures; in return she rewarded him with her love and then called to her court many knights and ladies to whom she proclaimed the rules. In this way they were made known and were spread throughout the world.[24]

The above account presents a general idea of the *De Amore* and of the author's method of handling his material. It now remains to examine the work in more detail in order to indicate the teaching of Andreas on various points as well as to grasp more exactly his interpretation of medieval love doctrine, so characteristically that of the late twelfth century, the period in which Provençal poetry reached its zenith.

A favorite idea that Andreas strives to bring home by frequent repetition is the troubadour notion of love as the source of all good, the fountain of all virtues and benefits; "qui omnium dicitur fons et origo bonorum," as is noted in the conversation of the noble man with the noble lady (81); "o, quam mira res est amor, qui tantis facit hominem fulgere virtutibus tantisque docet quemlibet bonis moribus abundare" (10). The same attitude is reflected in only slightly different fashion in this statement: "Sed amore in orbe nihil appetibilius reperitur, quum ex eo omnis boni procedat instructio, et sine eo nihil boni aliquis operetur in orbe" (87–88). The idea receives frequent mention, but there is no need to multiply these examples.[25]

Closely akin to this view is that of love as an ennobling power, a force able to transform a man of low birth into one of true nobility of spirit. This is mentioned as one of the first effects of love: ". . . infimos natu etiam morum novit nobilitate ditare" (9–10). In another passage it is declared to be superior to beauty, riches, and all other things: ". . . morum atque probitas sola est, quae vera facit hominem nobilitate beari et rutilanti forma pollere. . . . Non forma, non corporis cultus, non etiam opulentia rerum, sed sola fuit morum probitas, quae primitus nobilitate distinxit homines ac generis induxit differentiam" (17–18); for just as there are many who, though members of the nobility, are in no other respects noble, so likewise are there many of humble birth who otherwise qualify as noble. At the very opening of the conversation between the ordinary man and the more noble lady ("plebeius nobiliori feminae"), it is stated very definitely that moral uprightness and virtue must atone for his lowly birth: "Verecundum namque nimis nobili videtur mulieri exsistere et in eius plurimum contumeliam redundare, si inferioris ordinis sibi desposcat amorem, superiori et medio praetermissis ordinibus, nisi morum probitas supereffluente valeat penso nobilitatis compensationem inducere" (54). Such instances as these might be multiplied almost indefinitely; [26] yet they are probably sufficient to show that, here again, Andreas has much in common with the troubadours. This is also true of the next point, love as the inspirer of great deeds. In the conversation of the more noble man with the noble lady (*nobilior nobili*), he prays God to send him deeds to perform which are worthy of her; nothing can keep him from this; all shall redound to her honor: "Et ego bona semper cuncta, quae fecero, vestris volo laudibus indulgere et per omnia vestro nomini deservire. Nam quidquid boni peregero, intuitu vestri et assidua contemplatione noveritis esse perfectum" (126). This concept is not expressed so definitely again, but it is implied throughout the book.

Andreas' views on chastity are of especial interest, for the charge is frequently made that the *De Amore* is a licentious work, that it is more or less a defense and glorification of sexual love.[27] There is slight basis for this point of view. The spirit of the book is entirely worldly, it is true, but that does not mean that it is therefore wholly the work of the devil. There are numerous passages scattered through it urging moderation and restraint and forcing one to the conclusion that the author had a high ideal of womanhood as well as considerable moral sense. For example, the twenty-ninth rule states: "Non solet amare, quem nimia voluptatis abundantia vexat" (311). Voluptuousness has no place at the court of love: "Et dicitur esse idem in femina facilis rei petitae concessio, quod in homine nimia voluptatis abundantia, quam constat ab amoris aula penitus exsulare" (234). And the sentence following this statement is of especial significance, for it denounces sensual pleasures and calls that man a dog who is moved by such thoughts: "Non amator sed adulterator vocatur amoris ac simulator et erit cane deterior impudico" (234). As if this were not enough, he goes on to call the man a dunce, a blockhead: "Inmo impetuosus meretur asinus iudicari, quem tanta corporis petulantia movet, ut unius se non possit affectioni astringere" (234). The general conclusion of all this is that the man, realizing the seriousness of the situation, should be on his guard and should keep away from any woman who may be too easily approached: "Ergo tibi evidenter apparet, quod nimiam voluptatis abundantiam prorsus teneris abiicere et mulieris, in qua facilem petitae rei concessionem cognoveris, amorem tibi non expedit postulare" (234–35).

In another passage Andreas praises love as the source of chastity, for it keeps the lover devoted to his lady and by making him think of her alone thus keeps him from temptation: "Est et aliud quiddam in amore non brevi sermone laudandum, quia amor reddit hominem castitatis quasi virtute decoratum, quia vix posset de alterius etiam formosae cogitare amplexu, qui unius radio fulget amoris. Est enim suae menti, dum de amore suo plenarie cogitat, mulieris cuiuslibet horridus et incultus aspectus" (10). Andreas is also careful to make a sharp distinction between chaste and impure love (*purus* and *mixtus*). The former springs from the affection which draws two lovers together: "Et purus quidem amor est, qui omnimoda dilectionis affectione duorum amantium corda coniungit" (182). This love is extolled, for it is the source of uprightness and of good: "Amor iste tantae dignoscitur esse virtutis, quod ex eo totius probitatis origo descendit, et nulle inde procedit iniuria . . ." (183). *Amor mixtus*, on the other hand, has its origin in sensual desires: "Mixtus vero amor dicitur ille, qui omni carnis delectationi suum praestat effectum et in extremo Veneris opere terminatur" (183). This love, however, is short-lived, hateful to God, and fraught with dangers (183); yet Andreas is unable to condemn it, for it too is true love (*verus amor*) and as such a source of noble works (*origo bonorum*); he has drawn these distinctions, he states, in order to show which kind of love is to be preferred. In all fairness to Andreas, it should be insisted that, although he admits the existence of two kinds of love and does not condemn the fleshly, yet by the very emphasis which he continually places on the chaste variety, he does much to exonerate himself from a charge of licentiousness.[28]

Andreas frequently points out the incompatibility of love and marriage. It is implied in the first of the longer rules: "Causa coniugii ab amore non est excusatio recta" (310) and expressed very definitely in the letter of the Countess of Champagne quoted above (p. 61); and a little further on in the same letter this decision is repeated: "Merito ergo inter coniugatos sua non poterit amor iura cognoscere" (154). This doctrine is quite in keeping with the troubadour teaching and practice as we have pointed out elsewhere.[29] No doubt it was the attitude of the Church which kept more romancers from incorporating this rule in their poems. Chrétien's *Lancelot* and the later Provençal *Flamenca* are the only two romances of any great importance in which the lover and his lady are not finally united in marriage; yet, as in the case of the *Cligés*, the extra-conjugal spirit, if one may use such a term, pervades many of them.[30]

There is so much of interest in the *De Amore* that this examination of it could be extended almost indefinitely. It would be especially instructive to point out the innumerable points it has in common with Chrétien's work, especially the *Lancelot*, but it is hoped that the discussions of both of these works have been sufficiently lucid for the reader to observe for himself what are, after all, very obvious facts.[31] Since the theory of love elaborated by Andreas is precisely the same as that of Chrétien, there is little point in repeating the conclusions reached in the previous chapter. It remains only to insist that, though the *De Amore* is one of the most Ovidian documents of the Middle Ages, it nevertheless owes a great deal to the troubadours, a fact which, along with the spiritual training of its author, helps to explain its many inconsistencies as well as its numerous departures from the teaching of Ovid. But in the final estimate, of course, we must think of it as neither Ovidian nor Provençal but rather as a remarkable document faithfully reflecting what may easily have been, in courtly circles, the usual social ideal (more or less lived up to) in northern France of the late twelfth century.[32]

V

ITALY AND
IL DOLCE STIL NUOVO

TALIAN literature as such cannot be said to have existed
before the thirteenth century. There is undoubtedly
some oral tradition behind the earliest poems, but so far
as may be inferred that tradition was not particularly strong
nor was it far-reaching in its effects. In most countries the
early literature is characteristically fresh and spontaneous,
but this is decidedly not the case with Italy. A great deal of
the early writing has no doubt been lost; but judging from
what remains, one may say that Italian poetry in its beginnings is sadly uninspired and disappointingly imitative.
There is none of the spirit and intensity so characteristic of
much of the early troubadour poetry; on the contrary the
poetry of the earliest writers, the so-called Sicilian school, is
little more than transplanted Provençal. It remained for long
something entirely foreign to the new soil.

This is not the place to discuss the work of the early north
Italian poets who wrote in Provençal. Geographical location
and linguistic affinity early favored intercourse between
Provence and Italy, and consequently it is not surprising to
learn that the troubadours came south as early as the end of
the twelfth century. Among the more prominent of these,
some of whom have been mentioned in chapter II, were Peire
Vidal, Rambaut de Vaqueiras, Aimeric de Pegulhan, and
Gaucelm Faidit. Of the oldest imitators of these poets, Man-
fred Lancia and Alberto Malaspina, scarcely anything survives; but there is extant a considerable part of the work of
Rambertino Buvallello, who wrote in the early thirteenth
century, as well as the later writers, Lanfranc Cigala, Simone

and Perceval Doria, Jacopo Grillo, Bonifacio Calvi, and others. Yet the work of all these men, inspired by troubadour models and written for the most part in the Provençal tongue, belongs to the history of Provençal rather than to that of Italian poetry. These poets contributed nothing new and consequently need receive no further consideration; study of their work would unnecessarily swell the evidence already presented in the chapter on the troubadour lyric without affecting the conclusions. These north Italian writers are mentioned here solely to emphasize the fact that there were in thirteenth-century Italy two schools of poetry practically contemporaneous; each wrote in a different language and, though both had a common ancestor, they were entirely separate developments.

Courtly love as an outgrowth and reflection of the feudal system is unknown in Italy for the simple reason that chivalry and the feudal system never took root in Italian soil. The importance of this fact is stated by Thomas F. Crane in these words:

The city, not the castle, was the seat of social life, and the rapid absorption of the feudal lords into the cities rendered Italian life from the beginning very different from life in Provence or the North of France. The love which was the expression of chivalry never became general throughout Italy, but was, like the imitation of Provençal poetry, a fashionable fancy. It is true that the early Italian poetry which was written in imitation of the poetry of the Troubadours accepted the conventional love of Chivalry. . . . Still, this was essentially a matter of imitation and was foreign to Italian modes of life and thought.[1]

For this reason the poetry of the Sicilian school never attained a vigorous growth but on the contrary, after a comparatively short time, nearly died out completely. It was at the court of Frederick II, King of Sicily, that the Provençal influence was most strongly felt; consequently we may pause here for a moment to characterize the work of this group.

Since Sicilian social life was itself an imitation, there is of course no reason for expecting that the literature reflecting that life should be other than imitative and artificial. Though the great literary monuments and traditions of other lands (the Arabian Nights, the Round Table, Tristan and Iseult, et cetera) had made their way into Italy and had become familiar to the people, yet they did not profoundly affect their inmost beings. The Sicilian love poetry, to single out one type, seems strange until its relation to the poetic production of other lands is fully understood. In this poetry the ladies and gentlemen are not individuals but types: the lady possesses all the stereotyped qualities of the conventional heroine of romance, while the man is the usual chivalric hero. Such poetry is finely wrought and delicately conceived; indeed, this very perfection of imitation makes other and more original work oftentimes seem somewhat inferior. Yet such poetry is too calm and detached; it is not impassioned and does not arouse any deep emotion in the reader. It is written too much according to certain rules and reflects personal and intense feeling scarcely at all. It is a very distinct type of poetry and is, as Bertoni points out, a kind of imitation that approaches the creative: "Abbiamo talvolta nella prima lirica meridionale una forma speciale di imitazione, che potrebbe dirsi, essa stessa, creazione, in quanto il sentimento del poeta, lungi dall'esserne compresso, ne trabocca. La gioia di imitare ciò che risponde ad esigenze proprie, la gioia di superare nella tecnica i modelli imitati, è anch'essa fonte di commozione." [2]

The native Italian poetry which sprang up at the Sicilian court possesses none of the invigorating qualities one expects to find in an incipient literature but is, rather, quite devoid of spirit, wanting in originality, almost totally artificial. There is no depth, feeling, or poignancy; it is not the outburst of a soul demanding expression but is, on the contrary, the conventional representation of pleasant conceits and commonplace ideas. The convention followed, that of the troubadours, was both the life and death of this poetry. This

opinion expressed by the distinguished critic of early Italian
literature, Adolf Gaspary, seems to be well founded:

Die provenzialische Poesie hat . . . der ältesten italienischen Lyrik
den Ursprung gegeben und einen sehr ausgedehnten Einfluss auf
dieselbe ausgeübt. Allein diese conventionelle Dichtweise konnte nur
ein vorübergehendes Dasein fristen, da ihr die Grundlage im wir-
klichen Leben fehlte, und für die Fortentwickelung der italienischen
Poesie bedurfte es eines neuen und frischeren Geistes, der die alten
Formen erfüllte und wiederbelebte.[3]

In both feeling and expression the early Italian lyric is completely Provençal. Frederick II as a patron of learning encouraged the writing of poetry in this manner and, setting
the royal example by composing poems in the most stereotyped troubadour fashion, might also be said to have imposed
that style on his court. Among the poets of the early school
there were, in addition to Frederick II already mentioned,
his son Enzo, King of Sardinia, Pier delle Vigne, Jacopo da
Lentino, Istefano da Messina, Rugieri d'Amici, and Guido
delle Colonne. The poetry of all these writers is so singularly
lacking in freshness and originality that there is no object
in presenting a detailed analysis of it. Gaspary's characterization of this group is so admirable that it is here given at
length:

The theme of the troubadour poetry, chivalrous love, now reappears
in the same forms that had previously served for its expression. . . .
This circle of ideas in which the Provençal love poetry moved, had in
Provençal literature itself given rise already to much that was conventional and monotonous. But in Provence it was at home; here this
conception of love had developed, having its origin in an actual though
artificial condition of things existing among the upper classes. On that
account the earlier poetic efforts, at any rate, do not lack warmth of
sentiment, and the absence of variety in the subject-matter is often
atoned for by the tenderness and delicacy of the treatment. But when
Provençal poetry was to bear new fruit in Italy, it had already passed
the period of its full splendor, and was rapidly approaching decline.
And the ideas and sentiments imported from a foreign country only
remotely resembled those current in Italy. There chivalry, in its ideal
signification, had never properly taken root. Splendid feasts were

given and tournaments were held; people pretended to be in love, after the fashion of the troubadours, and composed songs in their manner; but all that was merely superficial imitation of foreign usages. In the Kingdom of Sicily there was a powerful and warlike feudal nobility; but these nobles were kept down by Frederick II, who endeavoured to put an end to feudalism, lawyers of civilian descent, like Pier della Vigna and Taddeo of Sessa taking precedence of them at court. As for the homage paid to ladies, this could not fail to become a mere fiction at a court where oriental customs still prevailed, where the emperor kept a harem and had his wives guarded by eunuchs, while he celebrated the fair ones in languishing tones.

Thus it is that the oldest Italian lyrical poetry gives us nothing but pale conventionality, both as regards subject-matter and expression. *Madonna*, the loved one, is always the same image of abstract perfection, without life or movement. Her charms and virtues are depicted only in the most general terms. She is the flower of women, the mirror of beauty, like the sweet-smelling rose and the morning star; her splendour surpasses that of pearls and jewels, every excellent quality is hers, and from her emanates every virtue that the poet may venture to attribute to himself. Love is also an abstraction, a personification which the poet addresses, and to which he complains of his sufferings. The relations between the lovers are colourless and without warmth, nearly always the same but for slight modifications: Madonna is cold and inexorable, the lover stoops and bends down, sighs and hopes, declares his eternal fidelity or prays for some mitigation of his fortunes. . . . The personality of the poet disappears, and it becomes almost a matter of indifference what name stands at the head of the songs. The life of the authors was often chequered and stormy, and full of poetry; but nothing of this passed over into their verses, because they wrote after a type common to them all, which had no connection with their individual sentiments.[4]

Thus, the early Sicilian poets deserve to be noticed not so much for their additions to the universal *corpus poeticum* as on account of their perpetuation of certain traditional ideas. It is for this reason that these writers are especially important. One should be careful not to make the easy generalization that because the Sicilians were not great innovators they are therefore of no importance. As transmitters of Provençal poetic theory and practice, they are distinctly significant, and an understanding of what they did (or should I say what they failed to do?) is essential to an understanding of subsequent developments. Vernon Lee seems to support this opinion when she writes: "The history of the Italian lyric before Dante is the history of a series of transformations which connect a style of poetry absolutely feudal and feudally immoral, with the hitherto unheard-of platonic love subtleties of the 'Vita Nuova.' " [5] In the brief space devoted to the Sicilian school I have attempted to make clear the characteristic features of the first of these transformations. There are numerous eddies in the main currents of the early literature, but these subordinate trends need not be considered. There are, however, three chief tendencies represented by Guinicelli and the school of Bologna, Cavalcanti and the Florentine group, and Dante himself in the *Vita Nuova*, which deserve to be characterized. This may be accomplished most successfully by indicating the development and pointing out the significance of each in the growth of the *dolce stil nuovo*.[6]

The Ordo Militiae Beatae Mariae was founded in Bologna in 1261; it was primarily an aristocratic organization formed for benevolent purposes, and its members were accorded special privileges. Its nickname, *frati gaudenti*, betrays what history reveals, namely, that it soon became a worldly and social group. Among the members of the order was Guittone d'Arezzo. I mention this order of the Blessed Virgin and Guittone together in order to emphasize two important facts: the *frati gaudenti* present a picture of thirteenth-century Bologna as a worldly city filled with a zest for life and much interested in the *joi de vivre;* Guittone is important as a transitional figure, one who served as a link between the Sicilian school and the north Italian poets best represented by the Bolognese group. His dull, uninspired, versified reasoning, deficient in both melody and charm, tends to minimize his importance. With Vossler we may say that by his almost completely ignoring sensuous beauty Guittone "prepared the way for the symbolic and mystical conception of the *dolce stil nuovo* and for the apotheosis of Beatrice." [7]

Tuscany became the new center of poetic activity and continued the Sicilian manner with all its slavish imitation of Provençal models. But this was of short duration; with the growth of political feeling, particularly the formation of the Guelph and Ghibelline factions, poets translated their feelings into verse and, adopting the Provençal *sirventes*, imbued the empty and rhetorical forms with new life. This remark may be applied with particular appropriateness to the love lyrics, save that in this case the inspiring force was the new scientific development which had its center in Bologna; the poet who most fully reflects the new movement is Guido Guinicelli (*circa* 1240–74). At first strongly influenced by the writers of the Sicilian school, he next became involved in the artificialities of Guittone, but finally found himself under the influence of the new intellectual life of Bologna. It is as student and teacher of that life that he is of importance to us; for, imbued with the "new science," he was the first to turn chivalric love into the spiritual, to endow Italian poetry with philosophical content. His thoughts carried him from the land of romance to that of philosophical speculation; this is at once the glory and the weakness of his writings. His interest in philosophy enabled him to improve upon the Provençal technique; for the loosely connected, undeveloped string of ideas characteristic of some of the troubadours, Guinicelli in his best work substitutes one topic only and proceeds to elaborate it. This is well illustrated in the famous lyric beginning, "Al cor gentil ripara sempre Amore," unquestionably Guinicelli's finest poem (though we would do well to remember that much of his work has not survived). [8] Since this poem embodies Guido's chief contribution to the new movement, it may be examined here in some detail.

Guido's theory is briefly this: love and true nobility always occur simultaneously; the one is inseparable from the other. In the opening lines of the poem he tells us that love dwells in the noble heart, like a bird in the forest green. Before the noble heart (*cor gentil*) there was no such thing as love:

nè fe' amore avanti gentil core,
nè gentil core avanti amor natura.

The fire of love is enkindled within the noble heart, like
virtue (i. e., its efficient property) in a precious stone. No
star will yield its excellence until the sun has purified it;
when the sun has drawn forth all that is bad, then the star
reveals its true worth. In the same way the heart, which by
Nature is formed noble and pure and gentle, becomes enamored of a woman, who acts upon it just as the sun does upon
a star:

> Così lo cor, ch' è fatto da natura
> eletto pur gentile,
> donna, a guisa di stella, lo inamura.

Fully to appreciate this poem a knowledge of scholastic philosophy is indispensable (not to mention the desirability of
such knowledge for the complete understanding of many
phases of medieval literature). This is particularly true when
studying such a writer as Guinicelli, whose chief claim to
fame is his successful fusion of two types of love heretofore
usually considered to have little in common: the love of God
and the love of woman. By elevating his lady, by transform-
ing her into a kind of spiritual being, he inaugurated a revo-
lution. The service of God and the service of woman are here
united; the poet interprets, defends, and explains the one in
terms of the other. That is why the poem, difficult enough
in the original, seems to lose much of its force in paraphrase
and translation; it is next to impossible to make clear the
fusion of thought which the poet has expressed so beautifully.

To continue our analysis: Love remains in the noble heart
for the same reason that the flame shines so clearly and
sharply at the tip of the candle: it is too proud to do otherwise! However, evil Nature stands in contrast to Love, as
water with its coldness may be contrasted to the warmth of
fire. Love takes its place in the noble heart; for like seeks
like, as the diamond in the mine finds its natural place in the

iron. The sun shines on the mud all day, but the latter still remains vile and the sun loses none of its warmth. The proud man says, "I am noble by birth." I liken him to the mud; the sun, to true gentility. High birth does not assure true gentility unless there is also a gentle heart; let no one think otherwise:

> chè non de' dare om fede
> che gentilezza sia for di corragio
> in degnità di rede,
> se da vertute non ha gentil cor.

God the Creator is mirrored more clearly in the celestial Intelligence than is the sun in our eye. As the soul operates in accord with God's desire, in like fashion must the lady infuse the truth in her lover's heart so that he may not cease to love her. The poet concludes by saying that when he dies and his soul appears before God, the Almighty will speak and accuse him of attributing to her what belongs only to God and to the Queen of Heaven. To this the poet states that he will reply: "I thought my loved one was an angel from your kingdom; wherefore, do not hold me to blame if I gave her my love":

> Dir li potrò: tenea d'angel sembianza
> che fosse del to regno,
> non fea fallo, s'eo li posi amanza.

What a change is here! The exquisite beauty, the childlike simplicity of the concluding lines more than compensate for the subtlety and the obscurity of some of the earlier stanzas. The seed of an idea found occasionally among a few of the later troubadours has sprouted and reached full growth here. Many of Guinicelli's poems are mediocre; the early ones especially are filled with the usual commonplaces. But this single *canzone* is the triumphant expression of an all-important philosophical concept. That is why it is so important to us; not only does it help us to understand Guinicelli, but without it Dante's treatment of Beatrice is scarcely comprehensible. Woman has now attained a lofty eminence; her deification is complete. Guinicelli, lawyer and podesta, lover and poet, is the father of a new school of poetry, "the sweet new style," *il dolce stil nuovo* as it is still called today.

Gaspary is somewhat misleading when, explaining Guido's theory of love in this *canzone*, he states that "an entirely new conception takes the place of this well-worn succession of phrases." [9] The doctrine expounded in this poem is inherent in the works of the later troubadours; for them woman had become a queen but still very much the queen of a feudal castle; for Guinicelli she had passed beyond all earthly bounds and was fit to be compared with nothing less than the Queen of Heaven. Gaspary makes the following judicious comment on this development:

> The earthly passion has become transfigured, and has been brought into contact with the sublimest ideas known to man; it is a philosophical conception of love, and the similes that serve to illustrate and to explain it in so elaborate and diversified a manner, show no traces of the old repertory. . . . And so this school is distinguished from the old by its endeavour to attain a greater depth of thought, by an increase of vigour and a fresh earnestness. Amore and Madonna remain abstractions, but they are imbued with a new significance. Madonna is still the sum of all perfection; but, at the same time, she becomes a symbol, the incarnation of something more exalted. The love inspired by her passes beyond her towards virtue, to the highest good; the chivalrous love of the Provençals has become spiritual love.[10]

Guinicelli has been rightly described as the first poet of this new movement. Few critics will find reason to take exception to the following statement by one of Guido's most discerning editors, Pietro Ercole: "La scienza divenne madre della nuova poesia che nasce, per così dire, in Bologna, ed ha in Guido Guinizelli il suo primo poeta. Al mondo cavalleresco succede il mondo scientifico e filosofico: oggetto della nuova poesia, che rimane pur sempre amorosa, non è più l'amore o il diletto delle gentili usanze, ma l'analisi e lo studio del sentimento." [11] The lyric of the "sweet new style" celebrates woman as an idealized being, a heavenly creature profoundly influencing all who subject themselves to her. Whoever has the *cor gentil* will be stricken by her celestial beauty and will be unable to resist her uplifting and ennobling charms. The expression of this feeling was profoundly influenced by the interest of the new poets in philosophical speculation, a fact already emphasized in connection with Guinicelli. Woman according to the Christian philosophy was now regarded as a means of moral elevation, a being midway between the human and the divine. This conception of woman produced a new mythology and resulted in a new mode of expression.[12]

Guido Cavalcanti (*circa* 1255–1300), contemporary of Dante and perhaps his most intimate friend, receives occasional mention in the works of the great Florentine. In the eleventh canto of the *Purgatorio* (xi, 97–99) he is referred to in this fashion:

> Così ha tolto l'uno all' altro Guido
> La gloria della lingua ; e forse è nato
> Chi l'uno e l'altro caccerà di nido.

The world has had no reason to reverse this judgment of Dante's, for it is certainly true that the one Guido snatched from the other *la gloria della letteratura;* it is Cavalcanti who should be regarded as the successor of Guinicelli and the perfect representative of the *dolce stil nuovo.* In his poetry, tenderness and feeling are finally united with philosophical speculation and academic profundity. Guinicelli had initiated the new movement; the lawyer, Cino da Pistoia, a rhetorician on the subject of love rather than a poet, was the workman of the school; Cavalcanti was the poet. Cavalcanti is more profound and serious than Cino; language and rhetoric are only the means to an end, philosophy. Yet despite his objective, Cavalcanti possesses genuine feeling and love for reality. The subjects he treats are all the same as those celebrated by the troubadours, but they are alive and real, not merely ornamented and prettified. It may repay us to examine one or two of his representative poems.

Probably the most important of Cavalcanti's poems is the *canzone* beginning "Donna mi prega, perch'io voglio dire. . . ." [13] It is of considerable significance since it sets forth in concise, if occasionally obscure, form the principal ideas of Guido on love. One of Cavalcanti's editors has written that it is not a genuine love lyric—in the sense that it is the expression of Guido's feelings for a lady—but rather an exposition of the entire theory which Cavalcanti had formulated about the nature and origin of love.[14] The opening lines state that the poem is being written at the request of a lady who wishes to know what love is; the *canzone* supplies a fitting answer to Guido Orlandi's sonnet, the first four lines of which are (Rivalta, 122):

> Onde si move e donde nasce amore?
> Qual è 'l su' propio loco ov' e' dimora?
> è sustanzia, accidente o memora?
> è cagion d'occhi o è voler di core?

The eight subjects which Guido proposes to treat are among the most frequent topics to be found in medieval love poetry: the dwelling place of love, its origin, nature, power, essence, its effects and manifestations, its visibility in the human body ("s'omo per veder lo pò mostrare").

Love dwells in the memory and has a double origin:

> In quella parte dove sta memora
> prende suo stato, sì formato come
> diaffan da lume,—d'una scuritate
> la qual da Marte vene, e fa dimora.
> Elli è creato ed à sensato nome,
> d'alma costume—e di cor volontate.

It may be a natural disposition or the result of desire. It springs from the image of the person seen and begins in the possible intellect, the *intellectus possibilis* of scholastic philosophy, that faculty which develops the image of the material object into the abstract idea or type:

Ven da veduta forma che s'intende
che prende—nel possibile intelletto,
come 'n subietto—loco e dimoranza.

Love is not a virtue like the natural and moral virtues, which
have their seat in the soul, but belongs rather to the passions
originating in the senses:

Non è vertute, ma da quella vene
ch'è perfezione, che si pone tale,
non razionale—ma che sente dico.

Love gives no rest, gives rise to conflicting sentiments, is
found for the most part only among people of quality, and
takes such complete command of the individual that it cannot be driven out (43–56). The next and last stanza (57–
70) tells us that love is an assured pleasure, that it cannot be
concealed, that the glances of both lover and lady are equally
beneficial, that fear discourages love, and that love cannot be
seen visibly, for it has no color of its own.

These lines are clothed in most obscure language and, despite the abundance of annotation to which they have been
subjected, are most difficult to interpret; but the above summary at least suggests what the poet was trying to say. Guido
realized perfectly well the difficulties of his verse and admitted this in the concluding lines addressed to the *canzone:*

Tu puoi sicuramente gir, canzone,
là 've ti piace, ch' io t' ò sì adornata
ch' assai laudata sarà tua ragione
da le persone ch' anno intendimento:
di star con l'altre tu non ài talento.

There is no denying the fact that these stanzas are what the
Germans would call "streng wissenschaftlich," but on the
other hand it must be insisted that they are priceless for the
insight they give into one side of the Florentine literary mind
in the late thirteenth century in general and into that of
Guido Cavalcanti in particular. Guido's other poems, like

Guinicelli's, are concerned with the psychology of love; this one is almost purely philosophical reflection.[15] In the words of Gaspary,

Here we have the apparatus of the scholastic philosophy, the logical divisions and distinctions, syllogisms and terminology of the schools. Image and sentiment, the foundations of all poetry, as we find them in Guinicelli's canzone, are here entirely lacking. Add to this the wearisome artificiality of the form, with its numerous difficult intermediate rhymes. . . . Here we have poetry entirely in the service of science, and overburdened with erudition, considered worthy of long commentaries, and requiring these, if it was to be understood at all; so that Guido's canzone concerning love appears as a forerunner of Dante's "Convivio," and, in a measure, of the "Commedia" too.[16]

Trustworthy as Gaspary is, yet I feel that the above is not a well-rounded description of the poem. Entirely lacking in sentiment? Wearisome artificiality of form? Cavalcanti is no Lord Byron wearing his heart on his sleeve nor do his lines possess the suppleness of Shakespearean blank verse. In many ways he recalls the early seventeenth-century school in England, especially John Donne, and in our own time, T. S. Eliot, though the comparison is not entirely accurate since Cavalcanti is so much superior to both in poetry as well as philosophy. Gaspary has described one side of Cavalcanti; Vossler, however, realizes that there is another:

He knew how to grasp both features of the new style, the mystical tenderness as well as the scientific profundity. For under his courtly and haughty demeanour he hid a soft, love-seeking heart. His mood is one of longing, unsated by scientific speculation; it is stronger than his will. His self-restraint put melancholy and longing for death into his desires, inward strife and agony into his sensuousness. But his sensuousness is not sober, his longing not gentle, his suffering not voluntary, his speculation not over-ingenious, his thoughts not playful, his pride not vanity. Hence the unevenness of his nature, which old Villani so well characterizes as tenderness with stubbornness, appears in his poems spontaneously and often artlessly direct and naked—and seems almost a hodgepodge.[17]

We may pause here a moment to observe some of these manifestations in a few of Guido's sonnets and *ballate*. The *canzone*, "Io non pensava che lo cor già mai" (Rivalta, 115–17), is a typical love lyric, picturing the lover suffering and languishing as usual. He can be lavish in the praise of his lady [18] and in particular of her unsurpassable beauty; this sonnet, for example, is far removed from the "Donna mi prega" (107):

Avete 'n vo' li fiori e la verdura
   e ciò che luce od è bello a vedere:
   risplende più che 'l sol vostra figura:
   chi vo' non vede ma' non po' valere.

In questo mondo non à creatura
   sì piena di bieltà nè di piacere;
   e chi d'amor si teme, l'assicura
   vostro bel viso, e non po' più temere.

Le donne che vi fanno compagnia
   assa' mi piaccion per lo vostro onore;
   ed i' le prego per lo cortesia

che qual più pote più vi faccia onore,
   ed aggia cara vostra segnoria,
   perchè di tutte sete la migliore.

The sonnet, "Una giovane donna di Tolosa" (170), has a good deal of feeling; so likewise has the one beginning "Ciascuna fresca, e dolce fontanella" (153), although it is more obscene and breathes an entirely different spirit. Another very fine sonnet celebrating the superiority of his lady deserves quoting in full (109):

Beltà di donna di piagente core,
   e cavalieri armati che sian genti,
   cantar d'augelli, e ragionar d'amore,
   adorni legni in mar forte correnti,

aire sereno quand' appar l'albore,
   e bianca neve scender senza venti,
   rivera d'acqua, e prato d'ogni fiore,
   oro, argento, azzurro in ornamenti,

passa la gran beltate e la piagenza
de la mia donna e 'l suo gentil coraggio
sì, che rassembra vile a chi ciò sguarda.

E tanto è più d'ogn' altra canoscenza
quanto lo cielo de la terra è maggio.
A simil di natura ben non tarda.

There is a certain amount of melancholy and sorrow in many of Guido's poems. The *ballata*, "Vedete, ch' io son un, che vo piangendo" (159–60), is a good example of this, and so likewise is the sonnet (103) in which Love appears to him in a vision as a dead figure that addresses him ("Certo mie rime a te mandar volendo"); the concluding tercet reads:

E tu conosci ben, ch'i' sono amore
E ch' i' ti lascio questa mia sembianza,
E portone ciascun tuo pensamento.

But though these verses quoted and referred to display Cavalcanti as a poet with considerable lyric ability, there is no denying that most of his poems are tinged at least, when not entirely saturated, with philosophical speculation. There may be but comparatively little of it, as in the sonnet, "Io vidi gli occhi, dove Amor si mise" (112), or it may reach the supreme exaggeration of those lines which recount the source and effects of love (148). Like the first *canzone* discussed above, this sonnet belongs to Guido's philosophical endeavors rather than among his purely lyrical attempts. Together with the *canzone* it is important in presenting his theory of love. Here Guido teaches that a glance from his lady enters his heart in the form of a spirit and arouses a number of other spirits each of which has a particular function:

Pe' gli occhi fere un spirito sottile,
   che fa in la mente spirito destare,
   dal qual si move spirito d'amare,
   e ogn' altro spiritel si fa gentile.

Sentir non po' di lui spirito vile,
   di cotanta virtù spirito appare:

quest' è lo spiritel, che fa tremare
lo spiritel, che fa la donna umile.

Poi da questo spirito si move
un altro dolce spirito soave,
che segue un spiritello di mercede,

Io quale spiritel spiriti piove;
chè di ciascuno spirit' à la chiave
per forza d'uno spirito che 'l vede.

One of Guido's editors, Pietro Ercole, describes the poem in these words: "In questo Sonetto si ha la spiegazione completa del sorgere e del progredire del sentimento dell' amore nell' animo dell' uomo con una fantasmagoria di *spiriti* che si succedono, si incalzano, si moltiplicano, l'uno dopo l'altro, con una pieghevolezza di pensiero ammirabile, con una facilità di versi, di rime e di lingua per quel tempo sorprendente"; and here the critic quite justly asks: "ma il vero sentimento, l'amore, dov' è?" [19] Indeed, where? Yes, this is precisely the difficulty not only with Cavalcanti but also with practically all the writers in the *dolce stil nuovo:* "il vero sentimento, dov' è?" The question may be answered in a few words: the true sentiment is to be found not in the many poems deeply philosophical and speculative but in the few lyrics which are chiefly the products of poetical fantasy. One of these has already been quoted; [20] this discussion of the many-sided Cavalcanti may be brought to a fitting close by quoting one of his most purely lyrical poems and surely his most delightfully conceived sonnet (108):

Chi è questa che ven ch' ogn' om la mira
e fa tremar di chiaritate l'a're,
e mena seco amor si che parlare
null' omo pote, ma ciascun sospira?

O Deo, che sembra quando li occhi gira
dica 'l Amor, ch' i' no 'l savria contare:
contando d' umilità donna mi pare,
ch' ogn' altra ver di lei i' la chiam' ira.

Non si poria contar la sua piagenza,
ch' a lei s'inchina ogni gentil virtute,
e la beltate per sua dea la mostra.

Non fu sì alta già la mente nostra
e non si pose in noi tanta salute,
che propriamente n'aviam canoscenza.

The *Vita Nuova*, the crowning glory of the *dolce stil
nuovo*, does not differ essentially from the work of Cavalcanti.
Dante makes no radical changes, uses the same poetic conceits, and shows himself in many ways a descendant of the
troubadours and a disciple of earlier as well as contemporaneous Italian poetry. The *Vita Nuova* contrasts with its
predecessors in only one important respect: it breathes, it is
a document infused with life, it is a record of personal experience on the part of the poet. Since this poem is so easily accessible in Rossetti's famous translation and in view of the
fact that its relation to the courtly love system has been sufficiently pointed out by Mott,[21] I shall dismiss the *Vita Nuova*
without further consideration; for it is a far cry from here
to the world of Boccaccio and Chaucer, the real subjects of
this investigation. In Dante's hands courtly love has become
so rarefied and idealized, is so entirely mystical and metaphysical, that it has passed far beyond the courtly love ideal.
"In the *Vita Nuova* the courtly homage to women changes,
unnoted and as if of its own volition, to saintly worship, and
the latter in turn to metaphysical speculation. The poet
gradually passes from knightly homage to mystical adoration
and philosophic contemplation." [22]

Courtly love is not a simple phenomenon but a very complex one. Its manifestations are multiform; its origins are
still the subject of much dispute; [23] the history of its development is not clear; [24] the story of its influence is yet to be
told; its relations to medieval philosophy and theology have
only been recognized in recent years.[25] In the preceding pages

an attempt has been made to sketch the development of the courtly love system from an early period down to its culmination in the poetry of the *dolce stil nuovo*. One may very well note the absence of a chapter on *La Roman de la Rose* and feel that there should have been included here some account of *Minnesang*, the trouvère lyric, and other equally important topics. I have preferred, however, to place the emphasis on certain trends which seem to me to be especially significant and have chosen to omit all else. The story is therefore necessarily incomplete, but I hope it is sufficiently adequate for the reader to obtain a reasonably definite idea about one aspect of medieval love. With the system in mind, then, as we have come to know it in these chapters, we are now ready to examine Chaucer and Boccaccio in this new light.

PART TWO
BOCCACCIO

VI

COURTLY LOVE IN
IL FILOSTRATO

N o one, I suppose, will dispute the statement that the *Filostrato* is in most respects a typical courtly love poem. That Boccaccio should order this work along courtly lines is readily understandable if we bear in mind his relations to Maria d'Aquino. In Naples, almost a foreign country, Boccaccio found himself penniless, unbefriended, of no social standing—facts which at first sight make it seem strange that he should become one of Maria's suitors; yet this is quite in keeping with the courtly love practice, for Maria's unhappy relations with her husband made the advances of the budding poet from the north of Italy all the more welcome. ". . . Like the troubadour of old, Boccaccio was single while his lady was married, stood beneath her in social rank, came as a stranger from afar to court her, and depended for success upon his skill in song." [1] Consequently it was highly appropriate that the *Filostrato* took the form which it did:

No poet of the later Middle Ages who undertook to compose a love story for the delectation of the upper circles of society could afford to neglect certain well-established rules of literary procedure which prescribed the nature of the relationship which should subsist between his hero and his heroine and the principles of conduct which should govern them therein.

There were in the circumstances in which Boccaccio found himself during his sojourn at Naples exceptionally urgent reasons why he in particular should have paid especial heed to the observance of these rules of Courtly Love, as they were called. For it was as the son of a Florentine money-lender that he had come there—not the best of recommendations for one who sought to win fame as a poet in that aristocratic environment. How better could he hope to overcome the prejudices certain to be cherished against one reared in the sordid atmosphere of trade than by showing himself a past master in the manipulation of a body of conventions with which only the gentle and highborn were supposed to be familiar? [2]

Griffin goes on to say that Boccaccio's interest in courtly love was more than literary: "There can, moreover, be but little doubt that the Italian poet's interest in Courtly Love transcended the bounds of literature and that he sought as far as possible to order his relations with Maria in accordance with its principles. . . ." [3] Following Hutton and other critics, he notes that Boccaccio's courtship of Maria, as allegorized in the *Amorosa Visione*, may be divided into four stages: uncertainty, trial, acceptance as suitor, acceptance as lover—a division which corresponds to the Provençal classification:

> Qatres scalos ha enamor
> Loprimiers es d'feignedor
> Elsegon es d'prejador
> Elo tersz es dentend'dor
> Ealqart es drutz apelasz. [4]

While all this fits the facts very nicely and provides a position which is perfectly tenable from most points of view, there is however no cogent reason for believing that in his wooing of Maria, Boccaccio depended solely on his dexterity in handling the courtly love conventions. Griffin's remark that his state in life as the son of a Florentine money lender was not the best recommendation he might have had [5] deserves consideration, but it may be nicely counterbalanced by noting that this same money lender was a frequent visitor at the Court of Naples and was described by the King as "Buccaccius de Certaldo de societate Bardorum de Florencia, consiliarius, cambellanus, mercator, familiaris et fidelis noster." [6] Della Torre, from whom this statement is quoted, regards this as conclusive evidence that Giovanni was introduced into the court circle by his father: "Con tutti questi dati di fatto non è lecito aver dubbio alcuno che Boccaccino fosse l'introduttore in corte del figlio Giovanni." [7] A plausible view seems to be that Boccaccio obtained his entree to the court of King Robert through his father but that his progress in the courtship of Maria was due to his own personality and literary ability. After all, there seems to be no good reason for trying to attribute everything to courtly love.

The *Filostrato* is a typical courtly love document. How Chaucer handled it will be the subject of the chapters which follow; for the present it will be profitable to devote our attention exclusively to the Italian narrative. In the very first sentence of the Proem, Boccaccio mentions a favorite topic for discussion in the courts of love: "Uno giovane ferventemente ama una donna, della quale niuna altra cosa gli è conceduto dalla fortuna, se non il potere alcuna volta vederla, o tal volta di lei ragionare, o seco stesso di lei dolcemente pensare. Qual' è adunque di queste tre cose di più diletto?" Boccaccio states that at first he argued that the delight of being able to think at times of the object loved was far greater than the other two. However, he hastens to add that when he was away the true answer (seeing his lady) became manifest: "la quale tanto fuori d'ogni dovuto termine m'ha l'anima constristata, che assai apertamente posso comprendere, quanta fosse la letizia, allora poco da me conosciuta, che mi veniva dalla vostra graziosa e bella vista." This notion of visual perception as an essential element in the genesis of love was first given prominence by the troubadours and became a commonplace in the amatory literature of later centuries. Boccaccio makes several references to this in the Proem and many times in the course of the poem. His beloved is so vivid in his mind's eye that she rules him (I, 5):

> Tu se'nel tristo petto effigïata
> Con forza tal, che tu vi puoi più ch'io.

When Troilo is smitten, he does not realize that the classical and Provençal are mingled in his medieval make-up (I, 29):

> Nè s'avvedea colui, . . .
>
> .   .   .   .
>
> Che amore dimorasse dentro al raggio
> Di que' vaghi occhi con gli strali sui.

Returned to his room, he recalls the pleasure he has had at the sight of Criseida (I, 33):

> E seco a rammentarsi del piacere
> Avuto la mattina dell'aspetto
> Di Criseida cominciò.

Addressing Love, he entreats him to obtain from her eyes that which will heal his soul (I, 39):

> Tu stai negli occhi suoi, signor verace,
> Siccome in luogo degno a tua virtute:
> Perchè, se 'l mio servir punto ti piace,
> Da que' ti prego impetri la salute
> Dell'anima. . . .

He feels that water from her eyes will soothe his ardor (I, 41):

> E da' begli occhi trarre immaginava
> Acqua soave al suo ardor severo;

but this serves only to increase his troubles:

> Perchè astutamente gli cercava
> Sovente di veder, nè s'avvedea
> Che più da quegli il fuoco s'accendea.

When Pandaro visits Criseida, he tells her of Troilo's complaint to Love, in the course of which he reveals how his soul is longing for the peace which only the eyes of his lady can give (II, 58):

> Chiamando sempre quella dolce pace,
> Che gli occhi belli e vaghi di costei
> Sol posson dar, caro signore, a lei.

Troilo, confiding in Pandaro, bemoans the part Criseida's eyes have played (II, 86):

> El m'ha Criseida sì la vita tolta
> Co' suoi begli occhi. . . .

In his letter to Criseida, Troilo states that along with her beauty, manners, modesty, et cetera, "lo splendore de' tuoi vaghi occhi" (II, 98) also played a part in his enamorment. In III, 36, Troilo devotes the greater part of the stanza to Criseida's eyes; they were responsible for his love in the beginning:

> Voi mi metteste nel cuor sì focosi
> Dardi d'amor, de'quali io tutto incendo;

and now they hold him prisoner:

> Voi mi tenete e sempre mi terrete
> Occhi miei bei nell' amorosa rete.

Troilo (III, 61) tells Pandaro of the fire caught from the fair eyes of Criseida and in IV, 51, elaborates the same idea. In V, 62, he points out that inability to see his beloved's eyes makes him go about groaning; and in the next stanza he tells Love that, separated from Criseida's eyes, death can be his only comfort:

> Non è amore al mio dolor conforto
> Fuor che 'l morir, trovandomi partuto
> Da que' begli occhi ov'io t'ho già veduto.

Another favorite courtly love precept which receives considerable emphasis in the *Filostrato* is the rule commanding secrecy in an amour.[8] When Troilo leaves the temple, he keeps his desire well hidden (I, 31), "tenendo bene il suo disio nascoso," fearful lest the abusive remarks he had formerly made about other lovers should now be applied to himself. Fully confirmed in his love, Troilo decides to keep it secret (I, 36):

> Pria proponendo di celar l'ardore
> Concetto già nell'amorosa mente

> A ciascheduno amico e servidore,
> Se ciò non bisognasse. . . .

This decision is of particular interest since it not only is fully
in keeping with the thirteenth rule just referred to but also
provides a practical illustration of the command decreeing
that a lover should not have too many confidants;[9] I shall
speak of this again when discussing the go-between.[10] Having
found it necessary to confide in Pandaro, Troilo begs him to
keep it secret (II, 8):

> e pregoti per Dio,
> S'alcuna fede al nostro amor tu hai,
> Ch'altrui tu non discopri tal disio,
> Che noia men potria seguire assai.

Pandaro likewise is fully aware of the importance of secrecy;
he urges Troilo most earnestly that he keep everything quiet
in order to protect Criseida's reputation (II, 26):

> Ma perciocchè 'l disio s' è impedito
> All' operare, e tutto simigliante
> Non conosciuto, parmi per partito
> Poter pigliar, che ciascheduno amante
> Possa seguire il suo alto appetito,
> Sol che sia savio in fatto ed in sembiante. . . .

Under the rules of the code there was nothing wrong in this
relationship; the real offense lay not so much in the actual
commission of the act as in its discovery. Pandaro goes on to
say that he will give each of them equal comfort provided all
is kept secret (II, 28):

> E a ciascuno donar pari conforto,
> Poscia che occulto il dovete tenere,
>
> .   .   .   .   .   .
>
>   e tu sii saggio poi,
> Nel tener chiuso tal'opera altroi.

Criseida too favors secrecy, but it is apparently not her reputation which makes her desire a clandestine attachment (II,
74); just as water acquired by stealth is sweeter than wine in
abundance,

Così d'amor la gioia, che nascosa
Trapassa assai, del sempre mai tenuto
Marito in braccio.

This is a complete reversal of the decision which she expressed
a few stanzas before this (69):

Se forse l' onestà questo mi vieta,
Io sarò saggia, e terrò sì celata
La voglia mia, che non sarà saputo
Ch' io aggia mai nel cuore amore avuto.

Criseida's vacillation continues until finally, at the end of
this soliloquy, it is regard for her reputation which makes her
renounce love, at least for the time being (77):

Che se si scuopre aperto, puoi tenere
La fama tua in eterno perduta,
La qual sì buona infino a qui è suta.

Criseida lived much grieved by her love but did not show it
openly (115); stanza 116 repeats the thought of 77. The
four concluding stanzas of Canto II further emphasize the
necessity of secrecy; Criseida begs Pandaro (II, 140),

Ma se alcun prego val nel tuo cospetto,
Ti prego, dolce e caro mio fratello,
Che tutto ciascun nostro fatto o detto
Occulto sia;

to which he replies (141):

Guarda la tua bocca,
Che el per sè, nè io, mai il diremo.

Pandaro's last words to Criseida are (143):

fa' pur ch'egli sia saggio
E sappia ben celare il suo coraggio.

In III, 9–10, Pandaro exhorts Troilo to observe the utmost
secrecy for the sake of Criseida's reputation. Troilo replies
that he has been much worried on this point (14) and swears
(15)

Ma nondimen per quello Dio ti giuro
. . . . . .
tu puoi sicuro
Viver, che a mio poter sarà interna
Questa credenza, e in ogni atto servato
L'onor di quella che m'ha 'l cor piagato.

At cockcrow, after the first night together, Criseida tells Troilo that he must go if their affair is to be concealed from the world (III, 43):

Ora si fa da doversi levare,
Se ben vogliam celar nostro disio.

Before Criseida is sent to Calchas, she tells Troilo during the last night together that if their love is to last it must remain hidden (IV, 153):

Perchè se 'l nostro amor vogliam che duri,
Com' or facciam, convien sempre si furi.

The correspondence of this thought with Andreas' rule already mentioned obviously does not require further comment.[11]

Another requirement of the courtly code is that expressed by Andreas: "Facilis perceptio contemptibilem reddit amorem, difficilis eum carum facit haberi." [12] There are several examples of Criseida's passiveness; in fact her attitude at first is one of almost complete apathy (I, 48):

Ma questo n'è assai chiaro ed aperto,
Che nïente pareva le calesse
Di Troilo e dell' amor che le portava,
Ma come non amata dura stava.

Five stanzas later (53) Troilo bemoans Criseida's indifference in these words:

Ma quella per cui piagni nulla sente
Se non come una pietra, e così stassi
Fredda come al sereno interza il ghiaccio,
Ed io qual neve al fuoco mi disfaccio.

Criseida of course does not always maintain this attitude of unconcern.[13] After the departure of Pandaro, she enters upon a long soliloquy in which her real feelings stand out in sharp contrast to the indifference just noted; here her advice to herself is to receive the lover and satisfy his desires (II, 74):

> Ricevi il dolce amante, il qual venuto
> T' è fermamente mandato da Dio,
> E sodisfa' al suo caldo disio.

Other examples of this frame of mind are to be found in II, 114, 116, 125, 128, et cetera. Criseida's letter to Troilo (II, 121–27) is an excellent example of this mingling of indifference with her real feelings, a fact which Troilo is not slow to recognize (129):

> se io costei intendo,
> Amor la stringe, ma siccome rea,
> Sotto lo scudo ancor si va chiudendo;
> Ma non potrà, pur che forza mi dea
> Amore a sofferir, guari durare,
> Ch'ella non vegna a tutt' altro parlare.

That Troilo was essentially right several passages go to prove. After Pandaro's talk with Criseida, Troilo goes to her house and watches in the hope of seeing if her manner is now any different. She was standing at her window, we are told (II, 82), and was no longer cruel to him:

> Non si mostrò selvaggia nè alpestra
> Verso di Troilo che le riguardava,
> Ma tuttavolta in sulla poppa destra
> Onestamente verso lui mirava.

In the next stanza the statement is made that Criseida's indifference vanished and she grieved much at the time lost when he was not her lover; and in stanza 84 Troilo is said to find that the pursuit of love is not a "cosa molesta," while Criseida is reported to have shown herself to him on many occasions "vaga e lieta." [14]

Loss of color, of appetite, and of sleep is usual among

lovers, according to Andreas; pronouncements to this effect are to be found in the longer code [15] and find frequent illustration in medieval literature. These notions, like so much else, are essentially Ovidian.[16] A typical example of the effect of love on Troilo's physical well-being is found in the first canto, stanza 47:

> Aveagli già amore il sonno tolto,
> E minuito il cibo, ed il pensiero
> Moltiplicato sì, che già nel volto
> Ne dava pallidezza segno vero.

Another very good description of Troilo's condition is to be found toward the end of the poem (VII, 19), after it becomes apparent that Criseida is not going to return:

> El non mangiava quasi e non bevea,
> Sì avea pieno d'angoscia il tristo petto;
> Ed oltre a questo dormir non potea
> Se non da' sospir vinto, ed in dispetto
> Là vita sua e sè del tutto avea,
> E come 'l fuoco fuggiva 'l diletto,
> Ed ogni festa ed ogni compagnia
> Similemente a suo poter fuggia.

Troilo is fully aware of the fact that his feelings are betrayed through his countenance as well as by his sighs. Pandaro reports to Criseida that Troilo opened his complaint to Love with these words (II, 57):

> Signor mio, già mi si pare
> Nel viso e ne' sospiri ciò ch'io sento
> Dentro del cuor per leggiadra vaghezza,
> La qual m' ha preso colla sua bellezza.

Other examples of these symptoms are to be found in V, 60; VII, 20; and VII, 90. But it must not be thought that this sort of thing is experienced solely by Troilo, for Criseida suffers the same reactions. They are not so pronounced, or rather the poet fails to emphasize them to the same extent as he did Troilo's. Thus, when Criseida is reasoning things out, she admonishes herself to be careful, to keep her love secret;

otherwise her hidden feelings will show themselves in her colorless face (II, 116):

> Che s' io il lascio in troppo grande arsura
> Moltiplicare, e' potrebbe avvenire,
> Che nella scolorita mia figura
> Si vederebbe il nascoso disire,
> Che mi saria non piccola sciagura.

And again, this time in the Greek camp, Criseida is described as spending her nights in weeping, for in the daytime she had to be more careful since her face had grown thin and pale (VI, 1):

> ed in lagrime amare
> Da lei eran le notti consumate,
> Che 'l giorno più le convenia guardare,
> Perchè le fresche guance e delicate
> Pallide e magre l' eran divenute,
> Lontana dalla sua dolce salute.

It now remains to consider an aspect of the *Filostrato* which is perhaps not quite as obvious as those which have already been pointed out. That is the conception of love as a great spiritual force above and beyond the senses, a power capable of changing and improving those whom it affected. This notion of love as a regenerating influence was first prominently elaborated by the troubadours and has been discussed in the section on the Provençal lyric.[17] That the *Filostrato* contains much doctrine of this type we are prone to forget. It is an essentially sensuous production, and consequently it is only natural to remember such a vividly portrayed scene as Troilo's first night with Criseida and to slight the less spectacular but more significant passages devoted to love as a spiritual quality.[18] By his mingling of the carnal and the spiritual in this poem Boccaccio proves himself a distinctly great literary artist, for it is done so skillfully that there is nothing incongruous about the combination.

That Boccaccio recognized love as an elevating and ennobling power is proved by his frequent elaboration of the

idea. He·makes a general reference to the good effects of love
in the opening stanza of the third canto, where he expresses
the hope that he may be able to describe the benefits of love
in every respect:

> Fulvida luce, il raggio della quale
> Infino a questo loco m'ha guidato,
> Com' io volea per l' amorose sale;
> Or convien che 'l tuo lume duplicato
> Guido l'ingegno mio, e faccil tale,
> Che in particella alcuna dichiarato
> Per me appaia il ben del dolce regno
> D'Amor, del qual fu fatto Troilo degno.

Troilo too recognizes the power of love, for in one of the
poem's most charmingly written stanzas, that describing
Troilo's joy following Pandaro's first visit to Criseida, he addresses Venus in this fashion (II, 80):

> Lodato sia il tuo sommo valore,
> Venere bella, e del tuo figlio Amore.

When Troilo becomes enamored of Criseida he praises her
dignity and bearing; furthermore, he believes her to be a person of very noble nature, "di cuor grandissimo" (I, 34). More
than this, he concludes that it would be a very fine thing to
love her and even better for her to reciprocate:

> e gran ventura
> Di cotal donna amar si riputava;
> E vie maggior se per sua lunga cura
> Potesse far, se quanto egli essa amava
> Cotanto appresso da lei fosse amato,
> O per servente almen non rifiutato.

From now on Troilo is filled with thoughts of his lady; we
are told that a thousand times a day he said to himself: may
the gods grant that you take pity on me, for you alone can
make me joyful and be of help to me (I, 43):

> Null' altra fuor che tu lieto può farmi,
> Tu sola se' colei che puoi atarmi.

During the period immediately preceding Criseida's return to her father, Troilo is seen at his best as the perfect lover, as one whom love has so regenerated and ennobled that he approaches perfection. His prowess is remarkable. Though in the midst of battle his thoughts are ever of love, nevertheless he very frequently performs remarkable feats of skill in the course of the fighting (I, 45); but it was not hatred of the Greeks nor the freeing of Troy that urged him on but rather desire of glory, a longing inspired by love (I, 46):

> E per amor, se 'l ver dice la storia,
> Divenne in arme sì feroce e forte,
> Che gli Greci il temean come la morte.

He was always victorious and, "se non erra la storia," the Greeks feared his strength and vigor. Love was responsible for this prowess which made him so superior a warrior (III, 90),

>   e questo spirto tanto altiero
> Più che l' usato gli prestava amore,
> Di cui egli era fedel servidore.

But when I spoke above of Troilo's regeneration, I was not thinking so much about the effects which love had worked on his valor as of the changes which were effected in his spiritual make-up:

> Era d'amor tutto il suo ragionare,
> O di costumi, e pien di cortesia;
> Lodava molto i valenti onorare,
> E simile i cattivi cacciar via:
> Piaceali ancora di vedere ornare
> Li giovani d'onesta leggiadria;
> E tenea senza amore ognun perduto.
> Di quale stato che si fosse suto.

The first two lines have been translated as follows: [19] "All his talk was of love or of gentle behavior, and full of courtesy." I feel however that this reading leaves much to be desired and should like to see it interpreted in this fashion: "All his talk was of love or of gentle behavior, and he was full of courtesy"—not courtesy in our modern sense but courtesy as the equivalent of the Provençal *cortesia*, that ennobling power of love which I have been mentioning. Taken in this sense, the stanzas immediately preceding and following these lines are much more satisfactory; for Troilo, viewed in this light, seems to me a far nobler conception than if he be regarded merely as a polished and courteous lover. Emphasis on his courtesy in the sense of affability and politeness comes very properly in the next stanza (93):

> Ed avvegna ch' el fosse di reale
> Sangue, e volendo ancor molto potesse;
> Benigno si faceva a tutti eguale,
> Come che alcun talvolta nol valesse;
> Così voleva amor, che tutto vale,
> Che el per compiacere altrui facesse;
> Superbia, invidia, ed avarizia in ira
> Aveva, ed ognum dietro si tira.

These two stanzas tell a good deal about Troilo and much more about Boccaccio; for his conception of the lover here is distinctly in the Provençal tradition and more directly, of course, in that of the *dolce stil nuovo*. Of particular interest is Troilo's feeling that everyone who lives without love, regardless of rank, is lost. This is somewhat of an advance on the earlier practice which taught that love could exist only among people of the upper classes. The pronouncement of Andreas on this point is very definite; for example, he states that the love of rustics and peasants is only a carnal relationship: "Dicimus enim vix contingere posse quod agricolae in amoris inveniantur curia militare, sed naturaliter sicut equus et mulus ad Veneris opera promoventur, quemadmodum impetus eis naturae demonstrat. Sufficit ergo agricoltori labor assiduus et vomeris ligonisque continua sine intermissione solatia." [20]

Another good example of the ennobling power of love is found in that passage in which Pandaro advises Troilo not to get so perturbed over the exchange of Criseida for Antenor: the city is full of beautiful and gracious ladies, any one of whom no doubt would be glad to assuage his pains if he will only become enamored of her (IV, 48):

> però se noi perdemo
> Costei, molt' altre ni ritroveremo.

But Troilo is not at all sympathetic to this suggestion; in fact, he would rather die than commit such a sin; he is her slave and belongs entirely to her, for it is from her eyes that the sparks of love entered into his heart. These sparks enkindled the fire whose heat has been the cause of all his bravery and excellence (IV, 51):

> Da' suoi begli occhi mosser le faville
> Che del fuoco amoroso m' infiammaro;
> Queste pe' miei passando a mille a mille,
> Soavemente amor seco menaro
> Dentro dal cor, nel quale esso sentille
> Come gli piacque; e quivi incominciaro
> Primiere il fuoco, il cui sommo fervore
> Cagione è stato d' ogni mio valore.

Much might be written about Boccaccio's treatment of the God of Love. Sometimes he speaks very definitely of a love deity as the all-controlling force, while on other occasions Criseida's eyes are mentioned as the cause of Troilo's sufferings. Professor Griffin sums up the facts in the case very neatly when he writes:

In view of what has been said of Boccaccio's representation of love as having been the cause of every excellent thing in Troilus, it would be natural to conclude that the reason of this lay in the divine origin of love as caused by the love deity. Plausible as this explanation may appear, however, it will hardly fit the case. For in Provençal poetry, where the conception of the beneficent effects of love originated . . . love is less often represented as of divine origin and occasioned by the eyes of the lady when gazed at by her future lover. In Italy the newly imported Provençal idea of the physiological genesis of love came into conflict with the old idea of a God of Love, inherited from the ancients, and many were the learned tensions to which this conflict gave rise as to

whether or no love possesses external existence. It is entirely in keeping with this difference of Italian opinion that in the *Filostrato* Boccaccio should so seriously blend the traditional anthropomorphic conception of a love deity with the more recent idea, imported from Provence, that love is generated upon the eyes of the lady, passes thence to
the eyes of her future lover, and finally penetrates his eyes to take up
its abode in his heart.[21]

Thus far most of our emphasis has been on Troilo, but this
should not blind us to the other two main characters of the
poem. Pandaro in particular deserves detailed consideration,
for Boccaccio's conception of this character is perhaps his
most original contribution. The go-between is an easily recog-
nizable type in medieval literature. He is the intimate friend
and devoted companion of the lover, wholly unmindful of his
own interests. He always shares the delights and softens the
sorrows of his friend, arranges assignations and rendezvous
for the lovers, bears messages between them and, of course, as
a genuine confidant he alone knows of their secret amour.
Concerning this general type of character in medieval romance Miss Barrow remarks:

Narration and courtly love need a faithful servant, a kindly host, a
spy, a fairy, an ambitious mother, a devoted friend, a rival, exacting
barons—somebody to advance or interpret the action, to illustrate a
principle or bring out the ideal qualities of the hero or the heroine, and
the romancer finds the proper person in the social environment of his
lovers, makes him serve the purpose and then lets him go, to pick him
up for reward or punishment at the end, or not, as the final situation
suggests. Here and there we catch glimpses of real personalities among
these creatures of narrative or sentimental convenience, and not in-
frequently a group of nameless men and women stand out from dead
convention with vivid reality.[22]

That Pandaro is far removed from this general type is at once
evident, yet it is clear that this is the literary tradition to
which he belongs:

Son rôle est emprunté à la tradition romanesque du moyen âge: il est
l'ami, le confident, le conseiller de l'amant désolé, quelque chose comme

Gouvernal à côté de Tristan, ou Galéhaut entre la reine Guenièvre et le timide Lancelot. Mais Boccace a donné au personnage une telle ampleur, il l'a traité avec tant de malice, de désinvolture et de légèreté que Pàndaro reste une des créations les plus originals du romancier.[23]

There is no reason for dwelling at length on the rôle of the go-between in ordinary life; he is a well-known character and a fundamental member of human society. Likewise there is no need to consider his function in prehistoric or ancient times. Even though in the Latin drama and especially in the comedies of Plautus we find a general resemblance to this type chiefly in the person of a faithful servant or old nurse, such a character bears only a remote relation to the go-between of later days.[24]

In view of his widespread popularity in medieval times Ovid perhaps deserves somewhat closer attention. In the *Ars Amatoria* I have found three references to what with some considerable stretch of the imagination might be conceived of as a very remote ancestor of the go-between. In one passage (I, 351–58) he recommends that the lover get acquainted with the lady's handmaid, for she will make his approach easy: "accessus molliet illa tuos." She must be a person who can be trusted with the most intimate secrets and who, if properly bribed, will help the lover to gain his end with ease. Then too (367 ff.) she will always talk about the lover to his lady, tell her how he is slowly dying because of his frantic love for her, and so on (367–72):

> Hanc matutinos pectens ancilla capillos
>   Incitet, et velo remigis addat opem,
> Et secum tenui suspirans murmure dicat
>   "At, puto, non poteras ipsa referre vicem."
> Tum de te narret, tum persuadentia verba
>   Addat, et insano iuret amore mori.

Furthermore he warns the lover against falling in love with the letter carrier, however fair she be. But all this is of no help whatsoever; aside from being a woman and a servant, the character lacks all that disinterested self-sacrifice which is one of the finer qualities of the confidant and adviser of later days.

In the lays of Marie de France there is scarcely anyone who looks or acts at all like Pandaro. Only in the lay of Guigemar is there a possible prototype and a lady at that. The sole reason that she, a niece of Guigemar's beloved, might be looked upon as a go-between is that she urges the knight to make known his love to the lady.

In the vast field of medieval romance there is a great deal of material, in presenting which I shall in the main follow the lines indicated by Professor Young in *The Origin and Development of the Story of Troilus and Criseyde*.[25] As he points out, friends resembling Pandaro are common in medieval literature: Natanell, the tutor to Generydes in the romance of that name, who acts as procurer in the hero's affair with Clarionas; the squire, in *Sir Eglamour*, adviser and helper of his master in his love of Cristabelle; and in *Claris et Laris*, Laris, who encourages Claris in his affection for Lydaine, wife of King Ladout and sister of Laris.[26] This last instance is more significant than the other two, for the go-between is not only a devoted friend but also a relative of the lady. But as Young puts it, "there is no evidence that any of the characters thus far mentioned had any part in the formation of the character of Pandaro." [27]

A more likely source is also a far more famous one than any that has been mentioned up to this point; I refer to the Italian version of the story of Tristan and Iseult.[28] The best studies of this romance as far as our present requirements go are those of Professor Savj-Lopez and Professor Young.[29] The latter points out that there is some resemblance between Pandaro and Governale, faithful companion of Tristano, in the varying rôles of "guardian, adviser, pander, and mere attendant or servant." There are indeed points in which the resemblance is striking; for example, when Tristano tells his friend about his dream of the stag, Governale answers that he should not believe in the vision he has had; visions are not to be credited because they are vain, and therefore he should not think about these things. This is much the same as Pandaro's advice to Troilo on a similar occasion (V, 32):

> I sogni e le paure caccia via,
> In quel che son lasciali andar ne' venti;
> Essi procedon da malinconia,
> E quel fanno veder che tu paventi;
> Solo Iddio sa il ver di quel che fia,
> Ed i sogni e gli augurii, a che le genti
> Stolte riguardan, non montano un moco,
> Nè al futuro fanno assai o poco.

And again in VII, 40, where Pandaro tells Troilo that it is folly to examine dreams too minutely, for no one can interpret them properly:

> Nessun ne fu, nè è, nè giammai fia
> Che possa certo ben significare,
> Ciò che dormendo altrui la fantasia
> Con varie forme puote dimostrare,
> E molti già credettero una cosa,
> Ch' altra n' avvenne opposita e ritrosa.

Again, Tristano's attempt to kill himself has much in common with Troilo's, though I suppose committing suicide heroically does not admit of much variation. Likewise Governale's advice to Tristano on this occasion is paralleled by Pandaro's to Troilo.[30] Another and possibly more amusing likeness, though certainly no more convincing, may be found in the scene which depicts Troilo's and Criseida's first night together. They undress and get into bed, whereupon Criseida, still wearing her last garment, says (III, 31):

> . . . speglio mio, le nuove spose
> Son la notte primiera vergognose.

Savj-Lopez and Young both point out that in the Tristan story Braguina gets into bed in place of Queen Isotta. To bring this about Tristano puts out the lights, and when the King makes inquiries he is told, "this is an Irish custom."

When a young lady lies with her lord the first night ("la prima notte"), the light is extinguished so that the lady need not be ashamed; young ladies are very modest ("perche le pulcielle si sono troppo vergognose").[31] The word "vergognose" appears in both versions and "la prima notte" of *Tristano* becomes "la notta primiera" of the *Filostrato*, but I doubt very much that Boccaccio is indebted to this passage. That Boccaccio deliberately adapted any of these passages seems to me extremely improbable. The three incidents mentioned are, after all, the sort that would very easily occur to any writer on such a theme. I do not think it is quite correct for Young to state that Governale is essentially different from Pandaro;[32] as Tristano's adviser he is most like him, perhaps more so than any other character in medieval literature. Though it cannot be denied that he does play more "the role of the faithful servant than that of the courtly 'amico' of Boccaccio's poem,"[33] nevertheless I cannot help agreeing with Savj-Lopez, who states that there is to be found in Governale "quella freddezza di giudizio, quell' amore costante pel discepolo, quella ferma superiorita morale che il Boccaccio ha dipinto in Pandaro."[34]

When Young made his observations on the character of Galehot,[35] the famous go-between of *Lancelot du Lac*, he was limited, so far as I know, to that portion of the Landsdowne MS 757 available in Paget Toynbee's *Dante Studies and Researches*.[36] Since that time the publication of a new and somewhat complete translation of the same romance from a manuscript in the Bibliothèque Nationale (Fonds français, 344) enables us to get a much more complete picture of Galehot, though not an essentially different one.[37]

Galehot has such great admiration for Lancelot, who heretofore has distinguished himself in combat with numerous doughty opponents, that he invites him to spend the night in his tent. The next morning he assures him of his complete devotion and assistance wherever he may need it.[38] Galehot promises to grant his boon, namely, that should he, Galehot,

win in the contest with King Arthur and his knights, he will
surrender and put himself entirely at his disposal. This he
does, to the astonishment and delight of the Arthurian forces.
When Lancelot sees him setting out to do this, he says to himself that this man is indeed a good friend and true comrade.[39]

Passing the next few days at court with Arthur and his
queen, Galehot makes daily visits to Lancelot, whom he has
left in his tent with the two kings, his prisoners. On his first
visit Lancelot begs him to stay with Arthur and do his every
request; he makes Galehot promise never to ask his name
until he sees fit to tell him. The kings tell Galehot that Lancelot has been sighing and weeping a great deal and, when
questioned, Lancelot makes various excuses and does not tell
him the actual reason for his sorrow.

Having returned to the court, Galehot spends the evening
visiting with Gawain and the Queen, who finally asks him to
arrange for a meeting with Lancelot. Galehot agrees to do all
in his power to bring this about. When he returns to Lancelot,
he makes known the Queen's request and gradually perceives
that Lancelot is in love with her. Lancelot entreats Galehot to
ensure all possible secrecy and he replies that he will do everything.[40] He returns to the Queen, who wishes to see Lancelot
that same evening; but Galehot, who seems much more easy-
going than Pandaro, makes no protest when Arthur asks him
to spend the night with him. Next morning he finds Lancelot
much improved—paleness gone and eyes no longer swollen
but restored to their usual beauty. Lancelot again begs secrecy, for he fears many at court will recognize him.[41] Going
to the Queen again, Galehot informs her this is the day of the
meeting; she, too, is very insistent on secrecy.[42]

That evening the Queen calls to her Galehot, the Lady of
Malohault, the maiden Lore of Carduel, and an unknown
damsel to walk to the meadow where Lancelot is to be found,
as Galehot has arranged. The seneschal summons Lancelot;
then he (i. e., the seneschal) and later Galehot retire to bear
the other ladies company. By repeated questioning she makes

Lancelot acknowledge his numerous acts of chivalry, and finally he confesses that he has taken all these risks for her sake. Galehot assures the Queen that Lancelot is the most worshiped and the truest of men; [43] he begs her to have mercy on him and requite his love. The Queen finally acquiesces. [44] Since Lancelot is apparently too timid to kiss the Queen, she raises his chin and bestows a lengthy kiss on him. She then informs Galehot that this knight is Lancelot of the Lake, the son of King Ban of Benoich; whereupon Galehot is most happy and they all go their several ways, Galehot and Lancelot sleeping together and talking all night long of those things "whereof their hearts had full great ease." [45]

Here we have the unprecedented example of a person who is so completely won over to his friend that he gives up all else, all worldly ambitions, in order to serve him henceforth as his devoted companion. From this synopsis it is clear how strikingly Galehot resembles Pandaro. He is unselfishly devoted to Lancelot, constantly serves as adviser and confidant, and frequently acts as messenger between him and the Queen. He arranges for their meeting and in fact engineers the love affair in very complete fashion. For the first time we have a person who meets all the requirements of a go-between as we know him in the person of Pandaro. He is an intimate friend willing to sacrifice all personal interests. He encourages both the Queen and Lancelot and is the agent who brings them together; in one qualification only is he lacking: he is a supernatural being. Since Dr. Paton is more conversant with this phase of the matter than I am, I quote the following paragraph from her introduction:

The role of Galehot is created by the exigencies of the story. He is an essential intermediary between the Queen and Lancelot, for the latter would never have dared approach her alone. This is a questionable part for any good knight to play, and it is therefore fitting that it should be filled by a person of supernatural origin, who, like the lady of the Lake, is not actuated by human scruples; moreover Galehot is almost as completely dominated by his love for Lancelot as Lancelot is by his love for Guinevere, and having no responsibilities toward Arthur, his only desire is to gratify his friend. His service is ended when the love of Lancelot and Guinevere is consummated, and Lancelot has definitely become a member of the household of Arthur. His death follows, therefore, as a natural dramatic conclusion.[46]

Though Galehot and Pandaro have much in common, this relationship does not mean much unless we can show that Boccaccio was familiar with the Lancelot story. Fortunately this is not particularly difficult to establish.[47] In the fifth canto of the *Inferno* (127–38) Dante hears the tale of Francesca of Rimini, who refers to Lancelot in this fashion:

> Noi leggevamo un giorno per diletto
> Di Lancelotto, come 'amor lo strinse:
> Soli eravamo e senza alcun sospetto. . .
> Ma solo un punto fu quel che ci vinse.
> Quando leggemmo il disiato riso
> Eser baciato da contanto amante,
> Questi, che mai da me, non fia diviso,
> La bocca mi bacio tutto tremante:
> Galeotto fu il libro, e chi lo scrisse:
> Quel giorno più non vi leggemmo avante.

We need spend no time connecting these incidents with the Lancelot story, though it may be helpful to remember that this last statement, "Galehot was the book and he who wrote it," probably means that the book and its author combined served to bring Paolo and Francesca together just as Galehot arranged the meeting of Lancelot and Guenevere; but I am not writing a Dante commentary, though strangely enough the next point concerns the first commentator on Dante. In 1373 the Signoria of Florence appropriated one hundred gold florins for a year's series of lectures on "el Dante," as the *Commedia* was known popularly in the Florence of that time. Appropriately enough, the man who was selected to give the lectures had written the best and only biography of Dante and had proved himself a close student and ardent admirer of the great poet; and probably no man living was better qualified for the task than Giovanni Boccaccio. On Sunday,

October 23, 1373, the first lecture was given in the Church of San Stefano in Florence. "Lecture" is almost too dignified a phrase to describe these detailed explanations, and it is hard to imagine their being delivered as addresses; they breathe more the air of exhaustive footnotes, but we are exceedingly grateful that they are what they are.[48] These lectures were cut short by Boccaccio's death; he got no further than the nineteenth line of the seventeenth canto of the *Inferno*, but fortunately the verses quoted above are found in Canto V.

The comment on these lines is somewhat detailed; indeed, so much so that it may be safely concluded that Boccaccio knew the Lancelot story intimately. He speaks of Lancelot as the man of whom the French romances recount so many and such praiseworthy deeds, "deeds, I am inclined to believe, composed more for delight than according to the truth." [49] The passage, "come l'amor lo strinse," is thus explained: "in the above mentioned romances it is written that Lancelot had become most fervently enamoured of Queen Guenevere, wife of King Arthur." [50]

His remarks on Galehot are of course most interesting and important, for he tells us that he was a prince in the story, a kind of giant, who was the first to become aware of the hidden love of Lancelot and Queen Guenevere. He was marvelously devoted to Lancelot and, by going to the Queen and talking with her, acted as the go-between in this love affair. Finally they came together and kissed each other.[51]

The evidence speaks for itself. Personally I cannot help regarding it as conclusive proof that Boccaccio was intimately acquainted with the Lancelot legend; [52] I therefore assume that if he took the notion of go-between from any piece of literature it was most probably from *Lancelot du Lac*.

Young notes that the account of Achilles wooing Hecuba, in the *Roman de Troie*, is a "more immediate, though less adequate, literary source for Boccaccio's Pandaro." [53] But the friend who goes to Polyxena and sues for her daughter's hand in marriage to his friend is only a messenger and has none of the earmarks of a go-between. Young admits that "such a figure is certainly only a very vague prototype for the scheming and courtly 'cugino' of Griseida and 'amico' of Troilo." [54] Consequently I do not think this possibility deserves further consideration, especially since we have seen that Galehot is a much more likely candidate.

Young concludes his study of Pandaro with a consideration of the *Filocolo* as a possible source for this character. [55] He would have us believe that Boccaccio distilled four of the personages in this story and from the remaining essence formed Pandaro. These four people are the Duke of Feramonte, who takes charge of Florio when he is separated from Biancofiore and sent to Montorio; Ascalione, who is Florio's tutor; Glorizia, Biancofiore's nurse; and the most faithful servant ("fedelissimo servidore"), who acts as letter carrier. He makes his point by presenting what he believes are parallel scenes: Feramonte urges Florio to confess his love just as Pandaro urges Troilo to do likewise (II, 1–20); secondly, Ascalione urges Florio to pay no attention to dreams, just as Pandaro makes the same suggestion to Troilo (III, 40); thirdly, the old nurse, Glorizia, urges Biancofiore not to cry so much when Florio departs lest her weeping cause Florio to kill himself; Pandaro admonishes Criseida in like manner in behalf of Troilo (IV, 106–7); finally, the servant carries love letters just as does Pandaro (II, 107–10, 118, 119, 128). Ascalione and the Duke of Feramonte are social equals and friends of Florio; the servant and nurse are inferior socially but perform services similar to Pandaro's. That Boccaccio had in mind the various functions of these four personages and from them took the hint for his Pandaro is entirely possible, but I think it far more probable that he was influenced by the Galehot type and possibly some unknown friend who helped him in his wooing of Maria d'Aquino. Let us briefly review the possibility of there having been a go-between in Boccaccio's own love affair. [56]

When in 1335 Boccaccio gave up the study of canon law

which he had begun in 1329, he turned to literature and, though he appears to have had no guide in this new field, he did at least have faithful friends whose counsel he sought. Among these were Giovanni Barrili, the jurisconsult and later seneschal for King Robert in Provence, and in particular Paolo da Perugia, a scholarly gentleman who became King Robert's librarian in 1332. Predecessor of the later humanists, he was much interested in history and poetry and even compiled a great encyclopedia of historical and mythological material which is now lost but which Boccaccio used in his work on the genealogy of the gods (*De Genealogiis Deorum*).

A friend whom Boccaccio honored with Pandaro-like devotion and intimacy was Niccolò Acciaiuoli, to whom, two years after he left Florence (1340), he wrote: "Nicola, if any trust can be placed in the miserable, I swear to you by my suffering soul that the departure of Trojan Aeneas was not a deeper sorrow to the Carthaginian Dido than was yours to me: not without reason, though you knew it not: nor did Penelope long for the return of Ulysses more than I longed for yours." [57] Again, most unhappy because of his return to Florence, he wrote Niccolò: "I can write nothing here where I am in Florence, for if I should I must write not in ink, but in tears. My only hope is in you—you alone can change my unhappy fate." [58] This is certainly interesting information, but it does not tell us enough. From the evidence at hand there is no way of knowing whether or not Boccaccio used a go-between to further his interests with Maria d'Aquino. However, we do know that the *Filostrato* is autobiographical, that Troilo and Criseida speak for Boccaccio and Maria. Does it seem unlikely then, especially since he had an intimate friend, that, having brought a third character into the story, he might have taken the suggestion from his own experience? This is of course pure conjecture, but I do not think it entirely idle.

I have endeavored to show the possibility of Boccaccio's having derived the hint for his Pandaro from medieval literature and from his own love affair. Yet, if he did not take the suggestion from either of these sources, the possibility remains that he might have obtained it from still a third source, the *De Amore* of Andreas Capellanus. From this, the most important treatise on the courtly love system, we may infer that the position of the go-between in the code is not prominent, but it is there. In a brilliant article entitled "Aspects of the Story of Troilus and Criseyde," [59] Professor Young has brought together some of the passages in which Andreas discusses the propriety of a third party in love-making. Since they throw a good deal of light on the problem at hand, we may examine them in some detail.

In the first chapter of the *De Amore* Andreas, speaking of the nature of love, sanctions the idea of a go-between when he tells the lover that, if his love seems to be getting the best of him, he may seek help and find a go-between; it is indeed significant I think that here almost at the very beginning he sanctions the *internuntium*.[60] One of the twelve precepts which he sets down is "do not have many secretaries for your love." [61] Almost as if elaborating this idea he recurs to it later on and explains that the law of secrecy is not violated when love is revealed to certain persons; these are a secretary (*secretarium*) for the lover, a female secretary (*secretariam*) for the lady, and for both a faithful go-between (*internuntium fidelem*), "by whom," as he says, "love may be secretly and justly guided." [62]

I have also found two other references which, though less specific, tend to confirm the idea. This all goes to prove that the go-between had a definite function in the courtly love system. Consequently it would seem that Professor Kittredge was somewhat in error when he wrote: "The system of courtly love had neither comfort nor excuse for Pandarus. Though Cressida's love for Troilus was blameless, or even meritorious, under the code, yet that same code, in its inconsistency, held no justification for the go-between." [63]

Perhaps the most important source for Pandaro is the most

obvious and therefore the least frequently mentioned: the creative faculty of one of the world's great literary artists. Certainly Boccaccio was entirely capable of originating and developing the character of Pandaro quite independently of literary tradition, courtly love theory, or actual life. Here we are dealing with that most intangible of problems, the creative process of a man of genius. Boccaccio has been dead for more than five centuries, the records are scant, and tradition helps us not at all; the problem is insoluble. Personally I feel that Boccaccio, one of the great scholars of his time and obviously an avid reader, knew a great deal more about ancient and medieval literature than most of his modern critics and undoubtedly derived an inestimable abundance of inspiration therefrom. He was directly acquainted with the Arthurian cycle; he may have had a go-between in his own affair with Maria; possibly he knew the work of Andreas. The sensible view, then, seems to be that, though all these elements were important, yet the most important factor was his own imagination, his own creative ability.

PART THREE

TROILUS AND CRISEYDE

VII

PANDARUS

BEFORE proceeding to that minute analysis of the *Troilus* which is the object of this study and which will begin with a detailed consideration of the characters of the go-betweens as portrayed by Boccaccio and Chaucer, we may well pause to say a few words about that delightful rascal whom the English poet so completely transformed. The passionate young rake of the *Filostrato* and cousin of Criseida has become in the *Troilus* a much more solid sort of person who, though he still likes a good time, has lost much of the vim and vigor of his Italian ancestor; if not considerably advanced in years, he is at least appreciably more mature. However, the mere fact that Chaucer has made him the uncle of Criseyde does not justify the usual assumption that he is a middle-aged person and all that this rather vague label connotes. Though probably older than either Troilus or Criseyde, he is still young enough to be Troilus' boon companion, and his advice to the heroine is obviously not that of a person far advanced in years; but this question will be more fully considered later on.

In the English poem Pandarus plays a far more important rôle than in the *Filostrato* since he has to deal with a woman quite different from her Italian prototype; much astute reasoning and many subtle speeches are required before Criseyde finally yields. In his illuminating introduction to the *Filostrato*, N. E. Griffin sums him up in this fashion:

Pandarus contemplates Troilus with the delight which an older man of more mature wisdom and riper experience beholds the fortunes of a youthful and still undisillusioned enthusiast—a visible reminder of his own vanished past and of the rôle which he himself would still play if he could. He is the outstanding example in literature of the man who finds a keener delight in the love affairs of another than in his own. That we have in Chaucer's Pandarus what Kittredge has happily styled "the sympathetic ironist" in place of the conventional "man about town" of Boccaccio, describes, if it does not explain, the nature of the transformation.[1]

Without further attention to the change which Chaucer wrought, let us see whether some satisfactory explanation may not be arrived at which will enable us to understand "the nature of the transformation." The only way we can do this is to scan the two poems rather minutely in order to find out exactly what Chaucer contributed of his own. Such a study will doubtless prove tedious by reason of its detail, but it is only by consideration of the minutiae that we may arrive at a better understanding of the larger aspects of the work.

Pandaro enters the story of the *Filostrato* in the opening stanza of the second canto. I shall analyze this personage in some detail in order to see just what kind of character Boccaccio has created. He tells us that one day as Troilo is resting pensively on his couch "a young Trojan of high lineage and of abundant spirits" appears suddenly in his room and solicitously inquires of Troilo just what the trouble may be. Troilo tells him that his woe is so terrible that he wishes to die without making known his sorrow. When Pandaro hears this, his pity increases and also his desire to know what the trouble is. He begs to be told what is wrong and points out that "it is not the act of a friend to keep anything hidden from his friend." He wishes to share his affliction and comfort his distress, if he may do so. Troilo agrees to tell Pandaro but only because he wants to please his friend by granting his request. When Troilo admits that he is in love, Pandaro very mildly reproaches him for not having let him know about it sooner so that he might have aided and advised him. We now learn that Pandaro himself is a lover and an unsuccessful one, too, and though Troilo questions the ability of another to help him when he cannot help himself, Pandaro nevertheless points out that a man who cannot protect himself from poison is capable of counseling another against like danger. Pandaro admits that he has loved unhappily and unfortunately still does so; this is entirely due to the fact that he has failed to keep his love secret. But he continues to assure Troilo of his devotion, urges that he have confidence in him, share his sorrow, and forget his troubles, if possible: "by talking assuage your grief." He then very suavely suggests that he may know the lady in question and thus may be able to render real assistance. This seems to be just what is needed to bring Troilo to the properly receptive mood, and he insinuates that the lady is one of Pandaro's relatives, that this is why he has been so hesitant about admitting the fact. Pandaro already suspects whom Troilo means and assures him that it will be but a short time before he will deliver him from his torment. After a bit more urging, Troilo tells him, "Love has seized me for your cousin . . . Criseida." Pandaro receives this announcement jovially and assures Troilo that he could not find a better person to love; her only fault is that she holds amorous affairs in contempt. But he promises Troilo that this is no great difficulty and that he will win her with his soft words. He says they are both deserving of each other and that he will employ all his ingenuity, but that they must exercise the utmost secrecy. Troilo is much pleased at this prospect but points out to Pandaro that Criseida does not recognize him nor requite his love; if he will only get her consent, Troilo will desire no more. Pandaro assures him that he will take care of everything, that he has undertaken much more difficult tasks before, and that now, though the work will be his, the resultant delight will be Troilo's. Pandaro now goes directly to Criseida.

From this introductory scene we have a very clear notion of Pandaro. He is a young man of noble birth and great courage, a worthy companion devoted to his friend, Troilo, for whom he is ready to sacrifice everything, so intimate is

their friendship. Furthermore, in common with Troilo he
is an unsuccessful lover, but he does not seem to take his
sorrow so much to heart. He is, I think, the gay-Lothario type,
a dashing man-of-the-world sort of person, somewhat vacil-
lating, quite sentimental, extremely clever and resourceful.
This is the Pandaro of the first part of the *Filostrato;* how
he lives up to the representation during most of the story
and also how he changes and seems to weaken become evident as the poem develops.

When Pandaro comes to Criseida, he manages the conversation artfully; at first joking and chatting as is usual
among relatives, he remarks that a certain young man admires
her and, in fact, is ardently devoted to her. She is somewhat
surprised at this but does remember that someone has been
gazing at her door a great deal of late. At the end of his
eulogy of Troilo, Pandaro names him and Criseida turns
pale; she insists that, since the death of her husband, she
has no desire to love anyone else; indeed, she seems to be
somewhat insulted, for she protests that if a near relative
tries to make her follow the precepts of Love, what will a
complete stranger attempt? Better far if Pandaro will strive
to comfort Troilo with pleasure and other diversions and
let her live the life she thinks Fortune has ordained for her.

Annoyed at these remarks, Pandaro is now ready to go, but
he stops long enough to berate Criseida for her heartlessness,
to remind her that her beauty will not last forever, and to
suggest that she make hay while the sun shines. Without delay, indeed with astonishing haste, Criseida yields to this
argument and wants to know how Pandaro first took notice
of Troilo's plight. With considerable skill Pandaro paints
a most sympathetic picture of Troilo walking in the forest
and talking of love to him; and for her benefit Pandaro
minutely recounts Troilo's complaint to Love. By this time
I would not say she is completely won over but she agrees to
see Troilo, ostensibly only to please Pandaro, but actually
her desire is perhaps more deep-set than that; at any rate,

it readily becomes so, for after Pandaro leaves she quickly persuades herself of the advisability of being in love again.

In the main, I think Cummings is correct when he observes that "Pandaro is, then, a player of shrewd histrionic ability. When a point is to be gained, he manifests an ingenuity and a faculty for simulation, which comport only with the most perfect of literary psychologizing. He has the skill of a master hand." [2] It is as the stage manager for this splendid melodrama that Pandaro shows himself at his best. Whenever Troilo needs help, he immediately turns to Pandaro. To his first plea (II, 89) Pandaro replies that he understands all and is ready to do everything possible, but that the principal thing to be done now is to write a letter. This accomplished, Pandaro bears it personally to Criseida and prefaces its delivery with the convincing persuasiveness we have come to expect of him. This is the first instance of this sort of thing, but before the story is finished Pandaro as confidential messenger has become a commonplace; even when Criseida has been exchanged, Pandaro visits her frequently during the truces and stays of conflict.

Pandaro's loyalty to his friend is indisputable; it is particularly striking as we follow the two during those fateful ten days after Criseida's departure. Having escorted her out of the city, Troilo returns to his palace and falls to weeping, bemoaning and cursing his fate. Pandaro joins him the next day and shares his sorrow; that he apparently is easily moved to tears we learn from the preceding canto (IV) when Pandaro brings a message from Troilo; having wept all the day with Troilo, he is again grieved on seeing her sad plight.

Pandaro now does his best to divert his friend's attention; he points out that others heretofore have suffered disappointment but that they have had hope and recovered; he should do likewise. The city is large and full of delights which will help him to forget his trouble. He finally agrees to some such plan, and they are entertained most delightfully by Sarpedon for five days. Pandaro apparently enjoys the hunts and par-

ties, but Troilo is too depressed to be even slightly comforted
by such diversions. He wishes to leave after the second day,
but Pandaro points out that going so soon might insult their
host and consequently they linger on for three more days.

But devoted though he is, Pandaro toward the last is quite
unable to cope with the situation. He fears that Criseida,
once gone, will never return, and when after the tenth day
it appears that her defection is to be permanent, his total
inability to remedy matters becomes more and more obvious
and pitiable. He tells Troilo (who has related to him the
dream of the boar that ripped out Criseida's heart) that
dreams and dream interpretation are all nonsense; but when
Troilo, illustrating by actual occurrences, shows that his
dream was minutely accurate and faithfully foreshadowed
succeeding events, Pandaro has no reply. His final words
condemn Criseida for her faithlessness and call on the gods
to punish her.

In both the *Filostrato* and the *Troilus* the go-between enters the story by unexpectedly coming upon the hero bemoaning his love in his room. In the former case he is described
as a "young Trojan of high lineage and abundant spirits,"
whose name is not mentioned until Troilo replies to him in
the next stanza.[3] Chaucer, however, fails to make any mention of his rank or "spirits" and presents him solely as "A
frend of his, that called was Pandare" (I, 548). Pandaro's
questions, "What is the matter dear friend? Hath the bitter
time already thus vanquished thee?" (which occupy but two
lines in the Italian), are not directly translated into English,
and it may be significant of the new Pandarus that he does
not ask what the trouble is but rather (I, 551–53),

> who causeth al this fare?
> O mercy, god! what unhap may this meene?
> Han now thus soone Grekes maad yow leene?

Now for the first time the great humorist makes his bow:
what are you doing here like this? Suffering from remorse

of conscience? Are you engaged in some devotion? Are you
crying because of your sins and are you now, because of fear,
contrite? God save those troops who by besieging our town
can in this wise turn the people to salvation! We are told
that Pandarus asked these questions solely to make Troilus
angry so that he would forget his sorrow for the time being
and display his courage. He well realized that (I, 566–67)

> Ther nas a man of gretter hardinesse
> Than he, ne more desired worthinesse.

The eight lines of the *Filostrato* are not enough to describe
Pandarus as Chaucer first conceives him; the English poet
requires twenty-one verses, but what a significant gain this
is! In the one case all that we know is that a solicitous friend
of high rank has come to inquire about Troilo's welfare; in
the other, however, we are informed at once that this friend
is Pandarus and, through additional conversation, Chaucer
makes us feel that here is a witty, voluble chap who does not
take life too seriously and who does not hesitate to mingle
friendly words with good-natured taunts.

The next nine stanzas (82–90) are largely translation;
I shall consider only the additions. Boccaccio tells us: "Pan-
daro's pity then increased, and his desire to know it" (II, 4);
Chaucer turns this into (I, 582–83):

> This Pandare, that neigh malt for wo and routhe,
> Ful ofte seyde: "allas! what may this be?"

Line 595, "Hid nat thi wo fro me, but tell it blyve," is but
little more than suggested by Boccaccio's (II, 4)

> Discuopri a me qual sia la crudeltade
> Che di morir ti fa tanto calere.

Stanzas 91 and 92 are not found in the Italian; Root notes
that the latter is from the *Roman de la Rose*, 22,562–74.[4]
These lines are of no especial significance, but they do reveal
Pandarus as a user of homely similes based on everyday experiences.

In stanza 93, line 646 is the only one taken from the *Filo-strato:* "Io ho amato sventuratamente" (II, 11). Minimizing Pandaro's activity as a lover, Chaucer fails to translate the following verse: "Ed amo ancora per lo mio peccato" (II, 11); he simply points out that he has had his share of troubles and consequently is the better qualified to advise (I, 646–48):

> I, that have in love so ofte assayed
> Grevances, oughte konne, and wel the more
> Counseillen the of that thow art amayed.

Boccaccio now comes directly to the point: "Therefore have confidence in me, my friend, and tell me who is the cause of this thy so grievous and hard living" (II, 12). Chaucer, however, requires four more stanzas (94–97). Lines 666–67 are suggested by Pandaro's statement (II, 13),

> Ed io, come tu sai, contra mia voglia
> Amo, nè mi può tor nè crescer doglia.

In like manner, lines 673–75,

> And of o thyng right siker maistow be,
> That certein, for to dyen in the peyne,
> That I shal nevere mo discoveren the,

are quite close to the Italian (II, 11):

> L' amore ch' io t' ho sempre mai portato,
> Ti porto e porterò, nè giammai fia
> Chi sappia che da te detto mi sia.

These stanzas reveal the intimacy existing between the two friends and also inform us that Pandarus is likewise an un-happy lover; but how differently he behaves! He is not at home bemoaning his fate but, so far as we are able to judge, has been about the city doing his best to forget his woes.

The next two stanzas (99–100) have no counterpart in the *Filostrato.* Here Pandarus reminds Troilus (I, 687–88) that it is equally wrong to mistrust everyone and to believe everyone, but he is sure that the happy medium is no vice:

"But wel I woot, the mene of it no vice is" (I, 689); and therefore Troilus will do well to tell his woe to someone (I, 691–93):

> and forthi wolde I fayn remeve
> Thi wronge conceyte, and do the som wyght triste,
> Thi wo to telle, and tel me if the liste.

He bolsters up this contention with a reference to the Bible (I, 694–95):

> The wise seith: "wo hym that is allone,
> For, and he falle, he hath non helpe to ryse";

and, as if this were not enough, he tells Troilus that rolling about and weeping is not the easiest way to be successful in love; take warning from the example of Niobe who, weeping for her dead children, was turned into stone, "Whos teres yit in marble ben yseene" (I, 700). These words are characteristic of the English Pandarus, for he revels in learned phrases, classical allusions, and wise sayings. In this respect he is radically different from Pandaro, whose persuasiveness is more effective but far less elaborately expressed; the one produces action while the second reveals character.[5] Pandarus thinks that the way to make a man do something that he does not want to do is not to tell him bluntly and baldly what course of action he should pursue but, rather, gradually to lead up to the main point, expanding on the notion in various ways and especially by quoting sufficient authority and testimony to show that his plan is the correct one, in fact, the only one possible.

The next three stanzas (101–3) provide an expansion of the thirteenth stanza of the *Filostrato*, which sets forth the idea that misery loves company. But Chaucer takes this opportunity to let Pandarus tell us a bit more of himself. He assures Troilus that he need have no fear of trickery or deception: ". . . thow woost I do it for no gyle" (I, 719); and therefore, because you trust me more than anyone else, tell me a bit about your troubles since you know all about mine. Pandaro comes to the point much more directly, I think, by attempting to persuade Troilo not of the wisdom of revealing his sorrow, abstractly considered, but by emphasizing the much more practical consideration: I may know the lady and perhaps I can fix it up (II, 14). But what Chaucer loses in directness here, in this one instance, he makes up in character portrayal in the next nineteen stanzas (104–22), which owe scarcely anything to the *Filostrato* except the statement that Troilo stood in some suspense—a point reëchoed in Chaucer's more powerful observation (I, 722–23),

> Yit Troilus, for al this, no worde seyde,
> But longe he lay, as stylle as he ded were.

Pandarus is much alarmed at Troilus' behavior and attempts to rouse him (I, 729–30):

> And cryde "awake," ful wonderlich and sharpe,
> "What? slombrestow as in a litargie?"

Strangely enough, as Root notes, Boethius defines lethargy as something "whiche that is a comune sykenes to hertes that ben deceived" (I, pr. 2, 14–15).[6] Far be it from me to suggest that all readers of Chaucer should be familiar with this definition, but it is strange that no one has attempted to prove that, in this fashion, Chaucer so early in the story is throwing out a sly hint as to the dénouement.

Troilus does not respond quickly to Pandarus' plea that he behave sensibly. He remembers that all that concerns love should be secret (I, 743–44):

> And, namelich, in his counseil tellynge
> That toucheth love, that oughte ben secree;

and he asks Pandarus to leave him alone with his sorrow (I, 755–60):

> "But suffre me my meschief to bywaille,
> For thi proverbes may me naught availle.

Nor other cure kanstow non for me;
Ek I nyl nat ben cured, I wol deye.
What knowe I of the queene Nyobe?
Lat be thyne old ensaumples, I the preye."

I can easily believe that Troilus was much annoyed at Pandarus' verbiage; he is in a frantic state and wants to be let alone, but Pandarus remains unabashed and is convinced, as ever, that it is his solemn duty to rescue his friend (I, 762–63):

Swich is delit of foles, to bywepe
Hire wo, but seken bote they ne kepe.

And he continues to make the suggestion which Pandaro did, with this difference, however, that while Pandaro intimates that he might know the lady, Pandarus suggests, in effect, "If you will tell me who she is, I shall not hesitate to get in touch with her at once; I shall tell her your trouble and urge her to be more compassionate."

In the next six stanzas (112–17) Pandarus continues his plea by pointing out the folly of Troilus' assumption that the lady will pay no attention to him. Furthermore, if his lady does not know of his love and he should die as a result, she will not impute it to his passion but rather to fear of the besieging Greeks. He who will not reveal his love to his lady must expect her to remain "Unknowe, unkist, and lost that is unsought" (I, 809). But some have loved twenty years without a kiss; then why should he be ready to kill himself on such short acquaintance? Let him be content to serve the damsel and consider this service his reward. These words finally make an impression on Troilus, for he realizes that suicide not only would help his cause not at all but, in addition to being a cowardly act, would also be a sinful one; whereupon he asks Pandarus what he would suggest. Pandarus replies, as brightly as if the idea had just come to him, "The beste is that thow telle me al thi wo" (I, 830). Troilus reminds him that it will be difficult for him to be of any help

in this case because Fortune is his foe; to which Pandarus
answers (I, 843–47),

> Wostow nat wel that Fortune is comune
> To everi manere wight in some degree?
> And yit thou hast this comfort, lo, parde:
> That, as hire joies moten overgone,
> So mote hire sorwes passen everychone.

Perhaps, says Pandarus, she will change for the better:
"Paraunter, thow hast cause for to synge" (I, 854). Leave
your sorrow and remember that whoever would be healed
by a physician must first of all uncover his wound. So devoted is Pandarus that, even if the lady causing all this
sorrow should be his sister, he is willing that she should be
his forever, though it would mean his (Pandarus') eternal
damnation. These lines are not to be found in the Italian
poem save for the reference to the sister (II, 16):

> Se quella ch' ami fosse mia sorella,
> A mio potere avrai tou piacer d' ella.

When Troilus still fails to confess his love, Pandarus proceeds to shake him; whereupon Troilus, almost frightened
to death, summons enough courage to admit that he is in
love with Criseyde. This "rough" scene is not even hinted
at in the *Filostrato*. True, the opening lines of the seventeenth stanza are very close to lines 862–64, but further
than this there is nothing; we are told that Troilo made no
reply "but each moment muffled his face the more closely"
(II, 18). No longer able to withstand Pandaro's urgings,
he takes two stanzas to make the admission which Troilus
made in two lines (873–74). Pandarus is overjoyed to
hear this and the next two stanzas (126–27) are expressions
of his feeling adopted from the *Filostrato*. Stanza 128, however, is Chaucer's invention and likewise the following one
(129); while Boccaccio explains that Criseida is so virtuous
that she is not interested in love, with the inference that

Troilo may have some difficulty, Chaucer does not offer much more than a hint (I, 902–3):

> Requere nat that is ayeyns hyre name,
> For vertu streccheth nat hym self to shame.

The next nine stanzas (130–38) owe but little to the Italian.

> Now loke that a-tempre be thi bridel,
> And, for the beste, ay suffre to the tyde

(I, 953–54) is but an adaptation of the *Filostrato*, II, 23. Otherwise, these stanzas offer us a view of Troilus not to be enjoyed in Boccaccio. True enough, he hints at Troilo's raillery (I, 21) and gives us three stanzas in which he speaks of the folly of love (22–24), but Chaucer, with his eye for detail, is quick to supply the deficiency. Troilus was wont to call on Love as, "Seynt Idyot, lord of thise foles alle" (I, 910). The servants of love "ben verray goddes apes" (I, 913). Troilus has joked about their lying abed suffering the pangs of love and has also made fun of the things they do (915–28). Pandarus, too, remarks that he could easily ridicule Troilus on these grounds, but he is quick to add that he considers him a different sort (I, 930–31):

> But natheles, though that I sholde deye,
> That thow art non of tho, I dorste seye.

Stanza 134 is a good-natured gibe which I shall come back to shortly. In the next stanza Pandarus points out that Troilus should be happy, for she who has heretofore been the cause of all his sorrow will now prove to be none other than his comfort and solace (I, 944–45):

> And thynk wel she, of whom rist al thi wo,
> Hereafter may thy comfort be also.

The very charming verses of stanza 136 are purely English in spite of the similarities to be found in the *Remedia Amoris*, the *Filocolo*, the *Mirour de l'Omme*, and the *Liber Para-*

bolarum.[7] Chaucer may of course have taken the hint from one or from all of these suggested sources, but he has made it into the singularly happy expression of an unusually common thought.

The probability that the first two verses of stanza 137 are from the *Filostrato*, II, 23, I have already noted; the rest of the stanza continues the fatherly advice we have come to expect of Pandarus. Stanza 138 is but an elaborate preparation for 139, in which Pandarus urges Troilus to be steadfast, and from now until the end of the book (sixteen stanzas) Chaucer is indebted to a considerable extent to his source. The metaphor that Pandarus uses ("for to good port hastow rowed," I, 969) is a clever one connected in no way with the Italian (cf. *Roman de la Rose*, 12,760: "a bon port estes arivez").[8] The idea expressed in 972–73 that, unless their efforts are spoiled by sadness or overhaste, he will succeed in his efforts as go-between, "I hope of this to maken a good ende" (I, 973), is adapted from the *Filostrato*, II, 24. The words which precede these in the Italian poem, "thou art worthy of her and she of thee" ("Tu se' di lei ed ella è di te degno"), are not translated, but the idea develops into the eulogy of Criseyde which fills the next two stanzas. Pandaro evidently has some qualms of conscience about acting as go-between (25–26), for he points out that affairs conducted in this fashion are not becoming to a lady of rank nor would it reflect much credit on him were it to become known. But everything will work out satisfactorily if the lovers will only be discreet in both action and appearance and cause no shame to those to whom shame and honor are matters of concern (II, 26). But Pandarus seems to take it for granted that the two lovers will play the game with him and so, after telling Troilus that he will be glad to do everything in his power, he notes that both of them have enough sense to keep the matter quiet (I, 991–94):

> for ye ben bothe wyse,
> And konne it counseil kepe in swych a wyse

> That no man shal the wiser of it be;
> And so we may ben gladed alle thre.

Stanzas 143 and 144 are Chaucer's; the first five lines of 145 are translated from the *Filostrato*, II, 29, lines 1–4. The prayer to Venus, however, which ends the stanza (1014–15) is original on Chaucer's part. The next stanza (146) grows out of the rest of the *Filostrato*, II, 29 and all of 30. In 147 Pandarus is apparently annoyed at Troilus' fears and doubts; at least the sarcastic tone of this stanza would seem to show that he is not in sympathy with the hero's useless worries. All he wants is to be let alone (I, 1027–28):

> For goddes love, I bidde the a boone,
> So lat malone, and it shal be thi beste.

The next five stanzas are largely from the *Filostrato*, II, 31–34. Lines 1042–43 are a splendid revelation of Pandarus' devotion to his friend:

> Yif me this labour and this besynesse,
> And of my spede be thyn al that swetnesse.

How completely Troilus has put himself under Pandarus' influence and power is revealed in stanza 151:

> "Now, Pandare, I kan no more seye;
> But thow wis, thow woost, thow maist, thow art al;
> My lif, my deth, hool in thyn honde I leye;
> Help now!" Quod he: "yis, by my trowthe, I shal."
> "God yelde the, frend, and this in special,"
> Quod Troilus, "that thow me recomaunde
> To hire that may me to the deth comaunde."

Hereupon Pandarus assures him that he will be successful and takes his leave; he goes off pensively, thinking about the best time, place, and manner for the meeting.

Just as the preceding pages have served to introduce us to Pandarus as he is found in Book I, so now we may continue to trace his development through the remaining four books of the poem. Thus far there has been very little in the way of action—true enough, the poem is very slight in this respect—but now the stage is all set, the drama is ready to get under way, and in spite of the poet's lingering manner and diffuse method the play will soon be over. As foreshadowed in the first book, Pandarus assumes a rôle of great importance as the instigator of the action; everything that takes place is due to his intervention; without his continual interference in the affairs of his friend, nothing would have happened; there could have been no poem—at least no poem at all comparable to the present masterpiece.

Most striking is the picture of Pandarus at the opening of Book II. This man who is so hardened to love affairs, so used to the disappointments of the world, so ready, so willing, so able to cure Troïlus of all his troubles, has himself been smitten. It is springtime, the third of May to be exact, the season, then as now, when a young man's fancy lightly turns (II, 61–63)—

> So shope it, that hym fil that day a teene
> In love, for which in wo to bedde he wente,
> And made, or it was day, ful many a wente.

But this is of short duration; the swallow Proigne awakens him; he is immediately mindful of Troilus' plight, assures himself that the time is astrologically favorable, and sets out for Criseyde's palace.

The first meeting of Pandarus with Criseyde (II, 50–595) is largely Chaucer's own; it of course follows the main outline of the *Filostrato* but is so greatly modified that it deserves especially close study. What Boccaccio related in thirty-four stanzas (II, 34–67, i. e., 264 lines) occupies twice as much space in the *Troilus* (545 lines). Pandaro goes to Criseida directly and comes to the point of his visit with as little delay as possible. Chaucer substitutes for this the leisurely opening of Book II, the new light on Pandarus as a lover, and the description of his arrival at Criseyde's palace —where the lady sat, how she greeted him, what they said to each other. While Pandaro loses but little time in leading up to the purpose of his visit and is almost equally direct in telling Criseida of Troilo's love, Pandarus acts quite differently. Of particular interest is Criseyde's reaction when he urges her to lay aside her book, dance with him, "and lat us don to May som observaunce" (112). Heaven forbid, exclaims Criseyde, are you mad? Is that becoming to a widow? You are so wild I am frightened; you seem to rave. It is more fitting for me to live in a cave and read "holy seyntes lyves"; let girls and young wives do the dancing. This is quite different from a similar scene in the *Filostrato* where Criseida, already informed of Troilo's love, declares that since her husband's death her wishes have been far removed from love; she still grieves for him and will continue to do so. She goes on to say that Troilo will easily find someone else to love and that she wishes to continue in her present state, the one Fortune apparently has marked out for her. It is with a minimum of persuasion that Pandaro finally gets her to agree to see Troilo, and at the conclusion of this first scene it is only too evident that she is very much in love; all her statements about revering the memory of her dead husband were platitudes, her resistance to Pandaro's eloquence apparently all sham.

Far different is Criseyde's conduct; in the end, of course, she behaves in much the same fashion, but just as she is a much more complex character, so likewise is a much more artful and ingenious Pandarus required to win her over. Properly rebuffed in his desire to do May "som observaunce," he immediately sails back on another tack (II, 120–21):

> "As evere thryve I," quod this Pandarus,
> "Yit koude I telle a thyng to doon yow pleye."

This is a very astute move on his part, for he immediately arouses her curiosity and holds it throughout the rest of the scene; instead of his trying to tell her something, she has taken the initiative and urges him to speak freely. But Pandarus realizes the importance of gaining momentum slowly and is highly successful in keeping Criseyde interested (II, 141–44):

> Tho gan she wondren moore than biforn
> A thousand fold, and down hire eyen caste;
> For nevere, sith the tyme that she was born,
> To knowe thyng desired she so faste.

After this they spend some time in pleasant conversation, and Criseyde finally inquires about Hector. Pandarus shrewdly seizes this opportunity to talk about his brother, Troilus, whom he calls (II, 158–61)

> The wise, worthi Ector the secounde,
> In whom that alle vertu list habounde,
> As alle trouthe, and all gentilesse,
> Wisdom, honour, fredom, and worthinesse.

These lines enumerate the virtues which the typical courtly lover should possess. Criseyde rejoices that they both are getting along nicely and remarks on their prowess and virtue (II, 167–68):

> For grete power and moral vertu here
> Is selde yseyn in o persone yfere.

Pandarus goes on to say that both Troilus and Hector are as "voide of vices" as any men under the sun; Hector's "vertu" is greater than his power and the same applies to Troilus. Criseyde rejoins that she knows this is true of Hector and is glad to hear the same said of Troilus, who everyone says is so worthy in arms and so gentle in conduct. Pandarus devotes two more stanzas (28–29) to describing Troilus' prowess and adds a few lines on his amiability and good nature. Pandarus is about to go, but Criseyde prevails upon him to stay and listen to her "tale"; exactly what this was we are not told but it must have been very pleasant, for Pandarus again wishes to dance and urges her to cast her widow's weeds to the devil (II, 223–24):

> What list yow thus youre self to disfigure,
> Sith yow is tid so glad an aventure?

Criseyde urges Pandarus to speak his mind to her (II, 246–49):

> But, for the love of god, I yow biseche,
> As ye ben he that I moost love and triste,
> Lat be to me youre fremde manere speche,
> And sey to me, youre nece, what yow liste.

But still Pandarus keeps Criseyde in suspense; he assures her of his friendship, promises to do nothing that seems "unsittynge" to him, and finally, after a plea on her part, breaks the news of Troilus' love (II, 319–20):

> The noble Troilus, so loveth the,
> That, but ye helpe, it wol his bane be.

After this, through four stanzas (47–50), he implores her to have mercy on Troilus, to bestow her favors on him if she wishes to save him from certain death. But Pandarus is very insistent on the part he is playing; he does not regard himself as the moral pervert which some of his critics hold him to be; on the contrary (II, 352–57),

> For me were levere thow and I and he
> Were hanged, than I sholde ben his baude,
> As heigh as men myghte on us alle se;
> I am thyn em, the shame were to me
> As wel as the, if that I sholde assente,
> Thorugh myn abet, that he thyn honour shente.

Pandarus wishes her to cheer him up, that and nothing more (II, 363–64):

> This al and som, and pleynly, our entente;
> God help me so! I nevere other mente.

I do not think that Pandarus strengthens his protestation of sincerity any by his verbiage in the next three stanzas (53–55). Here he assures Criseyde that there is nothing for her to be disturbed about, for people will only think of their meeting as "love of frendes"; and when she asks him what she should do about it, he replies (II, 390–92):

certein, best is
That ye hym love ayeyn for his lovynge;
As love for love is skilful guerdonynge.

In Boccaccio's words he urges her to lose no time, to remember that death or old age will soon rob her of her beauty. Criseyde, however, much disturbed that her best friend would not only urge her to love but even attempt to justify her doing so, bursts into tears and is much upset; whereupon Pandarus declares that if he is mistrusted so, he will not come there again that week: though you apparently care nothing about us dead or alive, yet it makes no difference about me if only Troilus might live! And once more he declares his innocence very emphatically (II, 437–41):

> So lat me nevere out of this hous departe,
> If that I mente harm or vilenye!
> But sith I se my lord mot nedes dye,
> And I with him, here I me shryve, and seye
> That wikkedly ye don us bothe deye.

But when he starts to go away, Criseyde jumps up and immediately causes him to stay. This scene will be handled in greater detail later on when we come to Criseyde, but here it may be noted that there is nothing spontaneous about her conduct; a certain amount of thought precedes all her actions here and makes us have doubts as to the heartiness of her acquiescence in Pandarus' request. But at any rate she agrees and urges Pandarus to tell her how he first became aware of Troilus' love. This he proceeds to do in the twelve leisurely stanzas (73–84) which follow, lines which do not derive a great deal from corresponding passages in the *Filostrato* (II, 56–64). He discovered it one day as they were walking in the palace garden and planning some strategy against the Greeks. When Pandarus heard him groan, he became silent and, listening carefully, heard Troilus' complaint to Love. And then again only recently he found him in a dreadful state; this time he told him the cause of all his misery. Though sworn to secrecy, he has consented to tell Criseyde only as a necessary step in saving his friend's life; and once again he emphasizes the rôle he is playing (II, 580–81):

> And sith ye woot that myn entent is clene,
> Tak hede therof, for I non yvel meene.

Pandarus then expresses the opinion that there were never two people so well matched as she and Troilus are and hopes that they will both soon be joined; then the following stanza, containing Criseyde's evasive reply, brings this first scene to a satisfactory end (II, 589–95):

> "Nay, therof spak I nought, a ha!" quod she;
> "As helpe me god, ye shenden every deel."
> "A! mercy, dere nece," anon quod he,
> "What so I spak, I mente nat but wel,
> By Mars, the god that helmed is of steel;
> Now beth nat wroth, my blood, my nece dere."
> "Now wel," quod she, "foryeven be it here."

It is significant of Chaucer's method to note that the additional details with which he elaborates this scene all tend to enhance the courtly love element. We see this especially, as has been noted, in the emphasis which is placed on the many fine qualities which distinguish Hector and Troilus, qualities which are commonplace in courtly literature and present in the typical courtly lover. The frequent attempts which Pandarus makes to justify his rôle of go-between are important additions which substantiate the impression that the changes introduced by Chaucer are for the most part corrections of and improvements on Boccaccio.[9] Pandarus' declarations of intention and his professions of innocence in bringing Troilus and Criseyde together help complete the impression we have of him thus far: that of a devoted friend and affectionate uncle; furthermore, they help to make him that kind of well-rounded *internuntius* that would have made Andreas Capellanus himself rejoice. A third improvement which Chaucer makes on his original, a change of which there

are numerous examples scattered throughout the poem, is his
habit of couching courtly love in the parlance of the Christian religion. This is suggested in the scene in which Pandarus relates his first knowledge of his friend's amour. In his
complaint to Love, Troilus begged mercy in these words
(II, 523–25):

> lord have routhe upon my peyne,
> Al have I ben rebell in myn entente,
> Now *mea culpa*, lord, I me repente.

This passage breathes a distinctly, in fact an almost exclusively, religious air; much condensed, it is unmistakably
the Act of Penance addressed to Cupid, and the *mea culpa*
is of course taken over directly from the *Confiteor*. The two
stanzas which follow, in which Troilus begs the God of Love
to guard him against despair, have all the sincerity and depth
of feeling one might expect to find in a hymn to the Almighty. It is quite as Root says: "He addresses Love in language suggested by words which Boethius applies to the supreme God, and prays to be defended against the mortal sin
of despair." [10]

We next meet Pandarus in Troilus' room whither he has
been summoned by the Trojan hero fresh from skirmish with
the Greeks. The beautiful stanza (139) expressing Troilus'
joy on hearing the outcome of the visit with Criseyde is
translated almost literally from the corresponding passage
in the *Filostrato* (II, 80), but the lines following are largely
Chaucerian. It is another excellent example of the English
poet's tendency to take a hint from his original and expand
it considerably. In the Italian poem, for instance, we are told
that Troilo embraced Pandaro a thousand times, kissed him
as much again, and was so happy that he could not have
been more so had he been given a thousand Troys. Chaucer
gains greatly in effectiveness by turning these words into
direct discourse. The four lines of the *Filostrato* which I have
just paraphrased become in the *Troilus* the much less effusive

statement (974): "And to Pandare he held up bothe his hondes." He then goes on to express his feelings in words that, save for the "thousand Troys," are all his own. He is so happy that his heart "It spredeth so for joie, it will to-sterte" (980). And what is he to do? How long before he shall see his beloved? Pandarus may tell him to wait but that will be of no help, for he (II, 986–87)

> That hangeth by the nekke, soth to seyne,
> In grete disese abideth for the peyne.

To this Pandarus devotes a 56-line reply (988–1043) in which he recommends to Troilus a policy of moderation ("Al esily, now, for the love of Marte!") and suggests that he write Criseyde a letter. This suggestion comes from Boccaccio, but otherwise the passage is largely Chaucer's own work. A significant change is Pandarus' profession of devotion to Troilus. Pandaro declares not only that he has never dissembled but also that he is ready to do for Troilo absolutely anything, without scruple and without being urged either by force or entreaty (II, 90). Pandarus, on the other hand, though he also makes profession of his faithfulness, is not so frank when it comes to saying that he will do not only what is fitting but anything at all; he simply states that, just as in the past he has worked for Troilus' pleasure, so he will continue to do (997–98)

> emforth my wit
> Don al thi lust, and shal with al my myght.

But he adds to this the command not found in the Italian: do as I say and everything will turn out all right (999–1001):

> Do now as I shal seyn, and fare aright;
> And if thow nylt, wite al thi self thi care,
> On me is nought along thyn yvel fare.

Now follows Pandarus' suggestion of the letter and the statement that he will be glad to carry it to Criseyde. The rest of the passage, entirely Chaucerian, portrays Pandarus the man of artifice: when you think I am there, ride by and you will find us sitting in a window gazing into the street; salute us and take a look at me if you wish, but do not linger there— "god shilde us fro meschaunce!"—ride on; preserve your self-control while I talk to Criseyde of things which I am sure will make your ears burn. Pandarus now proceeds to give Troilus practical advice about the letter: do not be scornful, avoid difficult arguments, and do not make it too much like a professional job; "biblotte it with thi teris ek a lite," and if you once get a good effect with a word, even though it is fine, do not repeat it too often. To emphasize the necessity of this, he devotes a whole stanza to the striking figure of the harper who, though the best one living, would bore his audience if he employed all his five fingers on only one string. And furthermore, Troilus, see that there is nothing discordant in your writing (II, 1039–43):

> hold of thi matere
> The forme alwey, and do that it be lik;
> For if a peyntour wolde peynte a pyk
> With asses feet, and hedde it as an ape,
> It cordeth naught; so nere it but a jape.

Chaucer now goes back to the *Filostrato*, though it should be noted that Troilus' protest against writing the letter is somewhat different from that of Troilo; the latter fears to do it because he thinks Criseida, ashamed, will reject it with angry words; while Troilus, in his innocence, fears that he will say something unwelcome to her or that out of malice or spite she will not receive the letter. Pandarus, quite impatient with Troilus, asks him to do as he has suggested so that he may bring back an answer; if he does not like that, why let it be (II, 1056–57),

> and sory mote he ben his lyve,
> Ayeins thi lust that helpeth the to thryve.

Troilus, like Troilo, invokes the God of Love to help him with the letter, and he also begs Minerva, Goddess of Wisdom, to aid him. Chaucer then tells us (1064) that he "sette hym down, and wrote right in this wyse," but he does not reproduce the letter; instead, the eleven stanzas of the *Filostrato* (II, 96–106) are condensed into three of indirect discourse in the *Troilus*. Chaucer probably felt as we do about Troilo's letter, i. e., "it axeth muchel space," and hence, particularly in view of the numerous additions already made, the English poem really gains by this condensation.

Pandaro apparently takes the letter to Criseida on the same day, but Chaucer tells us specifically that the above action takes place at night and that when Pandarus starts for Criseyde's palace it is "by tyme a morwe." He is in a jovial mood as usual and blames his early visit on his inability to sleep, a characteristic lover's plaint (II, 1098–99):

> I may nat slepe nevere a Mayes morwe;
> I have a joly wo, a lusty sorwe.

Criseyde's reception of Pandarus is somewhat different from that in the Italian story. There they come together almost immediately; she asks him why he has come, and in the same stanza he speaks of the letter he bears. Criseyde, however, not only asks why he has come but begs him to tell her of his "joly wo": to which he roguishly replies, "By god . . . I hoppe alwey byhynde." He then reports that a Greek spy with new tidings is in town, and at his suggestion they go into the garden so that, in full privacy, he may tell her at length about all this. This device, together with Pandarus' own love affair, is an addition by the English poet. Much alike, however, is the reception of the letter by the two heroines, though Criseyde is much more vehement in her rejection of the proffered writing. Criseida's request, "Have some respect for me as well as the young man," becomes in Chaucer (II, 1130–34):

> scrit ne bille,
> For love of god, that toucheth swich matere,

> Ne brynge me noon; and also, uncle deere,
> To myn estat have more rewarde, I preye,
> Than to his lust; what sholde I more seye?

That Criseyde is obviously marking time is perfectly clear from the lines which follow. Criseida takes the letter at once and hides it in her bosom; our English Pandarus, however, provides a decidedly more vigorous scene (II, 1154–55):

> "Refuse it nat," quod he, and hente hire faste,
> And in hire bosom down the lettre he thraste.

From now on, it seems to me that Criseyde is a different person. She seems to have stopped her outright connivance with Pandarus and apparently is quite in love with Troilus. Otherwise it is difficult to understand her sudden readiness to read the letter. When they come into the hall, she tells Pandarus that they will dine soon, but first she goes directly to her room, her sole purpose being "ful pryvely this lettre for to rede" (1176). The rest of this scene is managed with far greater dexterity than in the *Filostrato*, where Criseida, portrayed as deeply in love with Troilo, writes him a long letter explaining that she cannot grant his request, since she seeks that which is most to be desired in the world, i. e., to live and die in good repute; Troilo of course is not slow to see that she is much enamored of him. In the English poem, on the contrary, we come up to this point in the usual leisurely manner: first dinner, then small talk at the window, and finally Pandarus' pseudo-innocent query (II, 1196–97):

> How liketh you the lettre that ye woot?
> Kan he theron? for, by my trouthe, I noot.

Criseyde is not at all communicative on this point. She blushed, began to hum, and then said, "so I trowe"; beyond that the reader has to guess. Fortunately the heroine has changed her mind and accedes to Pandarus' request that she write Troilus at least a few lines thanking him for the good will he has manifested. Chaucer tells us that this is the first letter she ever "wroot"; possibly that is the reason he keeps

it from us, for in the Italian poem Criseida's epistle fills seven
stanzas (II, 121–27). "As fer" as Chaucer "kan under-
stonde," the context of the letter, which he relates in a single
stanza (II, 175) was this: she said she did not love him but
that she would always like to act as a sister to him, "to doon
his herte an ese." Boccaccio does not even suggest this sisterly
relation here, though on another occasion (II, 134) Criseida
tells Pandaro that because of Troilo's great goodness and
noble nature, she will love him like a brother, "come fratel."

When Criseida finishes her letter, she gives it at once to
Pandaro, who immediately proceeds to set out in search of
Troilo. In the English poem, on the contrary, eleven stanzas
(176–86) intervene between the letter scene and Pandarus'
departure. This makes possible Troilus' ride by the window,
an incident no more than hinted at in an earlier part of the
Filostrato (II, 82) where we are told that Pandaro and
Troilo ride by Criseida's window to admire her beauty. Now
of course it is the crafty Pandarus who sits gazing down into
the street; Criseyde naturally comes to the window and joins
him, thus giving Pandarus an excellent opportunity for two
stanzas (177–78) of commendation before Troilus passes.
As they talk, he approaches and she blushes deeply; he too
is affected—"oft his hewes muwe"—and rides by, after sa-
luting her and nodding to Pandarus. The author now gives
us his comment on this incident, the sum of which is: thank
Heaven, she has fallen and fallen hard! It is now like a thorn
in her side (II, 1273–74):

> She shal nat pulle it out this nexte wyke.
> God sende mo swich thornes on to pike!

Pandarus cannot wait to learn Criseyde's reaction and asks
her very bluntly if a woman would be doing right to let
Troilus die just because she showed him no pity; and her immediate reply is, "nay, by my trouthe." Pandarus urges her
to forget her scrupulousness and to speak with him in order
to ease his heart. However, it is too soon to grant him any

such liberty; her intention is to love him unknown and to reward him with nothing but her sight. Though Pandarus does not approve of such an attitude, he preserves a discreet silence and tells himself that this shall not happen if he may do anything about it; such a notion shall not be held for two full years. This last remark is fully in keeping with Andreas' teaching that a widow may not love again until two years have elapsed after the husband's death.[11] At this point Chaucer feels there is no need for discussing things further, and so he abruptly asks: "What sholde I make of this a long sermoun?" Whereupon Pandarus apparently agrees with Criseyde for the time being and then at evening "roos and toke his leve" (1302).

Returning to Troilus, Pandarus finds him in bed like a lover in a trance, tossed between hope and despair, "betwixen hope and derk desesperaunce" (1307). This is in marked contrast to the Italian, which relates that Pandaro simply gives the letter to Troilo, who reads it hastily, sighing and suffering change of heart according to the words (II, 128). Chaucer, expanding this account by putting it into direct discourse, recounts the conversation between the two and then tells us how Troilus, at first satisfied with or, rather, resigned to, the suggestion in her letter, soon finds his desire increasing with his hope; under Pandarus' guidance "fro day to day," he writes her of his sorrow and performs the other "observaunces" proper to a lover under these conditions. What these duties were he does not bother to tell us, for doubtless he felt that his readers were sufficiently familiar with the courtly conventions to picture for themselves the conduct of a typical lover in this state. The cast of dice in stanza 193, a striking metaphor of the vicissitudes of Fortune, is a Chaucerian addition; Root notes that "dice were actually used as a method of divination to foretell success in love." [12]

Troilus is well-nigh desperate and beseeches Pandarus to help and succor him. The latter, though he "wex wel neigh

ded for routhe" on hearing this, promises to do something
about it at once (II, 1362–65):

> And, by my trouthe, or it be dayes two,
> And god to-forn, yet shal I shape it so,
> That thow shalt come into a certeyn place,
> There as thow mayst thi self preye hire of grace.

To this Pandarus adds another stanza (in his best advice-to-
the-lovelorn manner), in which he tells us that, according to
those who are expert in love, one of the things that helps a
man most is the opportunity of talking and revealing his
misery (II, 1372–73):

> For in good herte it mot som routhe impresse,
> To here and see the giltlees in distresse.

Then follow nearly four stanzas of philosophizing in which
Pandarus, well fortified with proverbial lore, assures Troilus
of the accuracy of this advice and impresses him with the fact
that the longer people are occupied accomplishing something,
the greater will be their delight (II, 1391–93):

> Men shal rejoyssen of a grete empryse
> Acheved wel, and stant withouten doute,
> Al han men ben the lenger ther aboute.

When Troilus admits that it is his brother Deiphebus whom
he loves the most, Pandarus immediately sets out to bring him
there, for it is he who will ease Troilus' heart, though he
shall remain "unwist of it hym selve."

The remainder of Book II is one of Chaucer's best additions
to the story. While Boccaccio required only eighty-eight lines
(II, 133–43) to bring Pandaro's efforts to a successful outcome, Chaucer saw fit to use fourteen hundred. These are accounted for by the notable invention of the dinner party at
the home of Deiphebus, an addition which fills the rest of
Book II and the first 231 lines of Book III (a total of 595
lines), and the supper with Pandarus (III, 505–1309),
which accounts for the remaining 805 new lines. On the for-

mer episode Root remarks, "Chaucer found a hint in *Fil.* 7. 77–85, a scene near the end of the *Filostrato* not otherwise utilized by Chaucer, which is laid at the house of Deifebo." [13] If the English poet found a hint in this passage, it was certainly of the most tenuous sort. Furthermore, unless I am very much afield in interpreting this section of the *Filostrato*, the scene is not laid at the house of Deifebo; the context of the passage lends full support to my view, though there is no denying that, grammatically considered, Troilo *might* have gone to Deifebo. The first part of the stanza tells us that from day to day Troilo's grief at Criseida's failure to return increased with the decline of his hope and that as a result he had to take to his bed, for he had no more strength. Now comes the perplexing couplet which runs thus (VII, 77):

> Ma pur per caso un dì 'l venne a vedere
> Deifebo, a cui molto ben volea.

The Griffin-Myrick translation (p. 465), however, lends full support to my contention: "But indeed by chance there came to visit him Deiphoebus, for whom he had much love." When they have finished talking, it is Deifebo who goes away (VII, 82):

> Troilo remase con gli usati guai,
> Deifebo a' fratei sen venne ratto,
> Ed ebbe a lor tutto contato il fatto.

Most of this incident is devoted to Deifebo's urging Troilo to join his friends in battle with the Greeks once more, an invitation which Troilo accepts. Deifebo, however, recognizing the cause of Troilo's condition, on his return related it to his companions. Accordingly they asked their ladies to go visit Troilo and try to cheer him with music and song. Thus it is that Polyxena, Helen, Cassandra, and several others come to comfort the love-sick Troilo. Consequently it seems clear that Chaucer is even less indebted to this passage than has been thought; indeed, with the exception of the friendly relations which exist between the two, and the statement

that the ladies filled Troilo's room with music and songs, the
English poet's indebtedness seems to be practically nil. If the
above remarks are sound, Mr. Griffin's footnote on this passage must also be revised in part, a task the reader may
easily do for himself:

It is instructive . . . to observe how different is the use which Chaucer makes of the hospitality of Deiphoebus from that made of it by the
Italian poet. In Boccaccio the visit was paid to divert Troilo from his
grief at the non-return of Criseida; in Chaucer it is paid so that Troilus
may offer the guest of honor his moral support against an unscrupu-
lous lawyer, who, in the absence of the heroine's father, has designs
upon her estate. Nothing could better illustrate Chaucer's detached
and humorous attitude toward the story as contrasted with the serious
and preoccupied attitude of Boccaccio.[14]

   The poet tells us that Deiphebus had always been Pandarus' great friend and that, except for Troilus, there was
no man whom he loved so much. Deiphebus employs a
stanza (202) reciprocating this feeling and, replying to
Pandarus' request that he be of assistance to him, states
that he never has been and never will be against anything
in which his opposition might displease him. Pandarus now
puts into execution a piece of very deliberate trickery, for
he tells Deiphebus that there are some men who wish to
oppress Criseyde and seize her property, and Pandarus asks
that he should be their friend, "withouten more speche"
(1421). Not only does he assent but he is also very willing
to follow out Pandarus' suggestion that he invite Criseyde
to come to him on the morrow; in addition, he decides to ask
Helen and requests Pandarus to invite Troilus to dine with
him.
   With all of this satisfactorily arranged the arch con-
spirator goes "as streyght as lyne" to the house of his niece
whom he finds just risen from her repast. He bursts out
heroically (1464–65),

> O verray god, so have I ronne!
> Lo, nece myn, se ye nat how I swete?

and goes on to relate how Poliphete is about to bring a lawsuit against her, something she naturally knows nothing about. She apparently does not care to do anything about it, but then Pandarus explains the interest of Deiphebus in her welfare and, while they are discussing the matter, that gentleman walks in. He asks her to come to dinner on the morrow and she accepts. With everything running smoothly thus far, Pandarus immediately repairs to Troilus, to whom he reveals his deception of Deiphebus; and before poor Troilus can get in a word, his loquacious mentor has spouted four stanzas anticipating the chief objection of Troilus and supplying the remedy for it with the suggestion that he go the night before: once arrived he can feign illness, go to bed, and remain there awaiting his adventure.

Everything works out as planned and going "right to theffect, withouten tales mo," as Chaucer saw fit to do, we next meet Pandarus describing to Deiphebus' guests the terrible crime about to be committed against Criseyde (II, 1615–17):

> He rong hem out a proces lik a belle
> Upon hire foo, that highte Poliphete,
> So heynous, that men myghte on it spete.

To Helen's question whether Hector and Troilus know of this, Pandarus gives an affirmative answer but adds that, if they assent, he thinks Criseyde should herself tell Troilus about Poliphete before she departs (II, 1632–33),

> For he wol have the more hir grief at herte,
> By cause, lo, that she a lady is.

Thereupon Pandarus dashes in to see if Troilus is sleeping or will hear anything of this; but what he whispers in his ear is something quite different: "God have thi soule, ibrought have I thi beere!" Pandarus returns to Helen and Deiphebus and reports that Troilus would like them to bring in Criseyde; however, he is quick to add, "the chambre is but lite" and, since even a few people would easily make

it warm, he coyly suggests that it might be better for her to
wait until later. As for himself, he can go to Troilus and in an
instant (II, 1656–59)

> Reherce hire cas, unlik that she kan seye;
> And after this, she may hym ones preye
> To ben good lord, in short, and take hire leve;
> This may nat muchel of his ese hym reve.

Fully won over by Pandarus' convincing words and entirely
unaware of his trickery, Helen and Deiphebus go to Troilus
and beg him to be a good friend to Criseyde in the legal
difficulties which threaten her. Pandarus again recites "hire
cas"; Troilus promises "hire cause to sustene" and then by
a very neat ruse gets Helen and Deiphebus to absent themselves in order that Criseyde may come in, ostensibly to "take
hire leve or that she go" but actually of course to make
possible the assignation so carefully planned by Pandarus.

With but few preliminaries Pandarus is able to get Criseyde away from the other guests and, as they go to Troilus,
he entreats her to save Troilus' life; he begs her to seize her
opportunity at once and to delay no longer, especially since
no one suspects them (II, 1749–50):

> Las tyme ilost, I dar nought with yow dele;
> Com of, therfore, and bryngeth hym to hele.

Another final stanza of no import for its light on Pandarus
concludes the book.

Book III continues this scene at the house of Deiphebus
and the ever-present Pandarus appears almost at the start,
accompanying Criseyde to Troilus; peeking through the
curtain, he announces their arrival thus (III, 61–63):

> god do boote on alle syke!
> Se who is here yow comen to visite;
> Lo, here is she that is youre deth to wite.

Naturally enough, we do not hear much about Pandarus during the first few moments of the lovers together. But then
all of a sudden comes that very tender scene in which Troilus

declares his love and asserts his willingness to die if it will please Criseyde; Pandarus was deeply moved on hearing this (III, 113–19):

> Therwith his manly sorwe to biholde,
> It mighte han made an herte of stoon to rewe;
> And Pandare wep as he to water wolde,
> And poked evere his nece newe and newe,
> And seyde: "Wo bigon ben hertes trewe;
> For love of god, make of this thing an ende,
> Or sle us bothe at ones, or ye wende."

These lines deserve to be remembered along with those occurring just before (78 ff.) which describe the timidity of Troilus; at sight of his lady he becomes so frightened that he is absolutely speechless and totally unable to give utterance to those feelings which he had intended to confess; they were quite "thorugh his wit ironne."

Pandarus takes no further part in this scene until the end when he offers a prayer to Cupid and Venus for the miracle they have worked. The stanza reveals so much of his true character that I quote it in full (III, 183–89):

> Fil Pandarus on knees, and up his eyen
> To hevene threw, and held his hondes hye;
> "Immortal god," quod he, "that mayst nat dyen,
> Cupide I mene, of this mayst glorifie;
> And Venus, thow mayst maken melodie;
> Withouten hond, me semeth that in towne,
> For this miracle, ich here ech belle sowne.

With characteristic vigilance he notes the return of Helen and Deiphebus and, before their entry, speedily arranges for the second meeting at his house. This whole scene has been managed with consummate skill and with remarkable fidelity to that requirement of the courtly love code demanding the utmost secrecy in the conduct of an amour.

With the departure of Criseyde, Helen, and Deiphebus, Pandarus returns directly to Troilus' room where (III, 229–31)

> on a pailet al that glade nyght
> By Troilus he lay, with blisful chere,
> To tale; and wel was hem they were yfeere.

But he does not lie there for long; when everyone has departed and the doors are shut, he gets up, sits on the side of
the bed, and talks to Troilus "in a sobre wyse." The next
fifteen stanzas (35–49) comprise a Pandaric monologue
in that diffuse manner we have come to expect whenever the
lovers' confidant gets the floor. Now for the first time Pandarus gives full expression to his feelings about the rôle
he plays; whatever he may have thought before, however
sincere his numerous protestations of innocence were, are
now beside the point. He is ashamed to say it but admits
that what he has now stooped to doing is something he will
never again do for anyone, even though he shall be a
thousand times his brother (III, 253–59):

> That is to seye, for the am I bicomen,
> Betwixen game and ernest, swich a meene
> As maken wommen unto men to comen;
> Thow woost thi selven what I wolde meene;
> For the have I my nece, of vices cleene,
> So fully maad thi gentilesse triste,
> That al shal ben right as thi selven liste.

The first three lines of this stanza are an elaboration of
Pandaro's simple statement, "for your sake I have become
a go-between" (III, 6). The next line, "for you have I thrust
my honor to the ground," Chaucer does not employ at all,
possibly because he has already anticipated the thought in
the passage just discussed. And the third statement, "for you
I have corrupted the pure breast of my sister and put your
love in her heart," becomes something quite different in
Chaucer's hands; for Pandarus' statement in lines 257–59,
though equally definite, is much less direct. This subtlety is
an important part of Pandarus' shrewdness, a quality which
helps to make the English go-between a far more interesting person. Pandaro is so much less penetrating and dis-

cerning that he is a very different character. The next stanza
(38) presents in much more polished form than in the *Filostrato* Pandarus' justification of his action: it was only, he
tells Troilus, to shorten that agony which he thought could
cause his death; he then goes on to entreat Troilus to behave
as he should, to keep Criseyde safe from slander, and always
to preserve her good name. He points out how despicable a
part he has played: if people should hear about it, they
would say it is "the worste trecherie . . . that evere was
bigonne"; and then he begs Troilus to preserve the utmost
secrecy about it all; the "firste vertu is to kepe tonge" (294),
as "wise clerkes" teach about such things. The request for
secrecy comes directly from the *Filostrato* (III, 10), but the
rest of the soliloquy seems to be original with Chaucer. Of
particular interest is the apostrophe to his tongue, a device
which Pandarus employs with great effectiveness to impress
on Troilus the necessity for the greatest secrecy. This has
the desired result, for Troilus, rejoicing at Pandarus' words,
arouses himself and states very emphatically that on the
morrow he will pledge himself to secrecy in all the temples
of the town. He also expresses his appreciation of Pandarus'
services by saying that, in return, he is ready to serve him
as his slave for the rest of his life wherever he may go.
Troilus' comments (365–420) on the rôle which Pandarus
himself has virtually admitted is that of a pimp are greatly
expanded from the corresponding passage in the *Filostrato*
(III, 16). There Troilo begs Pandaro not to apply to himself
the ugly name of procurer, when it is a question of coming
to a friend's relief; let it be preserved for miserable creatures
whom gold induces to such service; Pandaro has acted
exactly as one should who is anxious to relieve the sufferings
of a friend. Troilus, however, is even more definite in his acquittal of his friend. You have implied by your words, Pandarus, that what you did for friendship's sake, I might
consider the act of a pander (III, 398–99):

> I am not wood, al if I lewed be;
> It is nat so, that woot I wel, parde.

Call him who acts for money by any name you will, while
(III, 402–3)

> this that thow doost, calle it gentilesse,
> Compassioun, and felawship, and trist.

Make this distinction, for it is widely known, as I have
learned, that there is diversity "bytwixen thynges like." As
further evidence that he does not regard Pandarus' service as
a joke or anything to be ashamed of, he offers to intercede in
his behalf with Polixene, Cassandra, Helen, or anyone,
howsoever fair or comely she may be. This scene ends with
an appeal from Troilus that, now that the enterprise is under-
way, it be carried through to the end, "for now is most
nede." This is much more direct and definite than Troilo's
request, "bring my desire to pass when opportunity pre-
senteth itself to thee."

The lines that intervene between this scene and the supper
with Pandarus (421–505) are of great significance for the
light they throw on the growth of the mutual infatuation of
Troilus and Criseyde, but since Pandarus is mentioned only
once in the course of this interlude we may pass it by for the
present. (The poet remarks that Pandarus continued faithful as ever, going back and forth between the two, carrying
letters, and in general manifesting a friendly devotion quite
unsurpassed.) Chaucer loses no time in getting on to his
next great scene, the meeting of Troilus and Criseyde at the
house of Pandarus.[15] The latter has expended no amount of
time and effort in arranging everything that "herto myghte
availle." Troilus spends most of his time in a temple of
Apollo while these preparations are being made. Courtly
love and the temple of Apollo are rather a striking anachro-
nism but of course no more so than the whole poem. This
scene is to be regarded as an illustration of the religious

piety proper to a courtly lover, though it is also to be noted
that Troilus' presence in the temple was part of his ruse in
deceiving his friends.

Everything being ready, Pandarus invites Criseyde to
have supper with him; he has carefully arranged it for a
rainy, moonless night in order to enjoy the utmost secrecy.
At both of Troilo's meetings the night was dark [16] but, considering the emphasis Pandarus places on the "chaungynge
of the moon," I see little reason to think Chaucer was greatly
indebted to the *Filostrato* for this idea. When Criseyde asks
if Troilus is to be there, Pandarus deliberately deceives her
by saying he is out of town, adding the pious protestation
(III, 573–74),

> For rather than men sholde hym ther aspie,
> Me were levere a thousand fold to dye.

And when she presses him further to be especially careful,
the poet describes his reply in these forceful lines (III,
589–95):

> He swor hire this by stokkes and by stones,
> And by the goddes that in hevene dwelle,
> Or elles were hym levere, fel and bones,
> With Pluto kyng as depe ben in helle
> As Tantalus. What sholde I more telle?
> Whan al was wel, he roos and took his leve;
> And she to soper com, whan it was eve.

After the supper a very heavy rain began to fall, a "smoky
reyn" that frightened every woman there. When Pandarus
urges Criseyde to stay, she hesitates for only an instant, long
enough to tell herself that she may as well agree at once as to
complain and then stay in the end. Pandarus is of course
much pleased when she tells him she was only joking when
she said she wished to go. When the guests retire for the
night, Chaucer again comments on the weather and its part
in the story; for it still rained and blew "so wonderliche
loude" that no one could hear another person speak, a condition most favorable to complete secrecy.

After escorting Criseyde to her bed, Pandarus bows himself out, assuring her that her women are sleeping just outside her door in case she might wish to call them. He then
goes to Troilus and acquaints him with the progress of affairs.
Once more emphasis is placed on Pandarus as a lover, for he
is described as one who (III, 694–95)

> wel koude eche a del
> The olde daunce, and every point therinne.

When Troilus finishes supplicating the gods and goddesses,
Pandarus ridicules his fear (III, 736–37):

> Thow wrecched mouses herte!
> Artow agast so that she wol the bite?

He then leads him into Criseyde's room through a trap
door. Again we are reminded of the storm and are told once
more that the wind blew so loudly that no one was able to
hear any other noise; and leaving no stone untouched, Pandarus takes the final precaution of shutting the door between
Criseyde's room and that of her attendants (III, 747–49):

> And Pandarus, with a ful sobre cheere,
> Goth to the dore anon withouten lette,
> There as they laye, and softely it shette.

The stanzas immediately following (750–952) recount his
conversation with Criseyde; though Troilus is in the room
all this time, he is not noticed until uncle and niece have
finished their talk. When she becomes aware of the presence
of Pandarus, she wishes to call someone immediately, but he
soon rids her of this folly by noting that that would only
serve to make people think things which would never have
occurred to them. He then begs her to have pity on Troilus
and gives a fictitious account of the latter's arrival: how he
has come to Pandarus' room well-nigh out of his head because he has heard that Criseyde loves Horaste. This fiction
of a rival lover is distinctly Chaucer's own addition to the
story and serves a very definite purpose by making possible

Criseyde's six-stanza disclaimer (799–840), which we shall revert to later on. The dialogue which follows (848–952) is skillfully managed by Pandarus so that finally she is very willing for him to introduce Troilus at once; his arguments that she should pity him, that the ring she wishes to send him must needs have a stone that can restore the dead, that his sorrow will be the cause of his death, and so on, all make her accede quite readily and willingly to Pandarus' wishes; her last words to him urge secrecy and reflect her general tendency to blame it all on Pandarus (III, 941–45):

> And, for the love of god, syn al my trist
> Is on yow two, and ye ben bothe wise,
> So werketh now in so discret a wise,
> That ich honour may have and he plesaunce;
> For I am here as in youre governaunce.

When Troilus enters immediately after this, he falls to his knees and, at the head of the bed, greets Criseyde "in his best wyse"; but she blushes and becomes so embarrassed at his sudden appearance that she cannot speak a single word. As if anticipating this situation, Pandarus ("that so wel koude feele in every thyng") immediately comes to the rescue of his niece first by joking and then by rushing for a pillow so that Troilus may rest more comfortably. When she finally kisses him and bids him sit down, it would seem that the time had come for Pandarus to hold his tongue and absent himself for a time; but the old rogue has to get in just one more bit of advice before withdrawing (III, 974–77):

> Now wol ye wel bigynne;
> Now doth hym sitte, goode nece deere,
> Upon youre beddes syde al ther withinne,
> That eche of yow the bet may other heere.

After this, the poet informs us, he went some distance away, took a light, and (III, 979–80)

> fond his contenaunce
> As for to looke upon an old romaunce.

Judging from the behavior of Pandarus thus far, I dare say he did not find the "old romaunce" so all-absorbing that he was entirely oblivious of everything else happening in the room! That this was exactly the case the lines almost immediately following are quick to prove. (In considering the meeting of the lovers at this point, I shall make mention only of those lines which have some bearing on Pandarus.) Thus, after Criseyde condemns the behavior of Troilus, he deems everything lost and lays all the blame on Pandarus (III, 1077–78):

> "O Pandarus," thoughte he, "allas, thi wile
> Serveth of nought, so weylaway the while!"

Directly after this Troilus swoons and his vigilant mentor of course rushes to the rescue. He cautions Criseyde to be still —"pes, or we be lost"—and then puts Troilus to bed. He then tells her that the only way he may be saved from death is by her telling him that he is forgiven: "Sey, 'al foryeve,' and stint is al this fare" (1106). Four stanzas are required for Troilus' resuscitation and then, when they are again happy together, Pandarus at last begins to act as a third party should under the circumstances: "I can not see that either I or this candle serve any useful purpose here, and light is not good for sick peoples' eyes; now that you two are together, may no sad thoughts burden your hearts." And so he "bar the candel to the chymeneye" (1141). Most people will heave a sigh of relief and breathe a *Deo gratias*, as I did when reaching that point in the narrative assuring me that Uncle Pandarus was about to go to sleep; but I was also confident that he would not do so without first making a characteristic remark (III, 1188–90):

> And Pandarus, with a ful good entente,
> Leyde hym to slepe, and seyde: "if ye be wise,
> Swouneth nat now, lest more folk arise."

We next meet Pandarus the morning after the meeting of the lovers. The visit which he makes to Criseyde at this time is a Chaucerian innovation; in the *Filostrato* Pandaro comes to Troilo. Pandarus greets Criseyde with the ironic statement that he fears the rain so disturbed her that she could neither sleep nor dream. In reply to "how kan ye fare?" Criseyde blames Pandarus for his trickery and makes him responsible for the events which have taken place. She covers her face with the sheet, then blushes. Pandarus peers under, apologizes to her in an artful fashion (III, 1572–73),

> nece, if that I shal be ded,
> Have here a swerd, and smyteth of myn heed,

and then kisses her. She forgives him and they amuse themselves together. Then (III, 1581–82)

> Whan tyme was, hom to hire hous she wente,
> And Pandarus hath hoolly his entente.

The visit of Pandarus to Troilus is paralleled in the *Filostrato* (III, 56–65), but while in the latter he apparently comes of his own volition, in the English poem Troilus "pryvely sente after" him. This scene, for the most part translated from the Italian, is chiefly concerned with Troilus' expression of appreciation to Pandarus for his services and the latter's reply, the substance of which is: if I have done anything for you, I am happy and rejoice with you; take heed now that you do nothing amiss. He impresses this on him with two stanzas of philosophizing in the Boethian manner, in which he tells Troilus always to restrain his talk and his desire; this is genuine courtly love doctrine and quite in keeping with those rules recommending moderation as formulated by Andreas.[17] When Troilus tells him of the happy night he has experienced and of the new feeling which has come over him, Pandarus replies that he who has experienced the heavenly bliss (III, 1658–59),

> He feleth other weyes, dar I leye,
> Than thilke tyme he first herde of it seye.

It is lines like these (which have no counterpart in the *Filostrato*) with their delightfully impersonal, disinterested, nonchalant air, rendered perfectly innocuous by the casual insertion of such expressions as "dar I leye" in the above instance, that reveal Chaucer's Pandarus as an utterly different individual from his Italian ancestor. Pandarus does not appear again in Book III and is mentioned only twice; once as bringing the two lovers together (1678–80) and the second time as the sole auditor of Troilus' hymn to Love (1735–43), the first being original with Chaucer and the second suggested by the *Filostrato*, III, 73.

From now on Chaucer follows his source much more closely. Book IV, in striking contrast to Book III, contains only one important new passage of any length, that on predestination (953–1085). It will also be noted that Pandarus' rôle from now on is a much less significant one than heretofore; this hints at, if it does not explain, Chaucer's change of technique. Up to this point Pandarus has been the instigator of all the action, the guiding spirit or presiding genius in most of the scenes of the drama. His function has been to draw the lovers together; that accomplished, there is little more to be done; hence Chaucer sticks pretty close to his original and hastens, as much as a poet with his tendency toward leisure and digression can be said to hasten, to the dénouement. In the closing books of the poem Troilus and Criseyde are the dominating figures, and Pandarus becomes just another actor; his duty done, he demands no more attention and is gradually forgotten.

Pandarus next appears after the conference which has decided on the exchange of Criseyde for Antenor (344 ff.). He is at his wits' end, crying tenderly and so upset he does not know what to say; when Troilus awakes he can say nothing but bursts into tears, and the two of them, powerless to speak, weep together. When Troilus asks Pandarus if he has heard the news about Criseyde, the latter replies affirmatively, first condemning Fortune and then endeavoring to comfort Troilus. This he does by pointing out, first of all, that he (Pandarus) is rather the one to do the weeping, for he has not had even so much as a cheerful look from his beloved; furthermore, there are plenty of other ladies about town who will do just as well and since new love chases out the old, as the saying goes, everything will turn out satisfactorily. Apparently, however, we are not to take this advice as heartfelt, for the poet tells us that he spoke thus all for the occasion, to help his friend lest he should die of sorrow (IV, 428–31):

> Thise wordes seyde he for the nones alle,
> To helpe his frend, lest he for sorwe deyde;
> For douteles to don his wo to falle
> He roughte nat what unthrift that he seyde.

This advice of Pandarus, Troilus rejects in twelve stanzas (63–74), first reaffirming his fealty to Criseyde and hers to him, then ridiculing Pandarus' inability to handle his own love affair, and concluding with an eighteen-line apostrophe to death. I quote the two stanzas in which Troilus taunts his counselor; though a close translation from the Italian, they are nevertheless of great significance in showing us Troilus' reaction to his friend's advice (IV, 484–97):

> But telle me this, syn that the thynketh so light
> To chaungen so in love, ay to and fro,
> Whi hastow nat don bisily thi myght
> To chaungen hire that doth the al thi wo?
> Whi nyltow lete hire fro thyn herte go?
> Whi nyltow love an other lady swete,
> That may thyn herte setten in quiete?
>
> If thow hast had in love ay yit meschaunce,
> And kanst it naught out of thyn herte dryve,
> I, that lyvede in lust and in plesaunce
> With hire as muche as creature on lyve,
> How sholde I that foryete, and that so blyve?
> O, where hastow ben hid so longe in muwe,
> That kanst so wel and formaly arguwe?

This concluding couplet, in its full implication so cutting, is severe, coming as it does from one who has enjoyed Pandarus' unfailing devotion; but in a way it foreshadows Pandarus' feeble rôle during the rest of the poem: he will argue well and formally, but it is to avail nothing; he has nought in the way of constructive suggestion that will be of help to Troilus.

At the end of this expostulation on Troilus' part, Pandarus at first is quiet and casts his eyes to the ground. Then he ponders and concludes that rather than let his friend die, he should speak to him again; indefatigable, he suggests this time that Troilus go and ravish Criseyde, then make her go away or keep her quietly in town; he urges him to get up, forget his sorrow, and show himself a man. Troilus replies that he not only has thought of all these things but much more in addition; he goes on to point out the folly of Pandarus' suggestion by showing that the adoption of such means would result in much publicity to the great detraction of her honor, which he holds more dear than his own self; he is torn between reason and desire (IV, 573-74):

> Desir for to distourben hire me redeth;
> And reson nyl nat, so myn herte dredeth.

He falls to weeping and bursts out again, exclaiming that love and his troubles increase as hope vanishes; he longs for death to give him peace, "for as in love is there but litel reste" (581). Pandarus' reply (which fills the next seven stanzas) is greatly improved over that found in the corresponding section of the *Filostrato* (IV, 74-75). The substance of Pandaro's advice is that, even if this action should displease her (and it probably will not, since she derives so much pleasure from loving), you will again enjoy your peace; and as for the loss of reputation, that after all is rather a minor detail; she can get along as well as Helen does provided she fulfills your desires; be courageous, pity yourself, and remember that I shall be with you at every turn. Chaucer, while clinging to the essence of this thought, greatly refines it. Pandarus too counsels Troilus to forget what people will say but qualifies it by pointing out (588) that such news never lasts but "nyne nyght." Then he advises him not to pay so much attention to reason and courtesy; let others do the weeping; get up and do something about it rather than die here like a gnat "withouten wounde." She may think you crazy if you do not save her from the Greeks; remember that Fortune favors the brave but punishes the cowardly. Pandarus goes on to say that, though Criseyde might be upset, Troilus can make his peace later; but he really does not see how she could possibly take it in the wrong spirit. At this point he leaves out Pandaro's words about reputation and Helen, only reminding Troilus that Paris has a love and so why should not he? Now follows an entire stanza (88) in which the idea is elaborated that if Criseyde loves Troilus as well as he loves her, she cannot be upset at any remedy which he may put forward; and if she does, "thanne is she fals." Pandaro's statement, "love cares for neither promise nor faith," is rendered "thorough love is broken alday every law," reminding one of Arcite's views on this topic.[18] Pandaro's pithy "have mercy on thyself" is made to fill four lines and is rendered much more tempting by Pandarus' reference to martyrdom; for if he dies a martyr in this trouble, he will go to heaven. In like manner Pandaro's single line promising his continual presence is made to fill one stanza, enriched, however, by the addition of a thought which many a reader through the centuries, no doubt, has marveled at his not expressing sooner (IV, 629–30):

> And if the list here sterven as a wrecche,
> Adieu, the devel spede hym that recche!

The outcome of this persuasion is the addition of just one more victory to the many already scored by Pandarus. When Troilus qualifies his assent "to ravysshe hire" with the clause, "but if hire self it wolde," Pandarus retorts, "Whi

so mene I . . . al this day" (638), words, like those which
immediately follow, not to be found in the *Filostrato;* when
Troilus replies negatively to his query about having seen
Criseyde, he wants to know why he (Troilus) is so convinced
that she will be ill pleased with the ravishing; did Jove
whisper it in his ear? This last is a revision in favor of the
classical, for the alpha text favors the Christian; there, instead of Jove appears "any aungel." [19] Pandaro next urges
Troilo to return to court, for now everyone will notice their
absence. Pandarus makes this more direct by suggesting
that Troilus go to the King at once, for he will wonder at
his absence; thus he leaves himself out of the picture entirely. Chaucer also makes Pandarus insist upon deception
(IV, 648–51):

> Thow most with wisdom hym and othere blende;
> Or, upon cas, he may after the sende
> Or thow be war; and, shortly, brother deere,
> Be glad, and lat me werke in this matere.

These last words are elaborated in the usual manner by the
addition of another stanza (652–58) telling how he will
arrange for a meeting between the lovers and how Troilus
will then know "al hire entente."

The scene immediately following is for the most part a
monologue recounting Criseyde's anguish at the thought
of leaving Troilus, and consequently we do not meet Pandarus again until he visits her at her house, whither he has
been sent by Troilus to arrange the meeting (806 ff.). When
Pandarus beholds her pitiful appearance, he is so moved
with pity that he can scarcely remain there. Though Boccaccio frankly admitted his total inability to recount Criseida's grief (IV, 95), Chaucer evidently felt no such qualms;
for Criseyde's lament fills four stanzas (119–22). This
meeting of uncle and niece is quite different from those we
have become accustomed to; this time there is no exchange of
greetings; they are in no mood to "pleye" and "jape" for
a time before proceeding to the business at hand. Instead,

Criseyde begins by doubting whether she can even say "welcome" to Pandarus who first brought her into the service of Love and who, though the original cause of her joy, is now equally the reason for her cruel sorrow. She then expounds a Boethian passage to the effect that sorrow follows close after happiness and presents herself as evidence of its truth. In the third and last stanza she pictures her state as the totality of all sorrow, pain, torment, woe, distress, and kindred evils; these lines are an interesting condensation of two passages in the *Filostrato* (IV, 96–97), one of which describes the pitiful sight which Pandaro beholds as he enters Criseida's room, while the other is his comment that everywhere he has gone that day, he has found grief, weeping, anguish, sighs, pain, et cetera. By having Criseyde express these feelings about herself, Chaucer makes the passage subjective and scores a distinct gain through the increased poignancy thus obtained.

Most of the rest of this scene is taken directly from the *Filostrato*, IV, 98–108. Since it is practically unchanged and sheds no further light on Chaucer's treatment of Pandarus, it may well be passed over. The outcome of it is of course that Criseyde agrees to meet Troilus again. The nature of this meeting is the only change I have noted; while Pandaro simply states that Troilo would like to be with her so that both may vent their sorrow together, Pandarus is more specific (IV, 887–89):

> And semeth me that he desireth fawe
> With yow to ben al nyght, for to devyse
> Remedie in this, if ther were any wyse.

The only addition Chaucer makes is at the very end of Pandarus' last speech. Having translated that stanza (107) in which Pandaro tells Criseida that Troilo would slay himself if he knew of her behavior, the English poet causes Pandarus to expand the thought to the extent of two additional stanzas. Criseyde promises to carry out her uncle's request that she cease weeping when Troilus comes and that she do everything possible "for to glade" him.

After this Pandarus goes away to seek Troilus, whom he finds in a temple where he is beseeching the gods (IV, 951–52)

> To doon hym sone out of this world to pace;
> For wel he thoughte ther was non other grace.

At this point intervenes Troilus' extended monologue on predestination (958–1082), at the conclusion of which Pandarus enters. It is not exactly clear how much of the soliloquy he hears, but it is sufficient to know that he came into the temple during the course of it and consequently must have heard the final petition to Jove either to take his life or rescue Criseyde and him from their distress (IV, 1079–82):

> almyghty Jove in trone,
> That woost of al this thyng the sothfastnesse,
> Rewe on my sorwe, and do me deyen sone,
> Or bryng Criseyde and me fro this destresse.

Pandarus' first words (1086) parallel those of Troilus, "O myghty god . . . in trone," though 1086 is earlier than 1079, according to Root.[20] Pandarus reëchoes Pandaro in asking Troilus if he will so destroy himself with fear that his eyes seem dead. Have you not fared well for many years without her? Are you born for her alone? Chaucer's improvement over Boccaccio in this instance consists in the addition of some plain common sense to Pandarus' reasoning: why are you so upset when you have not seen her and do not know but that she herself may be able to do something to prevent her going? Pandarus adds that he has been a long time with Criseyde (suggested in *Filostrato*, IV, 110), but Chaucer greatly enhances the effectiveness of this statement by making Pandarus say that he feels Criseyde has "in hire hertes privete" some means by which she can prevent everything that he dreads so much. Pandarus' concluding stanza is only partly suggested by the corresponding passage in

the *Filostrato* (IV, 112) cited by Rossetti; there Pandaro
states that he has arranged for Troilo to go to Criseida that
night when he will be able to explain his plans, learn her
feelings, and find some relief for their mutual anguish.
Chaucer's figure, however, as usual gains greatly in directness, though at the same time being much more gracious:
my advice is for you to go to her at night and make an end
of all this (may Juno send us grace!); my heart tells me
that Criseyde will not go, so put your heart at ease for
awhile (IV, 1119–20):

> And forthi put thyn herte a while in reste,
> And hold this purpos, for it is the beste.

Troilus fully agrees and at the proper time sets out to visit
Criseyde.

Pandarus does not appear again until the morning after
the departure of Criseyde when Troilus, completely dejected
and practically disconsolate, sends for him (V, 280 ff.). Boccaccio tells us that Pandaro was unable to visit Troilo that
first day nor could any other person come. In his usual ex-
pansive manner Chaucer not only states this fact but goes
on to explain the reason for it: Pandarus was busy with
King Priam all day and, though he had sworn at the risk of
his head to visit Troilus, he simply was not at liberty to go
anywhere. Why does Chaucer make this long explanation
and then cap it with these words (V, 286–87):

> but on the morwe he wente
> To Troilus, whan that he for hym sente?

If we are to take them literally, the whole explanation has
no point, for the reason he goes to Troilus is not that he is
free to do so but because he is sent for. He would probably
have found it possible to come the day before had his presence been requested; there is nothing in the story up to this
point to indicate that he is either an intimate friend or in-

dispensable adviser of Priam. Pandarus is well aware of
Troilus' state and of the reason for his wishing him to come
(V, 288–91):

> For in his herte he koude wel devyne
> That Troilus al nyght for sorwe wook;
> And that he wolde telle hym of his pyne,
> This knew he wel ynough withoute book.

The implication is perfectly clear that, realizing this and
being fully aware of his own inability to do anything to help
matters, Pandarus has no reason to hasten to Troilus' side
any sooner than he does. He is entirely cognizant of the fact
that he is utterly powerless and wholly incapable of doing
anything, on which account the poet adopts this artful means
of suggesting the fact. The succeeding events of the story
all serve to bear out the validity of this assumption, a point
I shall revert to later.[21]

Troilus believes that he is dying and gives brief directions
to Pandarus as to the disposition of his effects. This section
(comprising four stanzas, 43–46) is a Chaucerian addition
not even hinted at in the *Filostrato;* for the colorless Troilo,
completely absorbed in his misery, does not have even so
constructive a thought as the desire to die. Pandarus' reply
to Troilus is developed for the most part from the corresponding passages in Boccaccio (V, 29–35), though considerably expanded as usual. Thus Pandaro points out to
Troilo that others have been disappointed in love but have
assuaged their grief with hope (*Filostrato*, V, 29–30); Pandarus incorporates this thought but goes on to elaborate it
by pointing out that every day one may note a man separated
from his love or his wife "of necessite," but he does not become so upset about it. And furthermore, what about those
people who see their loves, victims of forced marriages, "in
hire spouses bed ybedded"?

> God woot, they take it wisly, faire, and softe.
> Forwhi good hope halt up hire herte o lofte,

And for they kan a tyme of sorwe endure;
As tyme hem hurt, a tyme doth hem cure.
—V, 347–50.

A minor change, but one which illustrates particularly well
Chaucer's tendency to be more concrete than his original,
is that found in the lines immediately following (351–52);
while Pandaro, after giving his advice, says merely, "You
should do the same," Chaucer causes Pandarus to speak
much more specifically: so should you bear up; let the time
slide and try to be glad and light-minded. He now goes on
to condemn dream interpretation, urging Troilus to forget
his dreams and expressing the opinion that no one knows
their real significance; this is taken over directly from the
Filostrato (V, 32), but there follow three stanzas (53–55)
in which Pandarus expresses himself further on the futility
of dream interpretation, pointing out how various authorities
differ in their opinions as to the nature of dreams and ending
with that perfect couplet (V, 384–85):

> Allas, allas, so noble a creature
> As is a man shal dreden swich ordure!

Pandarus' skepticism is not representative of his time, for
there was really very little difference of opinion about
dreams among men of the Middle Ages; as Curry points
out at the end of his study of medieval dream-lore,
". . . among philosophers, astrologers, medical men, and
theologians there are neither essential differences of opinion
nor grounds for controversy. There is only a variety of emphasis. . . . It is Chaucer, the man of philosophical mind,
who is quick to see the practical and almost insurmountable
difficulties in the way of determining precisely the nature
of any present dream that has not already been proved true
or false by the event." [22] One should note, however, that
Chaucer is not necessarily revealing his own views on dreams
but rather is only developing a hint found in the *Filostrato*.
The rest of this scene (V, 386–435) is modeled closely

after its Italian original, to which Chaucer makes no additions. Pandarus successfully persuades Troilus to visit King Sarpedoun at his palace where he will be able "the tyme wel" to "bygile." They go almost at once and are entertained most lavishly by Sarpedoun. Troilus, however, is not at all affected by the pleasant diversions and, weighed down with the thought of Criseyde, is ready to leave at the end of the fourth day (Troilo was ready to leave after two days had passed); but Pandarus, no doubt reveling in the luxurious entertainment provided by their host, immediately ridicules this idea: have we come to fetch fire and rush home with it while the coals are burning? I know of no one more delighted to have us than Sarpedoun and if we should hurry off like this, "I holde it vilanye" (490). Pandarus as usual, needless to say, succeeds in getting Troilus to stay the week as they had promised their host, but at the end of that time they take their leave and return to Troilus' palace.

This return journey, though hardly more than mentioned, breathes quite a different air in the two poems. The Italian poet tells us that after leaving (to the displeasure of Sarpedoun) they go back to their own homes, Troilo saying, "O God! shall I find my love returned?" Pandaro, like one knowing fully the whole intent of Calkas, spoke otherwise with himself saying that unless he is deceived, Troilo's fierce and fiery wish may be cooled by something he heard even while Criseida was there; and he expresses the opinion that the tenth day, the month, and the year will pass before he sees her again. Chaucer treats all this very differently. There is no mention of Sarpedoun's displeasure; the question "shall I find my love returned?" becomes a prayer (V, 502–4):

> now lord me grace sende,
> That I may finden at myn hom comynge,
> Criseyde comen!

And Pandarus acts quite differently. "Ye, haselwode!" he thinks on hearing these words and then, curiously twisting the Italian, expresses the hope that "this hote fare" may cool before Calkas sends Criseyde to Troilus. But nevertheless he keeps on joking, amusing himself, and swearing his heart promised him that she would come as soon as she might. Arrived at the palace they talk together about Criseyde—what they say is not even hinted at—and then, after supper, they seek their rest. This is a variation of the *Filostrato* account, for there (V, 50) after they have talked for a time, they go off to view Criseida's palace; in the *Troilus* this does not take place until the following morning (V, 519 ff.). Pandarus is not prominent in this scene; in fact, we are simply told that Troilus tells him of his "newe sorwe, and ek his joies olde" (558). During all this time of lamentation, until after the ninth night, Pandarus is as faithful as ever; this passage is practically identical with that in the *Filostrato* (V, 682–86):

> And ay bisyde hym was this Pandarus,
> That bisily dide al his fulle myght
> Hym to conforte, and make his herte light,
> Yevyng hym hope alwey, the tenthe morwe
> That she shal come, and stynten al his sorwe.

The action now shifts to the Greek side and Criseyde, and Pandarus does not reappear until those final tragic days at the end of the poem are nearly over. It is on the morning of the tenth day that Troilus sends for Pandarus (V, 1110) and they go together to the town walls to watch for Criseyde. They think everyone whom they see is the heroine but are always mistaken. Troilus ventures the opinion that she would come but that she probably is dining with her father and hence experiencing some difficulty in getting away. Pandarus admits the possibility of this and suggests that they dine and return in the afternoon. Chaucer thus gains once more in exactness, for Pandaro says merely, "Let us depart and then we shall return again." The fifth book follows the Italian closely for the most part and practically all the changes in Pandarus are of this character. Thus,

while the two are waiting, Pandaro laughs to himself at
Troilo's assuming every approaching figure to be Criseida;
but in order not to make him more sorrowful, he appears to
believe him and says, "This wretched youth expecteth a
wind from Mongibello" (VII, 10). Pandarus, on the contrary, openly assents when Troilus expresses his hopes: "It
may be wel ynough" (1170), noncommittal though he is.
Even though his real feelings do not differ essentially from
Pandaro's, they are presented much more vigorously; for
he says to himself "ful sobreliche" (V, 1174–76),

> From haselwode, there joly Robyn pleyde,
> Shal come al that that thow abidest heere;
> Ye, farewel al the snow of ferne yere!

Would that Pandarus had given us further and more definite
indication of his acquaintance with François Villon!

Almost two months later Troilus has the famous dream
about the boar and interprets it as an allegory of Criseyde's
unfaithfulness. He relates it to Pandarus (1245–74) and
asks what he should do. He replies in much more orthodox
fashion, as Root notes,[23] that dreams deceive because men
misinterpret them, "for folk expounden hem amys," and
urges Troilus to forget about it: "Thou canst no dremes
rede"; whereupon he points out that the dream might as
easily be taken to represent the death of Criseyde's father.
In this manner Chaucer makes something definite and concrete out of what was more or less vague, for Pandaro points
out that what Troilo interprets as hostile may prove to be
beneficial to him and will do no harm. I have already suggested that Pandarus is now more orthodox on dreams;
Pandaro, however, is very decidedly not, for he states explicitly, "No one there was nor is nor ever will be who can
with certainty well interpret what fancy can show forth
with varied forms in the sleep of another, and many indeed
have believed one thing while another opposite and contrary thereto came to pass" (VII, 40). Pandarus now ad-

vises Troilus to write Criseyde a letter and thus find out what the situation is; he proceeds to do so.

Pandarus' last appearance is very near the end of the poem. He has been listening to Troilus' last complaint and at the end of the monologue is able to utter no word of denial (1725). He is sorry for Troilus, ashamed of Criseyde, and so astonished for these two reasons that he stands "as stille as ston; a word ne koude he seye." Pandaro's feelings are much the same (VIII, 22). Boccaccio tells us that, on the one hand, love for his friend inclines him to remain while, on the other, shame of Criseyde's error invites him to leave; he does not know how to decide what he ought to do and both facts torment him greatly. In tears he finally speaks (23–24), telling Troilo that he blames Criseida, that he will offer no excuse for her great sin, and that he never again wishes to go where she may be; leaving behind his honor, he acted as he did only for Troilo's love. Pandarus says practically the same thing but is perhaps even more emphatic than usual; "blame" becomes "hate": I hate her and shall hate her for evermore; and (a touch not in the *Filostrato*) what you prayed me to do, I performed; without regard to my honor or my rest, I did everything that you desired. Save in one important respect, the two men express the same sentiments in their remaining words: If I did anything that pleased you, I am glad; this treason is a sorrow to me and if I knew any way of making amends, I would gladly do so. And then come the words that mark the difference between Pandaro and Pandarus; indeed, they sum up rather neatly the difference in outlook between Boccaccio and Chaucer; for the one begs punishment for the heroine so that she may not sin again in this fashion, while the other is content to implore divine mercy. This powerful scene, depicting the great comic figure at a moment of high tragedy, showing his complete helplessness, his utter inability to do anything further to help his friend and yet, with it all, his great generosity and mercy, is the last in which Pandarus appears.

Appropriately enough, as so often heretofore, the last words
spoken in the poem are his; summarized above, they deserve
to be given in full at this point (V, 1731–43):

> My brother deere, I may do the no more.
> What sholde I seyn? I hate, ywys, Criseyde!
> And, god woot, I wol hate hire evere more!
> And that thow me bisoughtest don of yoore,
> Having unto myn honour ne my reste
> Right no reward, I dide al that the leste.
>
> If I dide aught that myghte liken the,
> It is me lief; and of this tresoun now,
> God woot, that it a sorwe is unto me!
> And, dredeles, for hertes ese of yow,
> Right fayn I wolde amende it, wiste I how.
> And fro this world, almyghty god I preye.
> Delivere hire soone; I kan no more seye.

From the comparisons drawn in the preceding pages I
think it is at once evident that Pandarus is not only a person who plays a much more important part in the story of
Troilus and Criseyde than does Pandaro but also that his
rôle is essentially different from that of his Italian predecessor. In discussing Pandaro and the go-between in medieval
literature, I pointed out that the *internuntius* is a perfectly
well accredited individual in the courtly love tradition.[24]
This is a fact which the older, as well as some of the more
recent, Chaucerian criticism frequently misunderstood; the
next few pages may, therefore, very properly be devoted to
a review of these opinions. One of the earliest of the modern
critics of the *Troilus* to acknowledge Chaucer's genius in
handling Pandarus is W. M. Rossetti: "To turn him into a
character has been, in one word, the great achievement of
Chaucer; and never was a creative act of the like kind managed with more splendid ease and instantaneous power." [25]
He goes on to state that this change is explained by the poet's
expedient of increasing his age and then remarks:

The brilliant young man of fashion (as we might term Boccaccio's Pandarus) becomes a battered middle-aged man of the world; his buoyancy and rapidity of character take on a certain aspect of fatal facility; his scheming approaches nearer to treachery—both because he more cunningly undermines the honour of Criseyde, and because his position as her uncle places him almost in the position of her "guide and philosopher" as well as "friend"; his loose morals, natural to a young man whose passions master him in his own as well as in his friend's cause, become a distinct blunting of the moral sense—a contented adoption of the ignoble as a rule to live and die by.

Taine describes Pandarus as

a lively rascal, who volunteers for a singular service with amusing urgency and frank immorality, and carries it out carefully, gratuitously, thoroughly. In these pretty attempts Chaucer accompanies him as far as possible, and is not shocked. On the contrary, he makes fun out of it. At the critical moment, with transparent hypocrisy, he shelters himself behind his "author." If you find the particulars free, he says, it is not my fault; "so writen clerkes in hir bokes old," and "I mote, aftir min auctour, telle. . . ." Not only is he gay but he jests throughout the whole tale. He sees clearly through the tricks of feminine modesty; he laughs at it archly, knowing full well what is behind; he seems to be saying, finger on lip: "Hush! let the grand words roll on, you will be edified presently." We are, in fact, edified; so is he and in the nick of time goes away carrying the light: "For ought I can aspies, this light nor I ne serven here of nought." "Troilus," says uncle Pandarus, "if ye be wise, sweveneth not now, lest more folke arise." Troilus takes care not to swoon; and Cressida, at last, being alone with him, speaks wittily and with prudent delicacy; there is here an exceeding charm, no coarseness. Their happiness covers all, even voluptuousness, with a profusion and perfume of its heavenly roses.[26]

Ten Brink characterizes the part of Pandarus as

a work of such intellectual boldness and assurance as can only be found equaled in the productions of the greatest masters. The more innocent Criseyde is, the more inexperienced and helpless Troilus is, the greater grows the rôle of him who brings them together. Pandarus is here properly adapted for a pimp, and his name has remained in the language as a synonym for this word. He is an elderly gentleman with great experience of life, uncle to Criseyde, not—as in Boccaccio —her cousin. It is the poet's intention to excuse, or at least to explain, the part he plays by the intimate friendship between him and Troilus. How far one can go out of friendship—especially to high personages —in the domain of moral concessions, how hard it is to make a halt at the right point, Chaucer himself probably found out well enough in his relations with John of Gaunt. He presents the matter in the most objective form, but yet in such a way that the aesthetic charm given to the character of Pandarus helps us over the impression of the offense to morality in the same way as in Shakespeare's Falstaff. To the insipid and somewhat cynical views of an old worldling, Pandarus unites a good dose of *naïveté*. And Chaucer makes him push his trade of pimp as naïvely as possible. . . . He commences his work, and carries it triumphantly through with the greatest mastery. He has the necessary talents and the necessary liking for the play of intrigue, and knows well how to hide his roguishness under the mask of a somewhat rough good nature and a paternal recklessness.[27]

Morley speaks of Pandarus in this fashion:

He is to be Cressida's garrulous uncle, humorous, lachrymose, tricky, worldly wise according to the wisdom of the base; the sentimental comradeship with Troilus being an oddity which we may refer, if we please, to the fact that Troilus was a king's son, who might have any form of parasite. . . . In Boccaccio, Griseida is represented as the cousin of Pandarus; Chaucer makes her his niece, and ascribes to him craft of age instead of the fresh valour of youth. . . . Outwardly graceful, inwardly graceless. . . . Chaucer is not content with having taken the generosity of youth and manly dignity out of the character of Pandarus: he also modifies the character of his first offer to help Troilus.[28]

Jusserand holds that

Chaucer transforms the whole drama and makes room for the grosser realities of life, by altering the character of Pandarus. He makes of him a man of mature years, devoid of scruples, talkative, shameless, wily, whose wisdom consists in proverbs chosen among the easiest to follow, much more closely connected with Molière's or Shakespeare's comic heroes than with Musset's lovers. Pandarus is as fond of comparisons as Gros-René, as fond of old saws as Polonius; he is coarse and indecent, unintentionally and by nature, like Juliet's nurse. He is totally unconscious, and thinks himself the best friend in the world, and the most reserved; he concludes interminable speeches by:

I jape nought, as ever have I joye.

Every one of his thoughts, of his words, of his attitudes is the very opposite of Cressida's and her lover's, and makes them stand out in relief by a contrast of shade. He is all for tangible and present realities, and does not believe in ever foregoing an immediate and certain pleasure in consideration of merely possible consequences.[29]

Legouis's criticism of the *Troilus* is on the whole unsatisfactory and is particularly bad when dealing with Pandarus:

Criseyde being such a pure heroine, the character of Pandarus becomes necessarily more repulsive. He is no longer content to be the accomplice of a wary coquette, but he is the corrupter of virtue. The character would indeed have been intolerable if Chaucer had not veiled its nastiness by ridicule. . . . Chaucer never wearies of recording at length his discourses, his anecdotes, his equivocal remarks, his oratorical wiles, in short, all the devious ways of his hypocrisy. . . . The verbosity of Pandarus is not his chief defect, from a literary point of view. In his remodelling, Chaucer included such diverse and incompatible traits that the character does not stand out clearly. His Pandarus is a compromise between the young knight of friendship as drawn by Boccaccio, full of zeal and discrimination in a peculiar part, and the Shakespearian Pandar, a corrupt uncle, the type of the benevolent go-between who brings young couples together out of senile depravity, a dotard and an obscene old man who makes no pretence to virtue, who sings a coarse song for the amusement of Paris and Helen, and who acts far less out of affection for Troilus than for love of his trade. . . . He is so complex that we cannot give him our unqualified sympathy, nor think him altogether ridiculous. It is impossible to judge him, to realise the character as a whole, for we see two figures, one a young man with a gift of humour as in Boccaccio, and the other a grinning old man as in Shakespeare. Chaucer's Pandar in fact makes us see double.[30]

Cummings answers this criticism adequately when he says:

M. Legouis should remember that complexity in character is admissible, psychologically speaking, and that there is such a thing as dualism in personality. It is possible for middle age, nay even for old age, to retain something of the facile spontaneity of youth. It is possible for a man to be a sentimentalist, and, at the same time, be capable of depraved tastes. And, crafty though he is, Chaucer's Pandarus is seldom other than a sentimentalist. He luxuriates in emotion. . . . His is one of those temperaments, which never rationalize their moods or their grounds for emotion, to detect their sincerity or their insincerity, which are prone to indulge the intensity rather than to consider the motives of their feelings. He never distinguishes between the simulated and the genuine qualities of his tears; and of both kinds he is lavish.[31]

Notwithstanding this, however, so recent a critic as Looten has expressed unqualified approval of Legouis's strictures.[32]
Kittredge writes with fine discernment:

Pandarus is Troilus' friend and Cressida's uncle. This double relation is the sum and substance of his tragedy, for it involves him in an action that sullies his honor to no purpose. Since Cressida is faithless, he not only labors in vain, but ruins his friend by the very success that his plans achieve. This humorous worldly enthusiast has two ideals, friendship and faith in love. To friendship he sacrifices his honor, only, it seems, to make possible the tragic infidelity of Cressida, which destroys his friend. The system of courtly love had neither comfort nor excuse for Pandarus. Though Cressida's love for Troilus was blameless, or even meritorious, under the code, yet that same code, in its inconsistency, held no justification for the go-between. . . . Pandarus is Troilus' friend. The middle ages liked to exemplify virtues and vices to the last gasp, as in the case of Griselda's patience, even if the conflict of duties was ignored. Pandarus, however, is too individual and lifelike to take sanctuary in a parable, though his conduct might well entitle him to some such refuge. It was an old theory, which Laelius repudiated with horror, that friendly devotion should know neither limit nor scruple:—*si voluisset, paruissem*. There was some excuse for this view in the middle ages, when men changed sides with a light heart and personal loyalty was much needed as a steadying element in politics and society. In Pandarus, no doubt, the ideal has gone astray in the application, but there is something pathetic in the intensity with which he errs. It is, in truth, the monomania of personal devotion, and that too on the part of a humorous ironist, who cherishes few illusions.[33]

Root condemns the rôle of Pandarus in these words:

For from the medieval point of view as well as from the modern, the role which Pandar plays is one of infamy and dishonor; and he clearly recognizes that were his actions to be known he would be regarded as guilty of "the worste trecherye" to his niece. She also regards his advocacy of Troilus' love as a breach of faith. The conventions of courtly love hold Troilus free of blame, and Criseyde so long as she remains true, but not so her uncle, whom circumstance has placed in the position of a father to her, or an elder brother, and who betrays his trust. Had he been merely the friend of Troilus, acting as confidant and messenger, it would have been different; but as Criseyde's uncle, he should have been her jealous guardian. His only defense is that he acts from motives of pure friendship. . . . Though Pandar sacrifices all to the ideal of friendship, he is not like Troilus an idealist. He does not sentimentalize his friendship, nor yet his own unrequited love. It is one of his outstanding traits of character that he clearly faces the facts, that he sees things as they are; if he deceives others, he never deceives himself.[34]

Another recent critic, W. W. Lawrence, speaks of Pandarus as "a humorous elderly man of the world, kindly but unmoral" and goes on to say,

The part played by Pandarus must be clearly understood in this connection. In theory the perfect love-affair admitted of the intervention of no procurer. Go-betweens were indeed common enough in those days, but they were usually servants, retainers, waiting-maids, and the like, persons of lower station, with whom a gentleman could not allow himself to be confused. Their services were a constant danger to the preservation of complete secrecy. As an experienced man of the world, Pandarus knows the risk in an episode of headstrong passion, which may become an open scandal. Then Criseyde's honor will indeed be stained, and he himself will suffer too. Such a disclosure would put him on the level of a common procurer or go-between acting for money, basely influencing the actions of his niece for his own gain. In a noteworthy speech in Book Three he expresses his fears to Troilus (239 ff.), and the latter reassures him, emphasizing the difference between "bauderye" and "servyse" in rescuing a friend from suffering, and, to show how far he is from holding such service "a shame or a jape," he ends by offering to gain for Pandarus the love of his sisters Cassandra or Polyxena, or of Helen. The claims of friendship, always so powerful in the Middle Ages, have a strong influence here. So in the romance of *Claris and Laris*, the knight Claris loves the married sister of his bosom friend Laris, and Laris aids him in furthering the affair. After the intrigue with Cressida has been carried to a successful climax, Pandarus has no regret for his conduct.[35]

Chesterton has written a very readable study of Chaucer but, so far as his remarks on Pandarus are concerned, he has little to offer. Not content to say that Chaucer has changed

him to an elderly uncle, he goes on to remark that "Pandarus
has become a funny old man. . . . But, for the moment of
medieval transition, the point is that Chaucer made the
young man old, because he wished to make the character at
once more ripe and more quaint, more experienced and more
fixed. In that sense the character of Criseyde's uncle takes the
new road as the first of the Canterbury pilgrims. . . ." [36]

Robinson notes that Chaucer, by making Pandarus a gen-
eration older, complicates his character:

> As an elder relative and supposed protector of Criseyde he has obliga-
> tions of which he is not wholly unaware, while doing his best to further
> Troilus's suit. In his relations with Troilus he combines the rôles of a
> valiant friend, ready for any sacrifice, and of a philosophical adviser.
> His comments on life—often phrased in proverbial language, of which
> he is a master—are wise and humorous. They sometimes express dis-
> illusionment, for which experience and observation had given him
> plenty of occasion, but cynicism, which has been attributed to him,
> was not in his nature. And in his own rôle of an unsuccessful old
> suitor who has always "hopped on behind" in the dance of love, he
> is an object of amused sympathy alike to fellow characters and to
> readers.[37]

Lowes appreciates fully the importance of the conventions of courtly love for an understanding of the poem. This
is reflected clearly in his remarks on Pandarus:

> It is not, then, Criseyde's *virtue*, in our conventional sense of the word,
> which must be undermined before she yields, and Pandarus has suf-
> fered with something less than even-handed justice the obloquy at-
> tached to his name. For Criseyde thinks, Hamlet-like, a little too
> precisely on the event to be capable of the over-mastering passion
> which gives all for love, and the world well lost; and Pandare's
> masterly dialectics are directed, not against her chastity but against
> the wary circumspection of a woman—not a maiden, but, though
> young, a widow—who knew her world, and knew it as a world of
> wagging tongues.[38]

De Sélincourt observes that Chaucer "found nothing
scandalous in the love of Troilus and Criseyde; his poem is
a tragedy not of immoral, but simply of inconstant love." [39]
He then goes on to observe:

Inevitably, this affects his conception of the character of Pandarus, who is thereby relieved of much of the odium which his name suggests to modern ears. For just as this chivalric love, with its insistence upon faithfulness to the death, and its regenerating effect upon the lover, differs from mere lust . . . so will those men differ who act as accessories to the one or to the other. . . . Pandarus accepted the code no less than Troilus, and it is noteworthy that most of its doctrines are placed in his mouth. He has no qualms of conscience when he asserts that it is his niece's duty to love and cherish a worthy knight, and that unless she does so he "holds it for a vice." But he is also a man of the world; he knows the risks and the dangers; and these, indeed, seriously trouble him, and in the end confound him. There is always the chance of discovery; and again there is the danger that one or other of the lovers may prove false to the ideal, so that, in the issue, he will have performed no knightly service, but betrayed his niece, and branded himself as a procurer. . . . But while Pandarus's attitude to the *amour courtois* is sympathetic, it is also ironical. Chaucer's consummate genius saw in this third character the novelist's golden opportunity for presenting the story from another angle. . . . Pandarus becomes in his hands the first great triumph of English humour, to whom, in all the great gallery of our comic characters, Falstaff alone is comparable for brilliance of conception and execution. He is sometimes spoken of as though he were a battered man of the world, a clever but unprincipled and cynical old jester. But Chaucer saw him as a man of youngish middle age, with principles of his own, even if they are not ours. . . . Nor is he a cynic, who regards love as mere sensual appetite, and derides an emotion he cannot understand. . . . Pandarus can laugh at his own thwarted passion, and accept with imperturbable good nature the jests of others at his expense; whilst he is realist enough to pierce through the subterfuges and illusions of lovers who, because they are conscious of the idealistic element in their passion, persuade themselves that it is wholly Platonic, and either refuse to recognize its physical basis, or think that they will be content, or indeed have the self-control, to stop short of its full satisfaction. But, above all, his irony exposes the lover's preposterous absorption in his own woes, as though nothing in the world existed outside them.[40]

Lewis calls attention to the fact that Pandarus is practical, good humored, faithful, discreet, and resourceful, and then continues:

What surprises us is to find in conjunction with this practical effi-
ciency, this merriment, and this warm, not over-scrupulous, affection,
all the characteristics of a fourteenth-century gentleman; for Pandarus is a lover and a doctor in Love's law, a friend according to the
old, high code of friendship, and a man of sentiment. The "ironic"
Pandarus is not to be found in the pages of Chaucer, and those who
approach him with this preconception will be disappointed as they
read how he "neigh malt for wo and routhe" at the sight of Troilus'
love-sickness; how "the teres braste out of his iyen" while he pleaded
with Criseyde; and how, while he heard Troilus pleading for himself
in the house of Deiphoebus, "Pandare weep as he to watre wolde."
I do not say that he did not in some way enjoy his frequent tears;
but he enjoyed them not as a vulgar scoffer, but as a convinced servant
of the god of Love, in whose considered opinion the bliss and pathos
of a gravely conducted amour are the finest flower of human life.[41]

Mr. Lewis has emphasized an extremely important point
and, while not minimizing the merit of Pandarus as a great
comic character, he appreciates more fully than most critics
the other side of Pandarus:

Pandarus is perfectly serious when he expounds the commandments
of Love—or even general philosophy—to Troilus. And Chaucer is
serious, too, to the extent that he seriously wishes to include all this
erotic, or other, instruction: what would a love-poem be without
"doctryne"? . . . . Pandarus combines with his comic role another
function equally necessary in Chaucer's eyes. Chaucer intends to teach,
as well as to paint, the mystery of courtly love; and the direct doctrine
which Love himself, or Frend, or the Vekke, would have spoken in an
allegory, is given to Pandarus. It is not what Pandarus says that is
comic, on Chaucer's view: it is the importunity, the prolixity, the
laughable union of garrulity and solemnity, with which he says it.[42]

Pandarus is by no means a simple character; he is a richly
endowed, complex individual: "There is fold within fold
to be disentangled in him, and analysis, with its multiple distinctions, will never exhaust what imagination has brought
forth with the unity of nature herself. But we must not substitute a neat satiric abstraction for the richly concrete human
being whom Chaucer has given us." [43]

In discussing our poem as a medieval romance, Young

recognizes that the critic may well maintain that Pandarus, by his practical nature, his joking, and his general behavior, serves to nullify the romantic element in the story:

To such inquirers I can offer no quick and comprehensive response, but only a few reminders. Let us agree, in the first place, that, with all his jesting, Pandarus is not ridiculing the courtly sentiment which is the essence of the romance. He can be grave enough over the amorous transaction which he is managing, and he loyally persists in an *amour* of his own. What he finds droll is not love, but lovers. He derides his own antics, and he derides the maneuvers of the younger pair. His derision of Troilus and Criseyde, indeed, has the peculiar charm of making them seem more youthful and childlike— more like the innocently sensuous lovers who dwell in the romances.[44]

He points out that the romances themselves supply the precedent for the "humorous irreverence" of Pandarus and stresses the fact—as obvious as it is generally ignored—that the medieval romances frequently contain reflections of ordinary life:

The abundant reflection of actual contemporary life, indeed, is the aspect of medieval romances which is most likely to astonish the reader who approaches them in the conventional expectation of finding only the marvelous and the beautifully remote. Many romances contain an element easily comparable to the reality and naturalness which Pandarus evokes; and it is precisely this element which enables the social historian to paint his detailed picture of polite life in the period during which the romances flourished.[45]

Judging from these excerpts the reader will see at once that the critics vary considerably in their interpretations of Pandarus. The older scholars seem to agree that he is a middle-aged moral reprobate, an amusing character but a figure out of place in a courtly love poem. The more recent critics have made some of the necessary modifications in this view. There is still much to be said, however. For example, there is nowhere in the poem a definite statement about the age of Pandarus. Lowes notes that Chaucer changes Pandarus from cousin to uncle of Criseyde, "leaving him still young." [46] De Sélincourt terms him "a man of youngish middle age." [47] Perhaps forty or forty-five? This is what most people understand by early middle age. If, however, we bear in mind that in the medieval period life did not begin at forty, we may go considerably further in speculating on the age of Pandarus. There can be no doubt about his youthfulness; his actions are those of a young man; his words to Troilus and Criseyde especially reveal the intimacy and affection of youth; personally I am sure that he is still in his early thirties.

Another point which Chaucerian critics have often failed to understand in making their evaluation of Pandarus is the conventional nature of the part which he plays. However, since the preceding chapter is partly devoted to a discussion of this very important element, it is sufficient to note that the rôle of go-between is sanctioned and approved by the courtly love code. The ethics of Pandarus' conduct, though, has not been exhaustively investigated. I do not profess to say the final word on this subject, but I feel that there are still several considerations which may very properly be brought up at this point. [48]

The conduct of Pandarus is not to be judged by present-day standards and contemporary codes of ethics but rather according to the code of behavior operating in the *Troilus*, i. e., the ethics of the courtly love system. Hence Lewis' assertion that "every reader must interpret Pandarus for himself" is essentially false. [49] He should not be judged according to every individual's whim, howsoever liberal or conservative one's moral standards may be, but rather, as I have just remarked, according to the ethical code of the courtly system.

The comparisons drawn between Pandaro and Pandarus justify the conclusion that in handling the story told in the *Filostrato*, Chaucer turned it from a narrative into a dramatic poem and that in order to make it good drama he greatly intensified the activities of Pandarus. In other words, by making him the protagonist of the drama, he has at the

same time made him a more active, more efficient go-
between, in fact, the best developed and most finished go-
between in medieval literature. This study has brought out
the fact that Chaucer greatly intensifies Pandarus' activities
in the first three books of the poem, while in the last two he
allows him to become more and more helpless; as the end
of the poem approaches, he simply drops out of the picture,
like all go-betweens; in this he is a typical courtly figure.
In this respect, then—and a very important one it is—
Chaucer has greatly enhanced the courtly love element in
his work. It is therefore all the more desirable that we try to
reach some definite and satisfactory conclusion about Pandarus. This is made difficult, among other reasons, by the
several contradictory statements which he makes in the
course of the poem, some justifying his rôle, others expressing remorse over the part he takes. We may therefore review
these statements, which have already been examined in detail in the preceding pages, and see what their cumulative
effect is.

In the first expression of his feelings (II, 352–57) Pandarus leaves us in no doubt about the part he is playing.
He regards his conduct as perfectly upright and proper,
assures Criseyde that he would rather be hanged than act as
Troilus' bawd, and notes how shameful it would be for him
as her uncle if he should be a party to the ruining of her
honor. This passage has no counterpart in the *Filostrato*.
Pandarus again expresses this same opinion, more mildly
perhaps but no less definitely, later in the same conversation
(II, 435 ff.) when he calls on the gods and furies to witness
that he never intended any harm or villainy in suggesting
that Criseyde and Troilus should meet. This statement likewise is independent of the *Filostrato*. And yet a third time,
just before ending this conversation, Pandarus urges her to
give heed to what he has suggested; for she knows his intent is honorable and that he means no evil.

The next occasion on which Pandarus expresses an opin-

ion about the function he performs is in Book III during
the course of his visit with Troilus. He explains that he has
started doing something for him that he would never do for
any other person (III, 250–52):

> For the have I bigonne a gamen pleye
> Which that I nevere don shal eft for other,
> Although he were a thousand fold my brother.

He then goes on to explain that for his sake he has become
a procurer (253–59) but justifies this by saying that he did
not do so out of covetousness but only to assuage his distress
(III, 260–63):

> But god, that al woot, take I to witnesse,
> That nevere I this for coveitise wroughte,
> But oonly for tabregge that distresse,
> For which wel neigh thow deidest, as me thoughte.

This contrasts rather clearly with Pandaro's statement (III,
10) that it was his fealty as a friend which led him to such
action. This is significant, for it is impossible to approve of
Pandaro's reasoning from the courtly love point of view.
Pandarus, however, exonerates himself completely; to relieve a lover's anguish was a real deed of mercy according
to the courtly belief. But Pandarus is so voluble and so
fully aware of the delicacy of the situation that in the very
next stanza he is worried about ruining Criseyde's good name
(III, 271–73):

> But wo is me, that I, that cause al this,
> May thenken that she is my nece deere,
> And I hire em, and traitour ek yfeere.

If this affair should become known, it would be fraught with
terrible consequences for all concerned (III, 274–80):

> And were it wist that I, thorugh myn engyn,
> Hadde in my nece yput this fantasie,
> To doon thi lust, and holly to ben thyn,
> Whi, al the world wolde upon it crie,
> And seyn that I the worste trecherie

Dide in this cas, that evere was bigonne,
And she forlost, and thow right nought ywonne.

This seems to be suggested by Pandaro's words to Troilo (III, 8) that if he should take advantage of Criseida and hurt her reputation, it would bring great shame to him (Pandaro), her relative and guardian.

In his reply to Pandarus, Troilus is very definite in his acquittal of his friend and adviser. I have already discussed the relation of these lines to the corresponding passage in the *Filostrato* and should like to emphasize that Chaucer makes Troilus absolve Pandarus in words far more in keeping with the courtly system.[50] These lines deserve to be considered an epitome and interpretation of the teaching of the courtly love code in this respect (III, 393–406):

> But here, with al myn herte, I the biseche,
> That nevere in me thow deme swich folie
> As I shal seyn: me thoughte, by thi speche,
> That this which thow me doost for compaignie,
> I sholde wene it were a bauderye.
> I am nat wood, al if I lewed be;
> It is nat so, that woot I well, parde.
>
> But he that gooth, for gold or for richesse,
> On swich message, call hym that the list;
> And this that thow doost, calle it gentilesse,
> Compassioun, and felawship, and trist;
> Departe it so; for wyde wher is wist,
> How that ther is diversite requered
> Bytwixen thynges like, as I have lered.

Pandarus' final statement at the very end of the poem (1731 ff.) does not deserve serious consideration. He states that everything he did for Troilus he did without any thought of his honor or his rest. This is not a very definite reproach and certainly contains no feeling of regret for what he has done; for in the very next lines he says very explicitly that if he did anything that pleased him (i. e., Troilus), he is glad. This is directly translated from the *Filostrato* (VIII, 24).

It is interesting to note that so long as everything is going along nicely with Troilus and Criseyde, Pandarus never has a single doubt about the propriety of his actions. As soon as events change for the worse, however, he is immediately disturbed; these qualms of conscience, it is worth mentioning, may all be traced to the *Filostrato*. The lines which justify his behavior are either added by Chaucer or else are so changed that they may well be regarded as Chaucerian. We may therefore conclude that the English poet fully understood what he was doing in his treatment of Pandarus; his only violation of the courtly code consists in the doubts which he allows him to express. Otherwise he is a typical courtly figure, and I feel that the correct attitude toward him, Chaucer's greatest character, should be that in keeping with the courtly love code, the generous view expressed by Troilus in the lines quoted above.

VIII

CRISEYDE

THE following pages, devoted to a comparison of Criseida and Criseyde, will follow the same method as in the preceding chapter on Pandarus. However, in order to avoid repetition as much as possible, passages already discussed will be considered again only in so far as they serve to help toward a better understanding of Criseyde. The very complexity of her character seems to justify this attempt to avoid complexity of criticism.

In Book I there is scant attention given to the heroine. Pandarus and Troilus monopolize the dialogue, and the only references to Criseyde are descriptions of her personal appearance and some hints as to her character. We may well pause over these sections and note what changes the English poet has made. Boccaccio's first mention of Criseida (I, 11) simply states the fact that, without letting her know of his desertion, Calkas left behind him a daughter who was a widow named Criseida, so beautiful and angelic to see that she appeared not to be a mortal; she was as discreet, wise, modest, and well-mannered as any other lady born in Troy. Chaucer, in turning this single stanza into two, notes first of all that Criseyde was in great sorrow; she was so much in dread of her life that she did not know what was best to do, for she was a widow and without a friend to whom she might voice her complaint. The negative statement that she appeared not to be a mortal becomes the positive assertion that she is like a thing immortal, a fact which is driven home by the beautiful Chaucerian couplet (I, 104–5),

As is an hevenyssh perfit creature,
That down were sent in scornynge of nature.

The next four stanzas (16–19) relate that she begged and
received from Hector full assurance of protection as long as
she should live in Troy and that she continued to dwell in
her own house, honored and respected by all. This account is
precisely the same in both poems. In fact, the only variation
appears at the very end; while Boccaccio states definitely
that it was unnecessary for her to concern herself on account
of a son or daughter, Chaucer deliberately says that he does
not know whether she had any children and he will therefore
pass over the fact. That the English poet gained anything
by this change is doubtful, for the definite assurance that
she was childless would have removed the possibility of any
disrepute accruing to her children as the result of her later
conduct; this is, however, a very minor point.

Criseyde is referred to again a few lines further on (169
ff.) as being among those present in the temple at the feast
of the Palladium. Both poets state that she stood there
gowned in black; but as if to emphasize her status as a
widow, Chaucer writes "widewes habit blak" instead of
"bruna vesta." And the statement that Criseida surpassed
the other ladies in beauty as the rose does the violet is
dropped entirely; instead we are told that she stood there
peerless in beauty just as "oure firste lettre is now an A," a
substitution which, if we accept Professor Lowes' brilliant
suggestion,[1] may be admitted to make up by ingenuity of
allusion what it loses in delicacy of literary flavor. Boccaccio goes on to say that Criseida made the festival joyous,
while Chaucer states that it was the crowd who were made
glad by her; he adds that there was never seen anything so
dearly to be praised nor so bright a star under a cloud as
Criseyde, a fact which everyone who saw her in her black
"weeds" remarked. Nevertheless she stood very humble and
quietly alone behind other people in a small space near the
door, always in fear of shame, simply attired, gentle in
appearance, with a self-possessed countenance and manner.
For these additional facts Chaucer requires an extra stanza;

Boccaccio simply states that Criseida stood in the temple, very near the door, "altiera, piacenta ed accorta" (I, 19), words which the English poet's circumlocutions render as satisfactorily as any direct translation.

When Troilus first sees Criseyde, a stanza (41) is devoted to a description of her personal appearance. From Boccaccio's account (I, 27) we learn that she was tall, that her limbs were proportioned to her height, and that she showed a womanly dignity. According to Chaucer she was not tall; her exact height we do not know, only that she was "not with the leste of hire stature" (281). Her limbs were all so suitable to her womanly nature that there was never a creature who seemed less like a man in appearance; and the very manner of her movements showed that, in her, men might imagine honor, rank, and womanly nobility—qualities all quite necessary to the courtly heroine. The next stanza, telling how pleased Troilus is with Criseyde's actions, is much the same in both poems except that for Boccaccio's statement that Troilo took great delight in gazing at her sparkling eyes and angelic face, Chaucer substitutes the couplet (I, 293–94):

> And after that hir lokynge gan she lighte,
> That nevere thoughte hym seen so good a syghte.

Root has very properly remarked that Book II "may be called the book of Criseyde. An overwhelming proportion of its lines is directly dedicated to the unfolding of her character, and to the subtle analysis of her heart as the figure of Troilus gradually establishes itself there." [2] It is therefore doubly important that we study this Book with care. However, the first visit of Pandarus to Criseyde has already been treated in such detail that there is no necessity for going through that material again, except in so far as it may be desirable to supplement the remarks already made.[3]

Toward the end of his conversation, when things apparently are not going the way he wishes them to, Pandarus

starts up and proceeds on his way until Criseyde catches him
"by the lappe." This scene is somewhat different from that
in the *Filostrato*, where Pandaro, thinking himself abused
when he heard Criseida's reasoning, got up to leave but then
stopped and turned to her; there is no mention of her trying
to detain him. The reason for this is not far to seek, I think;
it is simply that Pandarus has been entirely successful in
frightening Criseyde into pity for Troilus and himself; she
was "the ferfulleste wight that myghte be," she perceived
the cheerless earnestness of Pandarus and the justice of his
prayer, and so (II, 454-55)

> for the harm that myghte ek fallen moore,
> She gan to rewe and drede hire wonder soore.

Thus moved to compassion, she begins to reason things out
for herself (II, 456-62):

> Unhappes fallen thikke,
> Alday for love, and in such manere cas,
> As men ben cruel in hemself, and wikke;
> And if this man sle here hymself, allas!
> In my presence, it wol be no solas.
> What men wolde of it deme, I kan nat seye;
> It nedeth me ful sleighly for to pleie.

This last line is one of the most perplexing in the whole
poem and on its correct interpretation a great deal depends.
Dodd states that he sees no tone of calculation in this line:

Criseyde encounters a difficulty, and she faces it fairly and squarely.
She is prudent and careful of her actions, and still cool-headed.
Shall we, for this reason, call her "calculating"? The truth is, she
is here showing—what comes out more clearly later in the poem—
one of her most noticeable traits, the ability and willingness to look
facts in the face. And so she succeeds in satisfying her crafty uncle,
without at the same time committing herself to any course of action
which will lead her into difficulty in the future. This done, she shows
the womanly side of her nature in her desire to hear more of the
new lover.[4]

This is all very true and quite in keeping with the view
again emphasized a few pages further on that Criseyde was

not "designing and calculating," [5] a position which Professor Kittredge upholds: "Cressida, then, is not a victim, as some have thought. Just as little is she, as others hold, a scheming adventuress. This view of her character is, indeed, so patently erroneous as to need no refutation. True, she keeps her eyes open, and takes no leaps in the dark. She has also the excellent mental habit of looking at a subject or a proposition from several points of view." [6] One can certainly have no quarrel with these opinions, for they are eminently sound. However, they do not say everything. It seems to me that line 462 is the first definite hint we have yet received as to what Criseyde really is—an opportunist. I mean no disparagement when I use this word to characterize her; it implies something quite different from the words "designing and calculating." As Professor Root states, "She does not so much fall in love as drift with her eyes open." [7] Exactly so: wide open, very wide open. Criseyde is not a simple soul but a very complex one; she is most decidedly not a sentimentalist; she sees exactly what is happening and coolly decides to face the facts. But more than this, as I feel the succeeding books of the poem fully demonstrate, she has quite decided to make full use of these "facts"; in this sense she might conceivably be called "calculating and designing" but not, as I hope I have shown, in the sense in which a "scheming adventuress" might be said to be. It remains to be seen if the succeeding events justify this point of view.

Criseyde is sad at the turn of events ("what me is tid a sory chaunce!") and laments (463 ff.) the fact that both her honor as a lady and her uncle's life are in jeopardy. But she decides that with the protection of God she will preserve her honor and also his life. "With goddes governaunce" may be taken in a literal sense of course, but it is equally probable that it refers to the God of Love; if so, it is a minor but effective courtly love touch. Weeping, she reflects further that "of harmes two the lesse is for to chese" and that she would rather cheer up Troilus in an honorable way than

make her uncle lose his life. When Pandarus tells her nothing more is necessary, she answers (II, 475–76):

> "Now wel," quod she, "and I wol do my peyne;
> I shal myn herte ayeins my lust constreyne."

I will not cajole him nor can I love a man against his will;
but, my honor safe, I shall endeavor to please him from day
to day (II, 481–83):

> Therto nolde I nat ones have seyd nay,
> But that I drede, as in my fantasye.
> But cesse cause, ay cesseth maladie.

But she protests that even if they go further with this affair,
she will never do more than have pity for Troilus, though
they both should die and though the whole world within one
day should become her foe. Pandarus agrees to this, and she
in turn protests that he will not have to keep after her to
make her do what she has promised. The rest of this scene
has already been so fully treated in the preceding chapter
that it does not require further attention at this point.

After Pandarus leaves, Criseyde retires to her room and,
sitting down as still as a stone, begins to go over every word
he has said. This is substantially the equivalent of what
Criseida does (II, 68), but the latter, Boccaccio adds, talks
joyfully to herself, sighs, and pictures Troilo in her mind
more than usual. Chaucer, however, proceeds along different
lines. He tells us that Criseyde was somewhat astonished at
this new affair but that after she considered it she found that
there was no reason why she should be afraid; for a man may
so love a woman that his heart breaks, but she need not love
him in return unless she cares to—rather a close approach
to the courtly love practice which gives the lady complete
sovereignty over her lover and makes no demand that she
return his affection unless she feels so inclined.

At this point a cry arises in the street, and we learn of the
victorious Troilus' triumphant return to the city after having put the Greeks to rout. Cummings remarks quite correctly

that "this passage, 604–44, contains one of Chaucer's finest artistic additions to the Troilus story, viz.—the figure of Criseyde at the window watching her hero ride by in triumph." [8] We need not consider this procession here but will stay in the room with Criseyde; she carefully observes the appearance of Troilus and lets it sink into her heart so that she says to herself, "Who yaf me drynke?" How perfectly this reference to a love-potion fits in at this point! The whole scene is in distinct contrast to the preceding and is one of the very few in which Criseyde's emotions almost get the better of her reason. She blushes deeply when she realizes that this is the man who her uncle has told her will die unless she have mercy and take pity on him. Ashamed, she draws in her head from the window and begins thinking about all the fine qualities of Troilus (II, 663–65):

> But moost her favour was, for his distresse
> Was al for hire, and thought it was a routhe
> To sleen swich oon, if that he mente trouthe.

As if anticipating criticism of this "sodeyn love," Chaucer here inserts several stanzas (96–100) defending Criseyde's conduct; whoever says she loved Troilus too easily at first sight (II, 670–72),

> Mot he nevere ythe;
> For every thyng, a gynning hath it nede
> Or al be wrought, withouten any drede.

He goes on to explain that he did not so much say she suddenly gave him his love as that she at first began to like him and that afterwards love began to spring up within her on account of his manliness and suffering. The result was that "by proces and by good servyse" Troilus won her love but in no sudden manner. This is excellent courtly love doctrine,[9] but, more than that, it does a good deal to explain Criseyde. I cannot pretend to interpret her character in a way that will be satisfactory to everyone, but there are one or two points that I feel should receive fuller emphasis than they have hitherto. One fact which most critics agree on is that Criseyde is a very complex character. Of course she is; then why do these same critics try to reduce her to a single type and endeavor to reconcile all her actions to a mode of conduct which they think befitting such a character? Criseyde is complex and it is this very complexity which explains and justifies the many contradictory elements in her make-up; it is this which makes her so radically different from the decidedly simple and correspondingly less interesting Criseida. These lines, then, are of particular interest not only as genuine courtly love material but also for the light they shed on another side of Criseyde's character, Criseyde in love. It is perfectly clear that she is undergoing a very distinct change, but it must not be inferred that there is anything objectionable in this nor that it is inconsistent with our characterization of her as an opportunist; on the contrary, it simply renders her more human. It is very clear that Criseyde views things somewhat differently now than she did when Pandarus first approached her. She is undergoing the first of the two great changes which come over her in the course of the poem; the dispassionate, detached, composed opportunist is falling in love and she, like everyone else, is profoundly influenced by the experience. From now until her departure from Troy we must bear this fact in mind and devote ourselves to a particular consideration of her character from this point of view.

The poet tells us that the time was astrologically favorable to Troilus and proceeds to devote his attention to Criseyde, sitting alone and trying to determine what she would finally decide to do in case her uncle should continue "Troilus upon hire for to presse" (693). With frequently changing sentiments she tries to determine what is best to do and what to avoid; these thoughts, the poet writes, he will try to describe as his author saw fit to express them. It is well to remember, as I have already mentioned, that this scene is of Chaucer's own invention. In spite of his promise to follow his "auctour," he is not greatly indebted to the *Filostrato* for the lines that make up the rest of the scene; the suggestions he takes are handled with great independence. After Pandaro's departure Criseida decides that there is no reason why she should not be in love, that she might as well take advantage of her opportunity, and that Troilo will make an excellent lover (*Filostrato*, II, 69–78). True, she also considers the other side of the question, wondering whether or not this is an enduring love and if it can remain hidden (II, 78):

> Dunque cotali amor lasciali stare
> A cui e' piaccion: ed appresso il detto
> Incominciava forte a sospirare,
> Nè si poteva già dal casto petto
> Il bel viso di Troilo cacciare,
> Per che tornava sopra il primo effetto
> Biasimando e lodando, e in tale erranza,
> Seco faceva lunga dimoranza.

Criseyde follows in general the same line of thought, but her reasoning is far more profound and so much more penetrating that it is something quite different from Criseida's. There are several points which she touches on in her soliloquy: (1) His "worthynesse," even though she does not grant him love, makes it desirable to be friendly with such a man both on her own account and for his welfare. (2) He is the King's son and might hold her in contempt if she avoids him; thus she would be in even a worse position. (3) He is of good habits, sensible, and not boastful; this last fact she minimizes with the consideration that she will never cherish him so that he will have reason to boast of her. (4) Practically considered, even if men should suspect their love, it would be no dishonor. (5) The life of this man, who might have the love of the most noble lady in Troy, is now entirely in her power. (6) It is no wonder that he loves her for, as men say, she is the fairest and best "in all the town of Troie." (7) She is independent, young, free from deceit, not jealous, not de-

sirous of a husband—for husbands are either jealous, mas-
terful, or in love of novelty; the implication is that such
novelties are not the "novelryes of propre kinde" mentioned
in the *Squires Tale* (619).[10] (8) If she bestows her heart on
this knight and preserves her honor and good name, there
can be nothing shameful about it. This conclusion is precisely the end and aim of all of Pandarus' arguments. Now,
however, she suddenly thinks of the other side of the matter:
(9) Since she is free, should her security and liberty be
jeopardized? Love is a stormy life, and something may happen to destroy her bliss; for women are powerless in ad-
versity and can do nothing but weep and sit and think about
it. (10) People are so ready to gossip. (11) Men are so un-
true; love ceases with their desire, and they are off to a new
friend. (12) If in love, she must busy herself deceiving those
who gossip about her. After all this her conclusion is "nought
venture, nought have" and, with mingled feelings of hope
and fear, she goes out to amuse herself.

The contradictory thoughts which fill Criseyde's mind
are perfectly natural for one in her position. They are quite
in keeping with her opportunist character and mark another
important step in her development. In the beginning she
will not even so much as listen to Pandarus' arguments.
Then she begins to think about them, weighs them pro and
con, and shifts from one opinion to another. There is nothing
objectionable about this vacillation; it is well reasoned and
considered. Her hesitation and the fact that she is beset by
contradictory sentiments are characteristic of one falling in
love, and it is for that reason, as has just been noted, that
these lines mark a definite stage in the change of her affections; it is perfectly clear now that she is falling in love
with Troilus.

Immediately following Criseyde's soliloquy comes the
scene in the garden with her three nieces and entourage, a
Chaucerian addition of unusual grace (II, 813–931). Notable is the Trojan song by one of the nieces, Antigone.[11] In the

opening lines of this hymn of praise she, like a vassal to a feudal lord, pledges loyalty to Love and, as a Christian sinner, likens it to a redeeming grace which will save her from fear and lead her to all joy and security. She goes on to praise love in a spirit much akin to Andreas, who called it the "fons et origo bonorum," [12] but the statement that she loves "withouten jalousie" counterbalances it, for Andreas was quite insistent on the necessity of jealousy; [13] Chaucer too makes use of this doctrine elsewhere. [14] She continues with praise of her lover as the mirror of everything noble and virtuous and goes on to express her gratitude to love for having banished all sin and vice (II, 853–54):

> This dooth me so to vertue for tentende,
> That, day by day, I in my wil amende.

He who condemns it as wrong is either envious, foolish, or powerless to love; such people revile love without ever having experienced it. An effective stanza (124) likening love to the sun, which is none the worse just because a man cannot gaze on it steadily, followed by one pledging unswerving loyalty to her lover concludes the lyric. The whole song is particularly appropriate and especially the final couplet (II, 874–75):

> Al dredde I first to love hym to bigynne,
> Now woot I wel, there is no peril inne.

When Criseyde asks who wrote the song, Antigone replies that it is by "the goodlieste mayde of gret estat" in the whole town of Troy; and when she inquires if there is really such bliss among lovers that they can really compose such words, Antigone answers affirmatively that all the people who are alive or ever have been could not fully describe the bliss of love. Criseyde is much impressed by Antigone's remarks no less than by the song itself and, taking both to heart, is less frightened by love than at first. The charming stanza (130) describing the approach of evening, together with the still more exquisite one relating the song of the nightingale, provides the proper atmosphere for ending this scene. This is done in a single stanza describing Criseyde's dream: how an eagle tore out her heart, left his own, not frightening her or causing any pain, and then flew away "with herte left for herte" (931).

The remaining events of Book II, in so far as they affect Criseyde, have already been discussed in the preceding chapter on Pandarus. It is well to remember that the book closes with the dinner party at the house of Deiphebus; Pandarus is escorting Criseyde into the room where Troilus is waiting (II, 1723–26):

> Al innocent of Pandarus entente,
> Quod tho Criseyde: "go we, uncle deere";
> And arm in arm inward with hym she wente,
> Avysed wel hire wordes and hire cheere.

It is necessary to point out that too much emphasis should not be placed on the words "al innocent." They do not refer to what is about to happen but rather to the words which have just preceded; Criseyde was innocent as to the meaning of Pandarus' words. If this be objected to, it may be answered that what actually happens is sufficient proof that Criseyde was not "al innocent" of the future; she acquiesces willingly, both her words and her expression are well chosen, and when she comes to Troilus, her behavior is certainly not that of one suddenly confronted by an unexpected situation. Troilus, completely aware of Pandarus' plans, is the one who is so abashed that he cannot utter a word; Criseyde, who, if she were "al innocent," would certainly be expected to be at least a little disturbed by this meeting with her lover, is indeed calm and collected; in fact, she is in complete command of the situation. But this is perhaps anticipating. At any rate we are ready to take up Book III, and I am confident that a close study of the opening scene between Troilus and Criseyde will substantiate this point of view.

The behavior of Troilus in the opening scene of Book III

has already been mentioned. It was caused by Criseyde's telling him that there are two reasons for her visit: first to thank him and then to ask for the continuance of his patronage. At this point, the poet tells us, Troilus became absolutely speechless and totally unable to say any of the nice things he had intended. Criseyde noticed all this, we are informed, "for she was wis." How are we to interpret these words? Separated from their context and properly declaimed they may be so twisted as to make almost any sort of adventuress out of Criseyde. But it must be remembered that this is her first meeting with Troilus and furthermore that this is Troilus' first "affair"; consequently what is more natural than that he should behave exactly in this fashion, particularly since it is precisely what a courtly lover should do? "For she was wis" simply means, then, that she, the worldly wise, the widow, the lady experienced in amorous affairs, was fully aware of Troilus' behavior and understood its significance, just as might be expected of a discerning courtly love heroine. She loved him none the less on this account, we are told, though he was not forward, persistent, or bold in speech.

When Troilus recovers sufficiently, he begs mercy of Criseyde and then, after a pause, goes on to declare that he belongs and always will belong entirely to her. This is fully in keeping with the courtly code, which demands undivided allegiance on the part of the lover. So too is the declaration which follows, that he will be glad to die if this will please her; now that he has told her something of his feelings, he does not care how soon he passes on. Then comes that finely acted interlude between Pandarus and Criseyde. Moved to tears by Troilus' protestations of fealty, the former urges her to do something. "I, what?" asks Criseyde, professing that she does not know what Pandarus wishes her to say. "I, what?" mockingly replies Pandarus; "have pity and do not make him die." The words that follow show that, even if she did not know what Pandarus wished her to say, she

knew perfectly well what she wanted to say herself. They are
not the spontaneous outburst of the moment but rather the
complete expression of what she has been thinking for some
time, a clear statement of the purpose of her visit (III, 124–
26):

> "Now thanne thus," quod she, "I wolde hym preye
> To telle me the fyn of his entente;
> Yit wiste I nevere wel what that he mente."

Troilus is not slow in grasping this opportunity to clear
up Criseyde's doubts and immediately declares (127 ff.)
that he hopes she will look kindly on him for a time and
then agree that he will be the one "alwey to don you my
servise." This is quite proper, for the courtly code counsels
against a too sudden love. He further declares his complete
devotion, his desire to do at any time anything she wishes,
and his willingness to endure cheerfully her every whim,
howsoever much it pain him. It is scarcely necessary to mention that this is excellent courtly love doctrine; the idea of
the complete sovereignty of the lady was a favorite notion [15]
(cf., e. g., Chrétien's *Chevalier de la Charrete*) and is one of
the ways in which Chaucer has considerably enriched his
poem. Criseida is quite different in this respect, for she certainly is not the type to insist on exercising sovereignty;
at least she does not do so, and I think Boccaccio was quite
right in not developing in her this aspect of the courtly heroine. Chaucer, on the other hand, adds greatly to the artistic
perfection of his poem, not to mention the complexity of his
heroine's character, by making her, among other things, the
sovereign mistress. True, she is in no sense the exacting lady
Guenevere is, but still she has absolute power over Troilus;
his confession is a complete admission of his mistress's supremacy. Chaucer's acquaintanceship with the work of Chrétien has never been proved (or disproved), but there are
many things in the *Troilus*, and especially this treatment of
sovereignty, which make it seem plausible that his ideas were

very possibly colored by a perusal of the French romances.

Immediately following Troilus' request that he be allowed to serve her (III, 127–47), Pandarus sarcastically observes that this is a hard request and a reasonable one for a lady to refuse (III, 148 ff.). He goes on to say that if he were a god, she should die very soon; for, though Troilus desires only her honor, she sees him dying and is loath to allow him to serve her. The statement, "This man wol no thing yerne but youre honour," is of considerable importance in that it implies a fundamental courtly love teaching, one that Pandarus repeatedly tries to impress on Criseyde; that is, that according to the code there can be nothing wrong in her bestowing her love on Troilus; there is no possibility of her honor's being defamed, and consequently she ought not to hesitate longer. Here, as in so many other instances, Pandarus is simply acting as the orthodox exponent of the courtly system. It might also be observed in connection with this remark that there seems little basis for the belief that Chaucer was trying, through Pandarus, to satirize the chivalric code. The joking, the lightsome mood, and the occasional mockery of the lovers' behavior which Pandarus indulges in are in no sense to be interpreted as satire. They deal with externalities and eccentricities. When it comes to fundamentals, Pandarus is orthodox and sincere.

In words which are at first apparently addressed to Pandarus and then intended for Troilus as well, Criseyde, with the usual insistence on her honor, agrees to accept him in her "servyse" and henceforward to "don hym gladnesse." Criseyde goes on to tell him that, even though he is a king's son, he shall not have sovereignty of her in love, a point hardly necessary for her to have mentioned since Troilus, as a courtly lover, would not even expect it. She now promises to do everything in her power to turn his sorrow "al into swetnesse," and taking him in her arms, she begins to kiss him. This definite pledge to Troilus is the third stage in her development. Once more she acts and with her eyes open; there is, in the whole

poem, probably no clearer proof that the person who seduces
Criseyde is Criseyde herself.

When Criseyde finishes speaking, Pandarus falls on his
knees and, raising his eyes to heaven, calls Cupid and Venus
to witness; it is a genuine miracle; he seems to hear each
church bell in town ringing. Mindful of the approach of
Deiphebus and the others, Pandarus invites the two lovers
to his house, where he promises them it will be easy enough
to ease their hearts (III, 198–99):

> And lat se which of yow shal bere the belle
> To speke of love aright.

Even if it be granted that Criseyde up to this point is just an
innocent girl who yields to temptation, it is perfectly clear
from the words of Pandarus that she goes to the meeting at
his house with full knowledge of what she is doing.

After Criseyde's departure Pandarus returns and spends
the night with Troilus; this scene has already been discussed.
It is followed by nearly one hundred lines (421–511) which
are for the most part Chaucer's own and which serve to give
the reader an idea of what the lovers did during the period of
several days which now intervenes. Troilus becomes a model
of exemplary conduct, avoiding rash deeds and angry looks
with such success that no living person could know what was
in his mind (III, 433–34):

> From every wight as fer as is the cloude
> He was, so wel dissimulen he koude.

In acting thus he was of course behaving as a courtly lover
should, and his avoidance of rash deeds and kindred acts is
not only part of his policy of dissimulation but also is due to
the regenerating power of love, a favorite conceit of the *dolce
stil nuovo* group mentioned above.[16] Troilus passes his days
in the performance of martial deeds and devotes his nights
to thinking how he might serve his lady best; the hint for
these lines probably comes from the *Filostrato*, III, 20, but
there is no literal connection between the two passages. Chau-

cer adds that Troilus was frequently distressed in his thoughts and often turned on his pillow; this typical lover's symptom is so common that it need scarcely be pointed out. It is a small detail, but so are many of Chaucer's improvements; their cumulative force, however, is very great.

During this period Troilus saw Criseyde sometimes, and she spoke to him when she dared and when she cared to. Cummings refers this statement to an earlier part of the *Filostrato* (II, 84),[17] but in spite of Chaucer's "as writen is in geste," this is scarcely necessary. At any rate the immediately following remark that they both conferred together about their procedure is certainly Chaucer's own; their talks are very short and very guarded so that no one may suspect them. But though they spoke little, Troilus felt that she knew his every thought, and hence it was unnecessary for her to request or forbid him to do anything. She in turn felt that, though love was late, it opened to her the gate of joy.[18] She is thankful that he is in her service; he is so discreet and reliable that she regards him as a shield from every "displesaunce." Fear besets her no more except, the author hastens to add, "as fer as oughte ben requered." From these lines Criseyde now seems to be heart and soul in love with Troilus; the stage is all set for the next great scene.

The meeting between Troilus and Criseyde takes place as scheduled at the house of Pandarus. The latter's conversation with Criseyde has already been considered in detail except for the disclaimer (799–840) occasioned by her uncle's fiction of the rival lover; this ruse (and therefore its denial) is Chaucer's addition to the story. Amazed she grows cold about the heart, sighs, and answers suddenly that it is a lie and that some wicked spirit has put the idea into Troilus' head. Then follows a Boethian apostrophe (813–40) to "fals felicitee" and "worldy joie unstable," ending with the stanza (120):

> Wherfore I wol deffyne in this manere:
> That trewely, for aught I kan espie,
> Ther is no verray weele in this world heere.

But O, thow wikked serpent, jalousie,
Thow mysbyleved, envyous folie,
Why hastow Troilus made to me untriste,
That nevere yit agilte hym, that I wiste?

The ideas expressed in these lines are closely akin to those in
the epilogue on the vanity of earthly things. Criseyde's statement that she will see Troilus the next day and assure him of
her loyalty is immediately seized upon by Pandarus, who
points out the necessity for immediate action; how he uses
this pretext so that everything comes about just as he has
planned has already been discussed. Consequently we may
now pass on to the meeting of the two lovers.

After the first moments of excitement Troilus calms down
under the influence of a soothing word and kiss from Criseyde
and listens to her expression of grief because of his jealousy
and the pain which it caused him. She begins by assuring him
of her undivided loyalty and of her desire to relieve all his
distress (988–1003) and then proceeds to denounce jealousy.
Her views are not orthodox, for she condemns it in wholesale
fashion; according to the code, "Qui non zelat, amare non
potest." [19] Concluding, Criseyde bursts into tears, covers her
head with a sheet, sighs and speaks no more. Troilus, we are
told, did not feel Criseyde's weeping as the stroke of a switch
but rather as the very cramp of death about his heart. He is
very despondent, bemoans the fact that he ever came there
and, finally, overcome by sorrow, falls in a swoon. The intervention of Pandarus at this crucial moment has been mentioned, and we need only add that Criseyde tries in vain to
arouse Troilus by swearing in his ear that she is not angry
with him. They rub his hands and temples, she kisses him,
and he begins to recover. She then asks (III, 1126–27):

is this a mannes game?
What! Troilus, wol ye do thus for shame?

This reproach is quite unfounded, for she knows perfectly
well that such behavior is typical of the courtly lover. How-

ever, she forgives him, and they comfort themselves with goodly words. In the course of the conversation she asks him to tell her all about the man who was the cause of his jealousy, saying that if he does not, she will consider that he was maliciously trying to put her to the test. He obeys and, as Chaucer says, "for the lasse harm, he moste feyne":

> He seyde hire, whan she was at swiche a feste
> She myghte on hym han loked at the leste;
> Noot I nat what, al deere ynough a rysshe,
> As he that nedes moste a cause fisshe.
>   —III, 1158-62.

Criseyde blames him for being jealous, especially since she meant no evil thereby, and reproaches him once more for his jealousy: "Wol ye the childissh jalous contrefete?" Troilus, fearing that she is angry and thinking his heart is about to die, begs her to have mercy on his sorrow and promises, if there was any wrong in his words, that he will sin no more. "Doth what you list, I am al in your grace" is an admission of the lady's sovereignty and his complete subjection to her. This courtly love aspect is emphasized, and the whole stanza brought to a more satisfactory conclusion, by adopting the variant for the last half line: "I put me in youre grace." [20] Criseyde forgives him once more, and the lovers embrace. When Troilus asks her to yield, since there is no other remedy, she replies significantly (III, 1210–11):

> Ne hadde I or now, my swete herte deere,
> Ben yolde, iwys, I were now nat here.

Dodd quite correctly interprets these words: "There is only one thing that can be said,—that they are a delicate way of stating the truth in the matter. If Criseyde had not already yielded in her mind, she certainly would not have been at the house of Pandarus." [21]

The rest of the scene (1212–1526) is filled with description of the lovers' delights and their amorous words to each other. Chaucer's admirable restraint in describing the purely

sensuous is nowhere more skillfully shown than in this passage; and the same statement applies to his precision in the
choice of words for the expression of the lovers' feelings and
the delineation of their innermost reactions. The various
descriptions of the lovers' embraces need not be considered,
for they have little to do with the problem at hand; they
could only lose their inimitable charm by paraphrase and
criticism. Suffice it to say that the poet's words can leave no
doubt in the reader's mind that he viewed their relationship,
in part, as a sensuous and physical one. This is of course fully
in keeping with courtly love practice for, though it recom-
mended chastity and the higher love, it also admitted and
approved of a carnal relationship; in Chaucer's words, love
"celestial or elles love of kynde" (I, 979).

Troilus utters a prayer of thanksgiving to Love (1254–
74), part of which (1261–67) is a translation of lines addressed, in the *Paradiso*, to the Virgin.[22] It is an excellent example of the use of ecclesiastical terminology for the expression of courtly love. Troilus remarks that in his loving of
Criseyde men may see that mercy surpasses justice (1282).
Root points out two other examples of this idea and notes
that "the language of courtly love has transferred to its own
use the theological opposition of divine mercy and strict
justice." [23]

The manner in which Criseyde addresses Troilus shows
that she has given herself entirely to him: "Myn owen hertes
lust, my ground of ese . . . al myn herte deere . . . my
knyght, my pees, my suffisaunce." Up to this point the scene
has been almost entirely Chaucer's own invention. Now he
returns to the *Filostrato* (III, 31–73, 90–93), which, however, he treats with considerable freedom. The lines (1352–
58) recounting the lovers' exchange of rings and Criseyde's
gift of a brooch are not found in the corresponding section of
the Italian poem. One need hardly seek a parallel for anything so common as the former; as to the brooch, it is mentioned only once in the *Filostrato* (VIII, 9) at the very end,

where it is the means of convincing Troilo of Criseida's disloyalty. Lines 1359–1400 are taken over from the *Filostrato* (III, 38–41) and are at the same time considerably expanded. The condemnation of avarice is quite in keeping with the courtly teaching which condemns that quality in a lover. May God give all such "besy wrecches" bad luck and advance every lover in his fidelity! The stingy "wrecches" are compared to Midas and Crassus (Chaucerian addition) to teach them that "coveytise is vice" and love virtue, though men call it foolish. Love as the source of virtue is a commonplace courtly idea, a favorite of the troubadours and elaborated to great extremes by the *dolce stil nuovo* school. Chaucer adds this same idea again in line 1400 where, noting that the lovers did not waste the night in sleep, he mentions that (III, 1399–1400):

> It was byset in joie and besynesse
> Of al that souneth into gentilesse.

The next two stanzas are a comment of particular interest by the author, for he says, in effect, that he has for the most part followed his source but has at the same time seen fit to add to the love material, which the reader may treat as he pleases (III, 1405–7):

> And if that I at loves reverence,
> Have any thing in eched for the beste,
> Doth therwithal right as youre selven leste.

If proof were needed that the *Troilus* is the work of the conscious artist, surely there could be none more convincing than this very definite statement by the poet himself.

Criseyde's address to night (1422–42) and Troilus' apostrophe to the dawn (1450–70) are Chaucerian additions. They are both traditional literary devices and neither is conceived particularly well. Troilus' aubade is sufficient proof that Chaucer had no firsthand acquaintance with the love poetry of the troubadours. Had that been the case, he would doubtless have produced something much finer. This great scene, of such consequence for the lovers (as well as the readers of the poem), is brought to an end by Troilus' leaving after a mutual exchange of expressions of loyalty and devotion, together with numberless final embraces.

After the departure of Troilus, Criseyde thinks about him. This stanza is suggested by the behavior of Criseida (*Filostrato*, III, 55), who, we are told, spoke of Troilo in her heart and, inwardly happy, gave boundless thanks to Love; it seemed to her a thousand years before her lover would return and she might embrace him as in the night just passed. Chaucer handles this statement much more skillfully by making it decidedly less obvious, if more concrete: Criseyde thinks of Troilus' worthiness, his desire, his wise deeds, his gentility, and of her first meeting with him. She thanks Love that he employed her so well and longs to have Troilus in such a situation that she might "make hym cheere."

The meeting between Pandarus and Criseyde has already been discussed; we need only mention that at its end Criseyde went home. The heroine does not appear again in Book III but receives frequent mention in the narrative account (1667–1715) of the lovers' happy meeting arranged by Pandarus in the same manner as the first one. This is only suggested in the *Filostrato* (III, 64–65), where it is said that Troilo's good fortune gave him an opportunity for his amours and that Criseida also came in her accustomed manner. After the exchange of greetings they entered her chamber with great delight and without hesitation they lay down. In Chaucer's account the lovers are still under the paternal vigilance of Pandarus, who brought them "abedde." Two stanzas of author's comment (241–42) explain the writer's inability to describe the joy which they had of each other (III, 1693–94):

> This joie may nat writen be with inke;
> This passeth al that herte may bythynke.

In the *Filostrato* the lovers become aware of the approach of day and curse angrily. Chaucer's scene is much more poeti-

cal—I refer to the thought and am not belittling the music of
Boccaccio's verse. The approach of day, which the lovers
recognize by "sygnes," makes them think they feel the wound
of death. Such woe is theirs that their complexions change
and once more they begin to despise the day (III, 1700–1),

> Callyng it traitour, envyous, and worse;
> And bitterly the dayes light thei corse.

In a brief *alba* (1702–8, Chaucer's addition) Troilus declares
that Pirous and the three swift steeds that draw the sun have
taken a short cut to spite him and thus have brought on day
ahead of time; further, since the sun thus hastens to rise he
refuses to sacrifice to him any more. Boccaccio tells us that
the lovers, after many sighs, took leave of each other in the
usual manner and that they planned in the future to turn to
their desires without any delay in order to assuage their sufferings and spend the season of youth, while it lasted, in
such happiness. Chaucer repeats this account of the lovers'
leave-taking and states that they set a time to meet again,
but he omits all the detailed explanation with which Boccaccio elaborated the simple statement. Chaucer makes only
this general remark (III, 1713–15):

> And many a nyght they wroughte in this manere.
> And thus Fortune a tyme ledde in joie
> Criseyde and ek this kynges sone of Troie.

After an account of Troilus' gallant conduct, including his
hymn to Love, Book III ends with the assurance that the
lovers are happy together (III, 1819–20): [24]

> And Troilus in lust and in quiete
> Is with Criseyde, his owen herte swete.

Book IV relates, as Chaucer puts it, how Criseyde forsook
Troilus, or at least how she was "unkynde"; he regrets that
people should find any reason to speak harm of her and says
that if they tell lies about her, they themselves should be
reproached. The English poet's merciful and generous atti-

tude is in definite contrast to Boccaccio's absolute and unqualified condemnation; but this topic will be considered in
greater detail later on.

After the decision of the Greeks to exchange Antenor for
Criseyde, the heroine makes her initial appearance alone.
This scene (659–805) is taken over for the most part from
the *Filostrato* (IV, 78–95) and consequently contains no
important Chaucerian addition or modification of significance
for the study of Criseyde. She has heard of the exchange but
is so afraid that the report is true that she dares not ask anyone about it. Boccaccio says that Criseida turned her desire
to Troilo whom she loved more than any other. Chaucer expands this statement to a full stanza by adding that the whole
world could not unbind her love nor cast Troilus from her
heart; she wishes to be his as long as she may live (IV,
678–79):

> And thus she brenneth bothe in love and drede,
> So that she nyste what was best to reede.

Then follows the very fine tragicomic scene in which several
gossipy women visit Criseyde, congratulate her on what they
of course accept as her good fortune, and try to comfort her
when she bursts into tears; in fact, seeing her weep and thinking it is on account of her love for them, they also weep for
her distress (680–730). But since all this lugubriousness
avails nothing nor do their words help, they leave after "al
this nyce vanyte"; by using this phrase Chaucer tempers very
considerably what Boccaccio calls the foolish cackling which
most women make (IV, 86).

After their departure Criseyde goes to her room and falls
on her bed as if dead, her intention being never to rise therefrom. She tears her hair, wrings her hands, begs pity of God,
and prays that death will come as relief to her sorrow. She
decides that she must have been born when the planets were
unfavorable and curses that day on which she first saw Troilus
with the two eyes that cause her such pain. This is a courtly

love touch not found in the *Filostrato;* the function of the eyes in arousing love was a favorite conceit with Chrétien and the troubadours. Criseyde's lament fills lines 757–98 and deals entirely with the thought that she cannot live separated from Troilus. Since she dare not take her life with "swerd ne darte," she will starve herself to death; until she dies, she will wear black in token that she has gone from the world and, in his absence, will devote herself to sorrow, lamentation, and abstinence. Their spirits will never be separated from each other but be happy together in the Elysian fields as are those of Orpheus and Eurydice. Addressing her words to Troilus she urges him to forget this sorrow and trouble and her as well; for, to tell the truth, "so ye wel fare, I recche nat to deye" (798). This is a Chaucerian addition; also added by the English poet are the decision not to take her life, the ascetic conduct she promises, and the projected reunion in the Elysian fields. Chaucer translates the question, who could tell in full what Criseyde said in her distress? (*Filostrato*, IV, 95), and says he knows not, for words fail him. Adding his own comment, he closes the scene thus (IV, 801–5):

> but, as for me, my litel tonge,
> If I discryven wolde hire hevynesse,
> It sholde make hire sorwe seme lesse
> Than that it was, and childisshly deface
> Hire heigh compleynte, and therfore ich it pace.

Troilus' visit with Criseyde (IV, 1128–1701) might well be considered the climax scene of the poem, for it is the last time that the lovers are together and is of momentous consequence in so far as the impending events are concerned. Boccaccio relates that Criseida, as was her custom, came to meet Troilo with a lighted torch. Chaucer ignores this detail (though he states that Troilus went to Criseyde alone, a fact the Italian poet does not mention) but otherwise the two agree in the main as to the meeting of the lovers: both are speechless with sorrow (1130) and it is only when Criseyde is able to control her fears that she utters the first words (IV, 1149–50):

> O Jove, I deye, and mercy I beseche!
> Help, Troilus!

Falling on his breast, she faints and seems to be dead. Troilus believes she has passed away, for she is cold and he cannot feel her breath; he therefore lays her out in the manner customary for a corpse and, uttering various imprecations and farewells, draws his sword and is about to kill himself when Criseyde, recovering from her swoon, cries out, "Troilus!" Needless to add, this stops the sword and the two embrace again. He tells her the reason for the attempt, and she replies that if she had found him dead she would have seized the sword and killed herself.

The additions which Chaucer makes to this scene are largely incidental: a simile here, a classical allusion there, various lines giving more accurate touches, and so on; but in the main the account is faithful to the corresponding section of the *Filostrato* (IV, 114–27). However, with Criseyde's monologue which follows (1254–1414), Chaucer deals more freely. He follows Boccaccio's statement that the lovers went to bed but that the night was not at all like those which had passed before; they weep and curse the day they were born until finally the practical-minded Criseyde tells Troilus that something ought to be done. The first seven stanzas of her speech (1254–1302) are added by Chaucer and are of considerable significance, for they show admirably how different Criseida and Criseyde are. It may be recalled that at the end of his visit Pandaro tells his niece to forget her anguish, to arise and control herself so that she may assuage and not increase Troilo's grief (IV, 107). Pandarus reëchoes these sentiments but adds that when he brings Troilus to her they both should devise some plan either to prevent her going or to assure her return (IV, 933–38):

Syn ye ben wise, and bothe of oon assent,
So shapeth how destourbe youre goynge,
Or come ayeyn soone after ye be went.
Wommen ben wise in short avysement;
And lat sen how youre wit shal now availle,
And that that I may helpe, it shal not faille.

Consequently, when Criseyde tells Troilus that it is time they
begin to seek a remedy for their sorrow, she is only following
out her uncle's suggestion. The reason we are sad is that we
must separate; what other remedy is there than that we should
arrange to meet soon? I am confident that I can arrange to
return, after I go, within a week or two and I shall show you
various ways in which it may be done. As I shall tell you my
conclusion in this matter directly, forgive my directness; it
is all for the best. You know that my going has been agreed on
by parliament and therefore may not be opposed; since it cannot be prevented, let us forget about it and find a better plan.
The separation will trouble us cruelly but those who serve
Love, if they will have joy, must also endure pain; and since
I shall not be so far from Troy but that I can return in a short
time, that should make us grieve less.

Chaucer now picks up the thread of the *Filostrato* account
and follows it for nearly six stanzas (1310–48). The substance of these lines is that when a truce is declared she can
return. When? Before ten days are over, surely. Even now,
Criseyde continues, we occasionally do not see each other for
two weeks at a time; why should ten days be impossible? My
father has no desire to see me except that he fears people
despise me because of him; if he knew how well I get along
in Troy, we would not need to worry about separation. Furthermore, the prospects for peace are very favorable. Chaucer
elaborates this fact in an additional ten lines (1349–58),
pointing out that then people may ride back and forth and
stay where they please. The next stanza (1359–65) is suggested in part by Criseida's statement that her father would
not keep her among the Greeks and therefore could do but one

thing: send her back. Chaucer does not mention Calkas in this connection but otherwise says practically the same thing. Save for Criseida's statement that her father is old and avaricious, Chaucer is quite independent of the *Filostrato* for the rest of the monologue (1366–1414). Criseida, by far the less resourceful of the two ladies, has no very definite plan to deal with her father: he is avaricious; therefore I shall tell him something about his property here, and he will send me back; for I shall show him that I may find a remedy for anything unexpected that may happen and, because of his avarice, he will delight in my return. What a contrast to this vague and confused notion is the adroit Criseyde's definite plan to exploit to the full her father's greed! She has some movable property which she will take to her father and say that it is sent by friends who beg him to send for the rest; but lest people should discover it, it may be sent by her alone. Furthermore, she will tell him of her standing with the court and how she can restore him to favor with Priam. If he discovers her deception through his divination, she will show him that (IV, 1405–7):

> He hath nat wel the goddes understonde.
> For goddes speken in amphibologies,
> And, for a soth, they tellen twenty lyes.

And if she does not change his ways and make him follow her advice, then may Troilus kill her: "I wol to you oblige me to deye" (1414).

Chaucer remarks that this was all said with good intent and that Criseyde was loyal and sincere (IV, 1415–18). When she went, she nearly died on account of her grief; she intended always to be faithful—thus write those who knew of her actions. As the poet states, these sentiments agree with those expressed by other writers who were properly informed: Boccaccio, Benoit, and Guido make no mention of Criseyde's disloyalty.

Paralleling Criseyde's extended monologue is the long section devoted to Troilus (1415–1526). He listens to Criseyde's plans, is of the same opinion, has misgivings, but finally decides to trust her. This hope relieves their sorrow and they are happy once more. Still, he cannot forget her departure and often begs her to be true to her promise. Thus far (1440) Chaucer has followed the *Filostrato* very closely; the rest of the scene, however, is treated with considerable freedom. Troilo tells Criseida that if she stays one moment too long he will kill himself; that he does not see how he can avoid bitter sighing when she is not there; and that, Calkas keeping her, he fears that what she has promised cannot be accomplished (IV, 140). Chaucer takes over only the threat of suicide in case of delay but plays with and elaborates it through three stanzas (1443–63). Troilus begs her to stay there and thus save him from death, for he is sure her trickery will not succeed; things planned ahead of time never work out, and her father is so crafty that she will not be able to deceive him. Troilus now repeats Troilo's suggestion that, even though there may be peace, Calkas will be too ashamed to return to the Trojan side and furthermore that he will find some Greek for her to marry. Then too he will say that the city is lost, for the Greeks have sworn not to lift the siege until the Trojans are slain and the walls razed. This is an expansion of Troilo's statement that Calkas will persuade Criseida that the siege will have a dangerous outcome (IV, 142). For these reasons Troilus fears that Criseyde will remain on the Greek side, especially since the polish of the Greeks will make her tire of the "rudenesse of us sely Troians" (1490). For all these reasons Troilus suggests they run away to some safe place; it may be noted that the suggestion of Troilo is identical, though he shows himself much less foresighted than Troilus. He points out that there are people who will be glad to receive them and honor them as members of nobility. Troilus, on the contrary, "vulgarly to speken of substaunce," suggests they take enough "tresour" with them so that they may live honorably and pleasantly until they die;

further, he has relatives and friends who, "though we comen in oure bare sherte," would not only provide gold and equipment but would also honor them while they dwelt there. This suggestion does not meet with Criseyde's approval (1527–96). She points out that if they should steal away and be unsuccessful, they would always regret it "ful soore." Criseida swears by the darts of Love that she will never be false to Troilo; Criseyde makes the same declaration but requires three stanzas (1534–54) to bring a sufficient number of deities to witness her solemn pledge. Both heroines agree in their reasons for not wanting to elope: (1) Troy needs all her brave men; (2) in case of peace, they never could come back to live on account of the attendant shame; (3) people would not say that it was love but voluptuousness and fear that made them flee—both his honor and her womanly virtue would be ruined forever. She reaffirms her intention of seeing him on the tenth day "withouten any faille," unless she is dead. Troilus says, in a stanza, he will wait until the tenth day since that needs must be, but he pleads once more that they steal away (IV, 1602–3):

> For evere in oon, as for to lyve in reste,
> Myn herte seyth that it wol be the beste.

Hearing these words Criseyde accuses him of distrusting her. Criseida's "why do you distrust me?" (*Filostrato*, IV, 157) is turned into (IV, 1609–10):

> Mistrust me nought thus causeles, for routhe;
> Syn to be trewe I have yow plight my trouthe.

She begs him to trust her and forget his sorrow, or she will not live till morning. Criseyde, like Criseida, promises that she will find a way to return and begs him to take such comfort and cheer that her heart will be set at rest; both pray that no other woman will occupy their lovers' fancies and thus supplant them. Criseyde declares that she perceives "alle trouthe" in Troilus and begs him not to be false to her (IV, 1651–52):

> and or ye cause fynde,
> For goddes love, so beth me naught unkynde.

Troilus replies that he has never been false to Criseyde since
he first saw her nor ever will be until he dies (IV, 1658–59):

> At shorte wordes, wel ye may me leve;
> I kan no more, it shal be founde at preve.

This differs from the account in the *Filostrato* where Troilo
indulges in several stanzas of explanation (164–67). The
lines are used, however, but Chaucer transfers them to Criseyde. After one of the usual prayers to Venus (Chaucerian),
she explains the reason for her love (1667–80); it was not
his royal state, vain pleasure, bravery in battle, nor pomp,
display, noble rank, wealth—none of these made her pity his
distress (IV, 1672–73),

> But moral vertu, grounded upon trouthe,
> That was the cause I first hadde on yow routhe.

Additional reasons were his "gentil herte and manhod," his
despising everything bad, and the supremacy of his reason
over his desires. This is a significant passage, for the idea of
"moral vertu, grounded upon trouthe" is hardly so much as
implied in the *Filostrato*. These virtues which Criseyde has
enumerated as present in Troilus make him the *ne plus ultra*
of courtly lovers; this emphasis on the moral qualities to the
exclusion of the less substantial, more external things shows
the influence of the *dolce stil nuovo*.

Criseyde remarks that their devotion to each other is something the years may not undo nor Fortune change. Chaucer
causes her to call on Jupiter, who helps the sad to rejoice, to
grant the favor that they may meet before ten nights elapse
(IV, 1686–87):

> So that it may youre herte and myn suffise;
> And fare now wel, for tyme is that ye rise.

In two more stanzas (1688–1701) Book IV is brought to an
end. With the approach of dawn the lovers separate. Whether

Troilus was sorry, the poet holds is no question; for it is impossible to imagine or relate the cruel pains of this despairing man (IV, 1699–1701):

> For whan he saugh that she ne myghte dwelle,
> Which that his soule out of his herte rente,
> Withouten more, out of the chaumbre he wente.

With Book V a new character, Diomede, enters the story. Almost the first two hundred lines (1–196) are devoted to Criseyde's departure and Diomede's profession of his love on the way to the Greek camp. Since our heroine is a decidedly minor figure in this scene, detailed consideration of it may be left until the next section, which is devoted to Diomede. Suffice it to note, as the poet tells us (176–89), that her sorrow was so great that she heard only an occasional word; when she saw her father, her emotion was such that she almost fell off the horse. Nevertheless, she thanked Diomede for his trouble and his offer of friendship (V, 186–89):

> And she accepteth it in good manere,
> And wol do fayn that is hym lief and dere;
> And trusten hym she wolde, and wel she myghte,
> As seyde she, and from hire hors shalighte.

Those lines are of great importance, I feel, because they demonstrate very clearly that she is still entirely loyal to Troilus. Were the opposite the case, that is, if she already looked upon Diomede as a potential lover, she never would have acted in this manner; such a willing spirit, such speedy acquiescence on her part would have been too flagrant a violation of the courtly love code for even so human a poet as Chaucer. It must be remembered that up to this point Criseyde's behavior is orthodox; Chaucer is not yet ready for the definite break which he is going to make with the code. Consequently her interest in Diomede is solely that of friendship; there is no question of her sincerity. If she were insincere, it would mean that she had already made up her mind about Diomede. If this were the case, it would follow that Criseyde had shown a rashness of decision entirely out of keeping with her previous conduct. But no, Criseyde was not that kind.

Boccaccio (*Filostrato*, V, 14) relates that Criseida's father welcomed her with great joy, although such affection vexed her and consumed her with sorrow, her heart being still faithful to Troilo; yet we are also told that she is soon to change and abandon him for a new lover. Chaucer does not follow this stanza at all closely in his account (190–96). According to him, Calkas took her in arms, kissed her twenty times, and bade her welcome. She in turn said that she was glad to meet him and stood there "muwet, milde, and mansuete." The suggestion that she will soon cast aside her lover for another is not even hinted at.

The intervening lines (197–687) are devoted to the activities of Pandarus and Troilus following the departure of Criseyde; line 687 begins a similar account of her life among the Greeks. This passage (687–770) is a rather free handling of the account in the *Filostrato* (VI, 1–8). She is lonesome in the Greek camp and, bemoaning the day that she was born, longs for death. She says she cannot change things for the better, for all is worse than she had ever imagined. Her father will not let her go despite her efforts to persuade him, while if she stays longer than agreed, Troilus will think her false, and she will have no thanks on either side (V, 699–700):

> Thus shal I have unthank on every side;
> That I was born, so weilaway the tide!

If she tries to steal away at night and is caught, she will be held as a spy or, what she dreads most, fall into the hands of some wretch. This is for the most part a Chaucerian passage. As Cummings very justly remarks on lines 694–707, "In this passage the poet very skillfully picks up the threads of *Troil.* IV, 1366–1414, and resumes the scheme of Criseyde to cajole her father through his covetousness. The able management of such details as this should raise Chaucer far above the suspicion of being merely a wearied translator in the Fifth

Book of his poem, with much of his enthusiasm for the work gone." [25]

Both poets agree in general on their heroine's conduct at this time (708 ff.). Criseyde spends the day, when she dares, gazing toward the town where she was born and "al the nyght wepyng." She sketches Troilus' great bravery and recalls all the words they have exchanged since the first meeting, but this serves only to inflame her heart. There is no one in the world so heartless as to refrain from weeping with her, she wept so copiously—"Hire nedede no teris for to borwe." Yet the worst of her trouble was that she had no one to whom she might complain (728). Confidants were not only tolerated but entirely approved of in the courtly system; the absence of any such person in the Greek camp is one of several good reasons for Criseyde's subsequent action. As she looks toward Troy, she wonders if Troilus still thinks of her and regrets that she had not gone off with him; who could have said that there was anything wrong to steal away with such a person as he is (V, 741–42)?

> But al to late comth the letuarie,
> Whan men the cors unto the grave carie.

Chaucer inserts a Boethian passage at this point in which Criseyde regrets that she lacks one of the eyes of Prudence; she could remember the past, see the present, "but futur tyme . . . koude I nat sen." The next stanza (750–56) parallels the *Filostrato* (VI, 7): she will steal off the next night, "bityde what bityde"; let people say what they will. Elaborating this, Chaucer adds 756–63; Criseyde reflects that whoever pays attention to what others may say and think will never prosper because of fear (V, 760–63):

> For that that som men blamen evere yit,
> Lo, other maner folk comenden it.
> And as for me, for all swich variaunce,
> Felicite clepe I my suffisaunce.

However, the poet adds, before two months had passed she was far from that decision to return to Troy without delay; both Troilus and Troy are destined to slip through her heart like a string without knots, for she has a reason to stay. Boccaccio is much more direct in telling us about Diomede's efforts to win Criseida: he uses every argument and finally is successful; in a short time all thought of Troilus and Troy, false or true, is gone from her. Only in the next stanza (771–77) does Chaucer mention Diomede and his plans for winning Criseyde. This passage will be considered in chapter IX.

Of the three descriptions which now appear, that of Criseyde (806–26) is the only one that need concern us at this point. Her portrait, like those of Diomede and Troilus, is not found in the *Filostrato* but is borrowed from the *Frigii Daretis Ylias* of Joseph of Exeter.[26] She was of medium stature and in loveliness unsurpassed. Her eyes were of such beauty that those who saw them say Paradise stood formed therein (V, 818–19):

> And with hire riche beaute evere more
> Strof love in hire aye, which of hem was more.

As to personal qualities, she was demure, modest yet wise, as well educated as "myghte be," and pleasant in her speech; charitable, stately, joyous, gracious, and never lacking in pity, tenderhearted, unstable in disposition—but as for her age, "trewely, I kan nat telle." The story thus far has, to a greater or less degree, brought out most of these qualities. Since the remainder of the poem is largely concerned with her instability, we may therefore pass on to the first meeting of Diomede and Criseyde.

Diomede visits Calkas on some pretext and is soon engaged in conversation with Criseyde; they talk of the war, the siege, the activities of the Greeks, and so on. When he asks why her father delays so in marrying her to some worthy man, she answers as well as she can, considering the pain she is suffering because of her love for Troilus; but of Diomede's intention she apparently has no idea whatsoever. Diomede now begins his energetic and persuasive wooing (871–924). Pointing out that the defeat of the Trojans is imminent, that Troy will be destroyed and no Trojan will be able to escape, he urges her to forget it, to substitute cheerfulness for sorrow, and to find another love among the Greeks; she will be able to find "a moore parfit" one before night (V, 922–24):

> And if ye vouchesauf, my lady bright,
> I wol ben he to serven yow my selve,
> Ye, levere than be Kyng of Greces twelve.

Now, somewhat belatedly I should say, intervenes a stanza (925–30) recounting some of the typical courtly love symptoms which he experienced; he blushed, became uncertain in his speech, stopped for awhile, and so on. Then he points out his royal ancestry and how, if his father Tideus had lived, he would now be a king. He regards her as his sovereign mistress —"syn that I am youre man"—and tells her that she is the first whose favor he has sought; for these reasons he wishes to serve her as long as he lives and begs for permission to return on the morrow to tell of his woe at greater leisure (930–45). This account follows the *Filostrato* (VI, 14–25) with a fair amount of accuracy, though with the inevitable amount of Chaucerian variation in matters of small detail. Of more significance is the way in which the English poet handles Diomede's pledge of service to Criseyde. In the Italian poem he is far more emphatic and decidedly more insistent in yielding complete sovereignty to her. Chaucer tones down his words very considerably; this seems to be part of a conscious effort on his part to present Diomede as a less courtly person. This, however, will receive further consideration in the chapter on Diomede.

Criseyde's speech now follows (953–1004). It is a strange mixing of patriotic devotion to Troy and Troilus along with an eye to practical affairs and definite assurance of interest in Diomede—Criseyde the opportunist to the fore again! She is not changing, degenerating, but is, on the contrary, simply behaving as her natural self. She swears to Diomede that she is not and never was in love with anyone except her dead husband; this is something decidedly different from the Italian account, which relates that she has not known love since her husband died nor did she ever care for Greek or Trojan *in such fashion* ("in cotal fatto," VI, 29). I take this as being Criseida's way of avoiding the necessity of deceiving Diomede; by saying she has never loved any Greek or Trojan in such a manner as she did her first husband, she avoids the difficulty very easily. Why then is not the same ruse employed in the English poem? Perhaps the poet simply forgot to fit in this additional fact; more probably he thought it would be better for Criseyde's interests to make Diomede believe that he has no rivals. Whatever the reason for it, Criseyde continues to insist, more emphatically than in the *Filostrato*, on her complete separation from love but, with an eye to the future, assures Diomede that if she were ever to love anyone, he would probably be the lucky person. Diomede has her permission to come again whenever he wishes, but love as a topic of discussion is to be taboo. And she concludes without making a definite promise either way (1002-4):

> I sey nat therfore that I wol yow love,
> Ny sey nat nay; but in conclusioun,
> I mene wel, by god that sit above.

Thus her last words express complete neutrality so far as her feelings for Diomede are concerned, and she is still loyal to Troy (V, 1006-8):

> O Troie town,
> Yit bidde I god, in quiete and in reste
> I may yow sen, or do myn herte breste.

In the Italian poem things are quite different. Criseida tells Diomede to wait until the expected victory takes place; perhaps she will then be content with the pleasures which now are not to her liking; a man ought to observe the proper time and season when wooing someone (VI, 31). This pleases Diomede greatly, for it gives him new hope; again pledging his loyalty and devotion, he departs. In the *Troilus* Diomede behaves in very different fashion. Encouraged by her words he "gan presen on" and eagerly sought mercy of her. He took her glove and when it was evening "and al was well," he departed. Is any particular significance to be attached to these words? The answer is in the negative, for they probably are to be understood as meaning simply that all was peaceful and quiet in the evening after the day's activities. It might possibly refer to Diomede and mean that all was well with him so far as Criseyde was concerned, but the context does not justify such an extravagant interpretation.

When Troilus suggested that she flee with him, Criseyde rejected the idea in no uncertain terms (IV, 1503–82). A significant indication of the desperate straits in which she now finds herself is the fact that she seriously contemplates flight (V, 701–3). She who was afraid to flee with her lover, the greatest of the Trojan warriors, is now able to consider stealing away from the Greek camp alone, to think of returning to Troy without guide or escort, presumably in the dark of night! Chaucer knew that such a complete change in his heroine, even in her extreme situation, would be too radical, too great a psychological inconsistency. Accordingly, when she accepts Diomede, she accepts him not as a substitute for Troilus but rather as the alternative to the utterly impossible course of action suggested above. Let me show the plausibility of this interpretation.

The lines in which Criseyde debates the Diomede question and finally decides to be faithful to him (1016–99) are entirely independent of the *Filostrato*. Diomede's words, his position, the peril of the town, her loneliness, and the need of assistance are the factors which help determine her final course of action (V, 1023–29):

> Retornyng in hire soule ay up and down
> The wordes of this sodeyn Diomede,
> His grete estat, and peril of the town,
> And that she was allone and hadde nede
> Of frendes help. And thus bygan to brede
> The cause whi, the sothe for to telle,
> That she took fully purpos for to dwelle.

Having thought the matter through, Criseyde thus makes up her mind to accept the situation and make the best of it. It is not surprising, then, to learn that when Diomede returns the next morning (V, 1033–36),

> So wel he for hym selven spak and seyde,
> That alle hire sikes soore adown he leyde.
> And finaly, the sothe for to seyne,
> He refte hire of the grete of al hire peyne.

Criseyde gives him a bay steed, a brooch, and a "pencel of hire sleve." The first and last are from Benoit, while the brooch appears in a later portion of the *Filostrato* (VIII, 9). Chaucer adds that he finds in other sources (and in these lines the same Benoit) the statement that Criseyde wept copiously when she saw Diomede's wounds, wounds inflicted by Troilus; she nursed him and "Men seyn, I not, that she yaf hym hire herte" (1050). The English poet goes on to add that "the storie telleth us" (and here it might have been Benoit or Guido) no woman made greater lamentation than she did when she was false to Troilus—surely peculiar conduct for a weak, fearful woman merely yielding to her lover! This expression of her feelings fills thirty-two lines (1054–85). She regrets and bewails the fact that her faithlessness in love will redound to her disgrace:

> allas! for now is clene ago
> My name of trouthe in love for everemo!

Her infamy will last "unto the worldes ende"; women will hate her most of all, for they will say that she has dishonored them. But she sees no better choice and, since it is too late to be sorry, decides to be faithful to Diomede:

> But syn I se there is no bettre way,
> And that to late it is now for to rewe,
> To Diomede algate I wol be trewe.

Yet even now she holds Troilus in memory, though no longer as her lover, and begs God to protect him. These, her last words, deserve to be quoted in full (V, 1072–85):

> "But Troilus, syn I no bettre may,
> And syn that thus departen ye and I,
> Yit preye I god, so yeve yow right good day,
> As for the gentileste, trewely,
> That evere I say, to serven feythfully,
> And best kan ay his lady honour kepe."—
> And with that word she brast anon to wepe.—
>
> "And, certes, yow ne haten shal I nevere;
> And frendes love, that shal ye han of me,
> And my good word, al myghte I lyven evere.
> And, trewely, I wolde sory be
> For to seen yow in adversitee.
> And gilteles, I woot wel, I yow leve;
> But al shal passe; and thus take I my leve."

It is well to point out here a fact that the earlier criticism tended to ignore too frequently; that is, that Criseyde has no regrets for the illicit relations she has had with Troilus; she condemns herself, and others should condemn her, solely because in granting her love to Diomede she offends against one of the cardinal principles of the courtly love system. The offense is further aggravated by the fact that she gives up the best of lovers for one who possesses but few of the outward graces and apparently none of the inner virtues associated with a genuine courtly lover. This, to my mind, is a point that should be emphasized, for it is not only her yielding but also the person to whom she yields that makes the offense so heinous. Diomede can in no sense be interpreted as a courtly lover; the implication seems to be perfectly clear that he is seeking a purely sensual relationship and nothing more. His words, like his manners, do not ring true; they are only skin deep. It may be reasoned that all this makes no difference, for Criseyde's behavior bars her from further consideration as a courtly mistress. This is hardly correct, however, because she does not change at all; except for her infidelity to Troilus, she deserves to be considered just as much of a courtly mistress as before; there is nothing to indicate that she will ever be anything other than loyal and true to Diomede. The amazing thing about Criseyde is not only her inconstancy but the fact that, with her intelligence, graciousness, and general superiority, she should yield to the addresses of such a person as Diomede; but *chacun à son goût!* Yet it is difficult not to regard this as an artistic flaw in her portrayal.

Before considering this problem further, attention should be given to Criseyde's two letters to Troilus (1422–35, 1590–1631). The first of these, written in reply to his long epistle (1317–1421), is developed from a later passage in the *Filostrato* (VII, 105), where it is related that Criseida wrote and explained how she loved Troilo more than ever, making many false excuses for her delay and asking further respite for her return, which, Boccaccio tells us, was never to be; he granted her this hoping to see her again, but he did not know when. Rossetti substitutes for this couplet in the Moutier edition the corresponding lines in the Baroni text, which he translates: "swearing always to be faithful to him—but she knew not when." [27] This is obviously much closer to Chaucer's lines which, however, do not mention the false excuses but relate only that she would come as soon as possible, though she knew not when. Her flatteries and protestations of love Troilus finds but empty promises, a fact which calls forth the following author's comment (V, 1432–35):

> But, Troilus, thow maist now, est or west,
> Pipe in an ivy lef, if that the lest.
> Thus goth the world; god shilde us fro meschaunce,
> And every wight that meneth trouthe avaunce!

The second letter is Chaucer's own invention and is of particular interest as Criseyde's last word. Its general intention is much the same as that of the first: she will come but she is in such peril that she is unable to name even the year or day; the real reason of her lingering she dares not mention lest the letter be intercepted and her secret discovered. She is sorry for his restlessness and tells him that he is not taking the command of the gods in a very good spirit, for the only thing he apparently thinks about is his own "plesaunce" (V, 1608). But she begs him not to be angry and says that her hesitation is all idle gossip. She evidently has heard rumors about their relationship, and even of how he does nothing but delude her with false hopes; however, she puts no stock in such talk and cannot fancy anything in him other than "alle trouthe and alle gentilesse." She assures him that she will always remain his lifelong friend and then, with apologies for her brevity, insisting on "thentente is al, and nat the lettres space," concludes, "la vostre C."

There are a number of deductions to be made about Criseyde as a result of the details presented in the preceding pages, but first of all it may be well to touch on one particular aspect which has been mentioned only in passing; that is her status as a widow. Professor Young in his illuminating study supports the view of Wilkins that Boccaccio made Criseida a widow because he regarded the widow as the ideal mistress.[28] From a decision in the *Filocolo* (Questione XI, in which the Queen discourses on the advantages of a maid, a married woman, and a widow in an amour) the widow is fixed on as the ideal mistress:

From this well considered utterance one cannot avoid at least a preliminary inference that the widowhood conferred upon Criseida represents not so much Boccaccio's attempt to allegorize the married state of Maria d' Aquino as his desire to portray an ideal *amie*. The *vedova* is superior to the *maritata* in her freedom from matrimonial entanglement; she surpasses the *pulcella* in her erotic desire and her immediate aptitude for an amour. It would appear, then, that the attributes of the ideal mistress are completely present not in the wedded Maria of actual fact, but in the widowed Criseida of actual fiction.[29]

He goes on to point out that by thus discriminating against married women Boccaccio diverges from the courtly code which sanctions adulterous love: "It should be remembered, nevertheless, that however alien the reasons for Boccaccio's choice may have been, the *result* of it may still be fully adequate to the circumstances of courtly love. Although the courtly code clearly discredits Boccaccio's aversion to the married woman, it can still readily accept, for its own purposes, the amorous widow of his preference." [30] This reasoning is equally valid when applied to the *Troilus*; so far as the courtly love code is concerned, the portrayal of Criseyde as a widow is fully justified.[31]

The conclusions justified by this study of Criseyde may be briefly summarized as follows: Criseyde exercises far more sovereignty than her Italian predecessor; by enhancing this quality Chaucer has greatly increased the courtly love element in the *Troilus* and has presented Criseyde as a more typical courtly love mistress than Criseida. The English poet has also caused his heroine to display much greater caution and to be much more solicitous that the whole amour be conducted with the utmost secrecy. In this connection it may also be remarked that Criseyde is much more independent in her thoughts and actions as well as far more intellectual than Criseida.

Chaucer intensifies the conception of love as a great regenerating force; this is not quite so obvious as in the case of Troilus (who will be discussed in the last chapter), but it is inherent in Criseyde's character as presented in the English poem. In a similar manner Chaucer omits entirely or else minimizes the various expressions of delight in physical passion which Criseida might be said to revel in. What is to be thought about Criseyde's dissimulation in her talk with Diomede? It is perfectly in keeping with the courtly theory and is paralleled by Troilo's words to Cassandra. In both instances the lovers are lying in order that their love may continue secret; such deliberate falsification is fully sanctioned by the

courtly code, which allows the lovers to go to any extreme
necessary to ensure the secrecy of their amour. In these ways
Chaucer greatly increases the courtly love material which he
found in the *Filostrato*.

On the other hand Chaucer may be said to minimize or
violate certain well-established courtly love practices. He
omits entirely Criseida's statement (II, 74) that hidden
love ever surpasses that of a husband held always in arms,
though the incompatibility of love and matrimony is implicit
throughout the poem. The most notable departure from the
code is of course Criseyde's infidelity to Troilus. In this one
instance Chaucer has rejected the artificiality of the courtly
love code for the naturalness of life. It must be insisted that
Criseyde is the same person at the end of the poem that she
was at the beginning. Her infidelity need never be com-
mended but it can be explained and condoned. Criseyde does
exactly what any other person *of her type* would do in similar
circumstances. She finds herself in a strange place, friendless,
indifferent to her father, fearful, amorous, beautiful, in-
tensely interested in men. She soon realizes the absolute im-
possibility of return and therefore decides to make the best
of things. What better proof than this is required to demonstrate that she is an opportunist and that in no pejorative
sense? A strong objection to her conduct is that, in yielding,
she did not bestow her affections on someone exhibiting a few
more of the courtly qualities than does Diomede. However,
Chaucer is fully justified in making her act thus because it
serves to intensify the tragedy of her conduct.

A point which must be borne in mind in any discussion of
Criseyde is the complexity of her character. Many critics have
underestimated the value of this fact; Cummings, for example, writes that Criseyde "is not so simple nor so direct as
are generally the heroines of medieval romance, but it is a
mistake to regard her as complex." [32] On the contrary it is
her complexity which is at one and the same time the cause
and the solution of most of the problems which she creates;

it certainly helps in understanding her conduct in the last book of the poem. As Lawrence finely writes,

Criseyde, the central figure, is so complex that critics still differ in their estimate of her character. But she is certainly treated sympathetically. The view which would make of her "a scheming adventuress" is, as Kittredge remarks, "so patently erroneous as to need no refutation. . . ." Chaucer treats Criseyde sympathetically throughout; even after she has proved faithless he does not condemn her, he only pities her weakness.[33]

Failure to appreciate the importance of this complexity is one reason that much of the criticism of the *Troilus* fails to offer an adequate explanation of the heroine's conduct.[34] De Sélincourt, for example, finds the secret of her behavior in the fact that she is "a woman pitifully weak, resenting the advances of Diomede, and in her sore straits using what seemed to her her only weapon of defence, her 'uncertain sickly appetite to please,' . . ." [35] Another recent critic, C. S. Lewis, believes that he has found the key to her character in her ruling passion, fear, and that everything is to be attributed to this quality in her make-up:

Fortunately Chaucer has so emphasized the ruling passion of his heroine, that we cannot mistake it. It is Fear—the fear of loneliness, of old age, of death, of love, and of hostility; of everything, indeed, that can be feared. And from this Fear springs the only positive passion which can be permanent in such a nature; the pitiable longing, more childlike than womanly, for protection, for some strong and stable thing that will hide her away and take the burden from her shoulders.[36]

In each of these quotations we have an answer to the problem of Criseyde's conduct, but neither provides *the* answer. Criseyde is a very complex individual, and consequently we must seek the key to her character, the explanation of her conduct, in the various elements which make up her complexity. Robinson suggests her many-sidedness when he writes:

Some have found the explanation of her, or at least of Chaucer's treatment of her, in the idea of fate, which undoubtedly pervades the poem. For some she is merely selfish and designing, but these forget her sincere affection. For others she is simply weak, the helpless victim of intrigue and circumstance; yet to a great extent she makes her own decisions. In spite of her tenderness and passion, as is not seldom the case with women, she is less sentimental and more practical than either Pandarus or Troilus. She has in her even something of the skeptical or disillusioned woman, a type in which Chaucer felt enough interest to portray it again in the Pertelote of the *Nun's Priest's Tale*. In the end circumstances are too strong for her and destroy her happiness with Troilus. Troilus, undeceived, but loving to the end, meets death bravely in battle. Criseyde, also loving and—we must understand—sincere in her bitter self-reproach, has made a practical compromise with fate and gone to Diomed. For in her nature tenderness was allied with *slidynge corage*, and not with the loyalty that suffers and endures. This was her condemnation and, in the moral sense, her tragedy.[37]

In the preceding pages I have called attention to various details which seem to me important to bear in mind in order to pass fair judgment on Criseyde. I do not propose to summarize these points and then speak the final verdict; I am confident that the final word on Criseyde will never be pronounced. However, I feel that this chapter has shown more completely than has been done heretofore that the key to the character of Criseyde is not to be found in any one element·but in the cumulative force of the various qualities with which she is so richly endowed. It is not merely fear nor pity nor affection, not destiny nor disillusionment nor lonesomeness, not beauty nor common sense nor passion, that provides the open-sesame to Criseyde; it is rather the combination of all these, and others, which helps us to condemn and condone our heroine; above all, to understand and appreciate her, the greatest of courtly love heroines, as Chaucer intended we should. In conclusion, it is important to notice that, though in the end Criseida is, to Boccaccio, "Criseida villana," to Chaucer her loveliness continues and he enters a plea for her in these words (V, 1093–99):

> Ne me ne list this sely womman chyde,
> Forther than the storye wol devyse.
> Hire name, allas, is punysshed so wide,

That for hire gilt it oughte ynough suffise.
And if I myghte excuse hire any wise,
For she so sory was for hire untrouthe,
Iwis, I wolde excuse hire yit for routhe.

IX

DIOMEDE

I N the account of Diomede's wooing of Criseyde (V, 92–
175) Chaucer differs considerably from the corresponding report in the *Filostrato* (V, 13). There it is related
that Diomede is secretly smitten with love for Criseida but
postpones his advances until the fourth day after her arrival
in the Greek camp (VI, 9). The English Diomede, on the
contrary, is decidedly more precipitate and in this respect,
therefore, strikingly less courtly than his Italian ancestor;
for by the time they arrived at the tent of Calkas he has freely
confessed his passion and declared himself Criseyde's devoted servant. This change is due to Chaucer's combining
the story of Diomede's wooing as given in the *Roman de
Troie* with that presented in the *Filostrato*.[1]

As they ride across the plain, Diomede tells himself that
all his work will not be in vain if he talks to Criseyde; at the
worst it may shorten the way. He reminds himself of the
adage, "He is a fool that wol foryete hym selve." These lines
(92–98) express a feeling quite different from that experienced by the Italian Diomede, for he (VI, 10) fears that
his trouble will be in vain: the lady is in love, and it will take
too much cunning to drive out the thought of her first amour
before he can make his own entry into her affections. It
should be remembered that this thought is expressed by
Diomede not on the occasion of his first meeting with Criseida
but four days later in the Greek camp. The English Diomede
almost adopts this point of view in lines 99–105 but then
alters it to a certain extent by his decision to find some method
of keeping her from knowing at first exactly what he intends.

This is one of the many ways in which Chaucer succeeds in discrediting Diomede as a lover. Dissimulation was countenanced by the courtly code but dissimulation toward the rest of the world, never toward one's beloved.

"Whan tyme was," Diomede began talking, asked Criseyde why she was in such discomfort, and expressed his willingness to do anything she might command to increase her pleasure (106–12); this offer is taken over from Benoit's account. Lines 113–19 of the *Troilus* reaffirm Diomede's previous offer: there is nothing he would not do for her with all his heart and all his strength "to don hire herte an ese"; for we Greeks as well as the Trojans, he adds, can also have the pleasure of honoring you. With these words (118–19) Diomede begins an address eight stanzas in length (18–25, i. e., ll. 120–75) in which he woos Criseyde in no uncertain terms. He tells her first of all that she will find among the Greeks one who is as loyal and as kind as any Trojan; and because he has sworn to be her friend and she is better acquainted with him than with any other stranger (V, 131–33),

> So fro this forth I pray yow, day and night,
> Comaundeth me, how soore that me smerte,
> To don al that may like unto youre herte.

In thus pledging himself to execute Criseyde's every wish Diomede acquits himself in approved courtly fashion, but the very suddenness of his avowal casts serious doubts on its sincerity and makes it singularly out of place.

Diomede continues his advances: treat me as your brother and do not despise my friendship; my heart takes great pleasure in easing your sorrow, though I do not know the cause of your grief, and if I may not relieve your suffering, I am very sorry for your "hevynesse" (136–40). Diomede now points out that they both serve the same god of love and begs her not to be angry with him (V, 146–47):

> For trewely, ther kan no wight yow serve,
> That half so loth youre wratthe wolde deserve.

Were they not so near the tent of Calkas, who may see them both, he would tell her his whole intention but this must be concealed for another day. Yet he swears loyalty to Criseyde in such a manner that she must know at once what he is getting at (V, 152–54):

> I am, and shal ben ay,
> God help me so, whil that my lyf may dure,
> Youre owene aboven every creature.

Again we may wonder just how heartfelt this avowal is. But there can be very little doubt about the insincerity of the lines which immediately follow (155–61). Here he swears that he never before loved a woman passionately "ne nevere shal no mo." These words certainly ring false. The only true statement in this stanza is his admission of ignorance and experience in the fine art of love (V, 160–61):

> Al kan I naught to yow, my lady deere,
> Compleyne aright, for I am yit to leere.

These lines are particularly worth remembering, for they are a definite admission by Diomede himself that he is no courtly lover, a point which I have already insisted on and shall return to again. He now tries to justify his sudden wooing by saying that he has heard of many a person who has loved something he has never seen before in his life; and furthermore he is not strong enough to struggle against the God of Love but will, rather, obey him always (162–68). His last words to her are that there are such worthy knights in the Greek camp and she is so fair that every one of them will endeavor to secure her favor; but he swears he will serve her better than any of them (V, 172–75):

> But myghte me so fair a grace falle,
> That ye me for youre servant wolde calle,
> So lowely ne so trewely yow serve
> Nil non of hem, as I shal, til I sterve.

As Young, Cummings, and Root have pointed out, the facts of this narrative come for the most part from the *Roman de Troie* and present a different situation from that found in the *Filostrato*, as I have already indicated.[2] Did Chaucer have any particular purpose in mind when he decided to follow Benoit's story of the wooing rather than Boccaccio's? I think so. Criseyde's reply (which has been discussed in the preceding chapter) is that she is too sad for love but, if she were to care for anyone, she would bestow her affections on Diomede.[3] Thus, by making the Greek warrior give vent to his feelings almost within sight of Troy and then by following his words with Criseyde's expression of willingness to consider him, Chaucer very greatly emphasizes the infidelity of his heroine and consequently makes her offense all the more objectionable when viewed in the light of the courtly love code of ethics.

Since Chaucer was not trying to make a courtly lover out of Diomede, it is not surprising to find that he did not change him radically. In only one respect did he enlarge on the courtly love element and that was by picking up and elaborating the various hints about Diomede's devotion to his lady and his willingness to be her slave; but as I have noted, these protestations all sound hollow and therefore minimize Diomede's claims to consideration as a courtly lover rather than enhance his status.

We next hear of Diomede in lines 771–98 where he expresses his determination to win Criseyde. His sole concern now is (V, 774–77)

> How he may best, with shortest taryinge,
> Into his net Criseydes herte brynge.
> To this entent he koude nevere fyne;
> To fisshen hire, he leyde out hook and lyne.

Nevertheless he feels that she has a lover in Troy, for not since she has been in the Greek camp has he seen her smile or appear joyful. He does not know how best to allure her but tells himself that it will do no harm to try, for he that "naught nasayeth, naught nacheveth" (784). Diomede questions the advisability of loving one who is sorrowing for another and tells himself that it may not be to his advantage to approach her now. This is substantially the same as Boccaccio's account (VI, 10). However, the Italian Diomede interprets her sighs as the sighs of constancy; the English Diomede makes no mention of her constancy and apparently thinks her conduct is due to her grief. He shows himself a bit more learned by quoting authority to substantiate his doubts (V, 790–91):

> For wise folk in bookes it expresse:
> "Men shal nat wowe a wight in hevynesse."

The enunciation of such doctrine by Diomede is strangely out of keeping with his conduct and character. He now goes on to consider that he who would win her from the man for whom she mourns both day and night might call himself a conqueror (792–94); then he thinks in his heart (V, 796–98):

> happe how happe may,
> Al sholde I deye, I wol hire herte seche;
> I shal no more lesen but my speche.

The *Filostrato* (VI, 11) relates practically the same thing, though there it is stated that Diomede decided to tell Criseida how the bitter attacks of love had made him feel toward her and also how he was first smitten with her, sentiments decidedly more courtly.

The description of Diomede which fills lines 799–805 is not to be found in the *Filostrato* but comes from the *Dares* of Joseph of Exeter.[4] According to Chaucer's words Diomede was quick in dangers, courageous, stern in voice and strong of limb, bold, headstrong, powerful, and chivalrous in deeds like his father Tideus; some men say he was free with his tongue; he was the heir of Calidoyne and Arge. It is noteworthy that in this description absolutely nothing is added to enhance Diomede's status as a lover; the emphasis is placed entirely on his qualities as soldier and warrior.

Keeping these details in mind together with those already noted in the preceding section, we may now try to reach some conclusion about Diomede. Whatever else may be said about him, he is not a courtly lover. He is the very antithesis of Troilus, and I have no doubt that Chaucer consciously or unconsciously tried to emphasize this distinction. The most strikingly uncourtly aspect of his behavior is the precipitate manner in which he rushes into his love affair; such speed is entirely at variance with courtly practice. There is nothing to indicate that Diomede ever experienced any of the regenerative powers of love or was in any way ennobled by his experience. In fact, his whole conduct shows that the fascination which Criseyde cast over him had but little to do with love in any elevated sense. He had no deep feeling for her, and all his professions of loyalty and devotion are quite lacking in sincerity. His bold and brazen manner stands in sharp contrast to Troilus' irreproachable conduct and unfailing humility. He apparently suffers none of the usual lover's pains and is not dependent on a go-between for the conduct of his amour. As Root observes,

He is no idealizing courtly lover, but a somewhat cynical man of the world, a medieval Lovelace, whose motto is:—
        He is a fool that wol foryete himself.
Diomede does not lose his heart; he merely improves a good opportunity to win a lady's.[5]

Diomede is even less courtly than his Italian and French models. Of his main characters Chaucer has changed him the least but he has, nevertheless, presented him in a very different light. In the story as told in the *Filostrato* he had at least some claim to consideration as a lover but in the *Troilus* he has none whatsoever. The conclusion is inevitable that just as in the case of Troilus, whom Chaucer sought to make the typical lover through the enhancement of his courtly love qualities, in the case of Diomede he strove for the opposite effect and presented him as an example of what a courtly lover should not be. This careful balancing of Diomede against Troilus I consider one of the finest additions to the English poem.

X

TROILUS

TROILUS plays an important part in Book I, a fact particularly worthy of note in the succeeding books of the poem; for there he is so subject to the whims of Criseyde or the advice and suggestion of Pandarus that the reader unmindful of courtly love conventions may easily be annoyed at his conduct. Consequently there is a certain satisfaction in recalling that, in the first book, Troilus was able to fall in love without any assistance. The two preceding chapters have dealt with the hero in his relations to Pandarus and Criseyde; the following pages therefore will be devoted to scenes in which he appears by himself and to such other passages as have not already been sufficiently studied.

Troilus first appears (183 ff.) with a number of his companions at the temple where the feast of the Palladium is being celebrated. He wanders about gazing on the various ladies present and praising or blaming them as it pleases him. Thus far this parallels Troilo's first appearance (*Filostrato*, I, 20), but Boccaccio's statement that Troilo rejoiced in his independence, praised the ladies or in like manner disparaged them, as if one were no more pleasing to him than another, becomes in Chaucer (I, 187–89):

> for no devocioun
> Hadde he to non, to reven hym his reste,
> But gan to preyse and lakken whom hym leste.

Already in his treatment of Troilus, Chaucer saw fit to enlarge upon his conduct as a courtly lover; sleeplessness and restlessness are typical symptoms.[1] As Troilus walks about, he observes if any of his company is attracted by one of the ladies and, if he is, proceeds to make fun of lovers. These lines (195–203) are condensed from the corresponding stanzas of the *Filostrato* (I, 21–24) in which Troilo ponders the fickleness of women, admits that he too has loved (though the pleasures he enjoyed were far exceeded by the sorrows), rejoices that he no longer loves and that he may now laugh at those who are ensnared. Troilus' words are simply mockery of lovers in general; there is no hint of the personal confession found in the *Filostrato*.[2] Troilus makes no statement as to his previous experience in love (though it seems reasonable to regard his affair with Criseyde as his first enamorment) but remarks to the knight that while his lady sleeps softly for love of him, he often tosses about—a minor courtly love addition. He goes on to say that he has heard of the life of lovers, their conduct and sufferings, and roundly condemns them (I, 202–3):

> O veray fooles! nyce and blynde be ye;
> Ther nys nat oon kan war by other be.

To punish him for his arrogance the God of Love strikes Troilus with an arrow. This corresponds in a general way to the stanza (25) in which Boccaccio comments on Troilo's raillery without a thought of what Heaven has in store for him, whom Love pierced more than any other before he left the temple. The Italian poet goes on without delay to describe Troilo's first glimpse of Criseida, but in the *Troilus* there intervene eight stanzas (31–38) of author's comment and advice. Chaucer remarks that Troilus falls in love just as suddenly as anyone else, even though he is a king's son; whereupon he urges everyone ("Ye wise, proude, and worthi folkes alle") not to scorn love, which can so soon take away the freedom of the heart; for love is irresistible and no man can resist the law of nature. The poet continues, lavish in his praise of the benefits of love (I, 241–44):

> Men reden nat that folk han gretter wit
> Than they that han be most with love ynome;

> And strengest folk ben therwith overcome,
> The worthiest and grettest of degree.

Furthermore, it has been the source of great comfort to those who have suffered most and has caused even noble people to grow in virtue (I, 251–52):

> And worthi folk maad worthier of name,
> And causeth moost to dreden vice and shame.

Since it cannot be withstood and is "a thing vertuous in kynde," the poet urges his readers to follow love that "yow so wel can lede." It is scarcely necessary to note that this entire passage is a courtly love addition of considerable significance. It is an excellent example of Chaucer's tendency to improve the tone of his original by placing emphasis on love as a great spiritual force that will transform all those who become subject to its power.

While wandering about gazing at the different ladies, Troilo's eyes light upon Criseida (*Filostrato*, I, 26). The part of the eyes in arousing love is a commonplace feature in courtly love poetry. Chaucer adopts Boccaccio's conceit and enriches its courtly quality (I, 271–73):

> And upon cas bifel that thorugh a route
> His eye percede, and so depe it wente,
> Til on Criseyde it smot, and ther it stente.

In an additional paragraph of his own, the English poet considerably elaborates his hero's courtly conduct by telling the reader that his heart "gan to sprede and rise"; he sighed softly lest someone might hear him and resumed his earlier playful countenance. The next two stanzas (41–42) have been dealt with in the chapter on Criseyde.[3] In an added stanza of his own Chaucer relates that Troilus' desire and affection grew so that the image of Criseyde became deeply fixed in his heart; he who had at first gazed around everywhere is now glad to pull in his horns like the snail, i. e., pursue a different mode of conduct; but "Unnethes wiste he how to loke or wynke" (I, 301). Chaucer now returns

to the *Filostrato* and follows it rather closely until the
end of this scene in the temple (302–29). Troilo did not
notice that love dwelt in Criseida's eyes, nor did he remember his scornful speech nor the arrow which pierced
his heart until it stung him. Chaucer translates the first
statement almost literally, the second is omitted entirely,
and the third is radically changed into a favorite courtly
love conceit: the lady's glance is so powerful that he feels
the spirit of his heart die. As Root points out in his note
on this passage, the spirit of the heart is the vital spirit
which controls pulse and breathing; a look from Criseyde
so affects Troilus that his heart ceases to beat.[4] After this
Troilus and his companions leave the temple; in both poems
the hero so conducts himself as to avoid any possible suspicion of his change in feelings.

Returned to his palace, Troilo dwells for a long time in
joyous living with his companions. Sometimes, in order to
hide the amorous cruelty he endures, he jeers at lovers; finally,
pretending that other matters compel him, he tells each of his
companions to go where he pleases. Chaucer expands this last
statement (*Filostrato*, I, 32, ll. 7–8) into a stanza (ll.
351–57) but the rest he adapts to his own purposes. He notes
that Troilus returned "right with hire look thorugh shoten
and thorugh darted"; furthermore the English poet is not
content simply to suggest Troilus' mockery but supplies
twenty-one lines (330–50) of direct discourse in order that
the reader may know all about his scoffing at love. Troilus'
remarks are couched in semi-ecclesiastical language, for he
addresses lovers as if they were members of a religious order,
ironically remarking that though all their "observaunces"
are uncertain except for a few unimportant details, yet nothing demands such great attention as does their law; for example, a lover will do something with good intentions, but
his lady will misconstrue his motives and consider it harmful, and if she is angry for some other reason, then he will
have cause to complain. Happy the man who may belong to

this order (I, 350): "Lord! wel is hym that may ben of yow oon!" Ironic though these words are, they nevertheless constitute an important addition to the courtly love material. Furthermore, it must be remembered that Troilus' irony is intended only as a sham to disguise his real feelings; it is an important factor in the permissible dissimulation necessary to preserve the utmost secrecy in the conduct of an amour, a practice fully sanctioned by the courtly love code.

Having discharged his friends, Troilus retires to his room and in typical courtly fashion sighs, groans, and thinks about his lady. This section of the poem (351–546) follows the corresponding passage in the *Filostrato* (I, 32–57) with a fair degree of closeness. Telling himself that it is great good luck to love such a person, Troilus argues that there would be nothing shameful about loving her even if it should become known (I, 377–78):

> Thus argumented he in his gynnynge,
> Ful unavysed of his woo comynge.

Thereupon, the poet tells us, Troilus decided to follow love's craft. Boccaccio merely notes that Troilo was disposed to follow such a love. Through the conception of love as an art the English passage takes on an added significance; the statement that Troilus decided to follow the art of love shows clearly that he considered himself a disciple of courtly love. The rest of the stanza telling of his determination to keep his plan absolutely secret (translated from the Italian) is of course genuine courtly material.

An important variation from the *Filostrato* is supplied by the so-called *cantus Troili*, a close translation of one of Petrarch's sonnets (88). In these lines Troilus questions the nature of love: If it is good, why does he suffer? If it is wicked, why does it seem so pleasant? Whence come his weeping and complaint if he burns in his own pleasure? If harm pleases him, why does he complain? How can there be so much of death in him unless he consents thereto (I, 414–20)?

> And if that I consente, I wrongfully
> Compleyne, iwis; thus possed to and fro,
> Al steereles withinne a boot am I
> Amydde the see, bitwixen wyndes two,
> That in contrarie stonden evere mo.
> Allas! what is this wonder maladie?
> For hete of cold, for cold of hete, I dye.

Again taking up the thread of the *Filostrato*, Chaucer makes Troilus reach a quick decision, apparently, for in lines 421 ff. he dedicates his spirit to the God of Love and thanks him for having brought this about. Whether his lady is a woman or a goddess, he knows not but is determined to live and die as her servant. This last is a courtly love touch added by Chaucer; by this statement Troilus yields complete sovereignty to the lady. The rest of the scene follows the *Filostrato* faithfully. The poet remarks that his royal blood afforded him no protection against the onslaughts of love but held him ever a slave. Troilus thinks about Criseyde always. His brave deeds are inspired not by hatred of the Greeks but by the desire to please Criseyde. The account of the lover's symptoms (484–97) is taken over from the Italian (I, 47–48) without modification by Chaucer. In the soliloquy which concludes this scene, Troilus chides himself for having fallen in love and reminds himself of what those will say whom he so enjoyed abusing. He goes on to state that it would be a great relief if he were already in the port of death to which his sorrow is leading him; but now he begs God (the God of Love?) and his lady to show him some mercy and save him from death; he swears he will love her more than he does himself and entreats her to favor him with a glance, though she never promise him anything else (I, 540–46):

> Thise wordes, and ful many an other to,
> He spak, and called evere in his compleynte

Hire name, for to tellen hire his wo,
Til neigh that he in salte teres dreynte.
Al was for nought, she herde nat his pleynte;
And whan that he bythought on that folie,
A thousand fold his wo gan multiplie.

The long first meeting of Troilus with Pandarus (547–1071) has already been discussed.[5] The three stanzas which follow and bring Book I to a close are Chaucerian and constitute a courtly love addition of considerable interest. Troilus conducts himself in typical courtly fashion: he is such a lion in battle that it is unfortunate for the Greek who happens to meet him, while in town his manner is so kindly and obtains such favor for him that he is loved by all who see him (I, 1079–85):

For he bicome the frendlieste wight,
The gentileste, and ek the moste fre,
The thriftieste, and oon the beste knyght
That in his tyme was, or myghte be;
Dede were his japes and his cruelte,
His hye port, and his manere estraunge;
And ech of tho gan for a vertu chaunge.

There is nothing new or unusual in these lines, for the spiritual growth of one subject to love is a common theme in courtly literature; but it is another and very excellent example of Chaucer's effort to portray love as a great regenerative force.

The various meetings with Pandarus as well as Troilus' other activities in Book II have already been discussed in chapter VII. Consequently the only lines which need be examined are those toward the end of the Book (1537 ff.) recounting the behavior of Troilus after the departure of Pandarus; this is but a part of a larger scene added by Chaucer, as has already been noted.[6] Troilus went to his palace, agreed to Pandarus' advice, and at night went to Deiphebus' house. There all his brother's efforts to cheer him were of no avail. One thing is certain, however: before Troilus lay down, Deiphebus had begged him to be a friend and helper to Criseyde; we are told, "god woot," he fully agreed to be "hire fulle frend with al his myght":

> But swich a nede was to preye hym thenne,
> As for to bidde a wood man for to renne.
> —II, 1553-54.

The next day Deiphebus entertains Helen, Criseyde, and the others as his guests at dinner. At frequent intervals he sighs "allas" and laments that his brother Troilus lies sick. Everyone was exceptionally kind and solicitous, especially Helen, and all proceeded to recommend various cures, all but one (II, 1581-82):

> But ther sat oon, al liste hire nat to teche,
> That thoughte: "best koude I yit ben his leche."

And after this, all wax eloquent in praise of his fine qualities. Not the least among these was Pandarus, who "naught forgat hire preisynge to conferme" (1589). Most of the rest of this Book has already been discussed in the preceding chapters on Pandarus and Criseyde. Passing mention might be made of the fact that when Pandarus rehearses Criseyde's supposed difficulties for the second time, Troilus expresses his willingness to champion her cause alone; to this Helen replies, "Good thrift have ye." Then Pandarus asks if he is willing for Criseyde to take her leave of him before she goes, and Troilus replies (II, 1690-91):

> "O, elles god forbede," tho quod he,
> "If that she vouche sauf for to do so."

He then gets rid of Deiphebus and Helen by pretending to want their advice on an official document and a letter which Hector had sent him. There is no further mention of Troilus until the very end when the author devotes lines 1751-57 to his predicament: Wasn't he in a pickle, lying there and hearing Pandarus' and Criseyde's whispering? He reasons, quite naturally:

"O lord, right now renneth my sort
Fully to deye, or han anon comfort";
And was the first tyme he shulde hire preye
Of love; O myghty god, what shal he seye?

Book III is chiefly concerned with the meeting of Troilus
and Criseyde, together with Pandarus' activities in arranging it. Since the preceding chapters have dealt with this
material, we may pass on to those lines which are devoted
more exclusively to Troilus (1716 ff.). The effect of love
on Troilus is described in words taken from two passages in
the *Filostrato* (II, 84; III, 72), where it is said that Troilo is
happy and lives his life in song and merriment; he is generous,
provides entertainments, and changes his garments frequently, as the occasion demands. To these statements
Chaucer adds the additional fact (1720–22) that he kept
about him a world of folk, "the fressheste and the beste"
he could find. The English poet states further that there
spread throughout the world such talk and rumor of his
honor and generosity that it "rong unto the yate of heven"
(1725). One need scarcely remark on the significance of
these additions. They are typical of Chaucer's attempt to
place greater emphasis on the finer aspects of love, a fact
which explains the greater part of the English poet's changes.
Generosity, which is stressed in these lines, was regarded as
a virtue particularly desirable in the courtly lover. Chaucer
adopts Boccaccio's statement (III, 72) that Troilo believed
that other men lived in sad misery compared with him, so
much did love please him; nor did the beauty of any other
lady attract him. Chaucer intensified this last statement by
comparing Criseyde to a net so closely enmeshed and knitted
around his heart that it will not be undone, whatever may
happen. This is a subtle way of emphasizing the courtly
teaching that the lover must have his lady always in his
thoughts, and it also emphasizes her complete sovereignty
over him; in both ways, then, it serves to enhance the courtly
love element.

We are told that Troilus frequently led Pandarus into the garden where he would praise Criseyde's beauty and womanliness so that it was "an hevene his wordes for to here." With the exception of these words in quotation marks, the lines (1737–43) are directly translated from the corresponding stanza in the *Filostrato* (III, 73). Now comes Troilus' hymn to Love, which follows Boethius (2. m. 8) closely; Troilo's song in the Italian version has already been used by the English poet for the Proem of Book III.[7] The hymn (1744–71) celebrates love as the great force which controls everything in the universe and without which all would be ruined and lost; wherefore Troilus beseeches God as the author of nature (III, 1766–71)

> That, with his bond, Love of his vertu liste
> To cerclen hertes alle, and faste bynde,
> That from his bond no wight the wey out wiste;
> And hertes colde, hem wolde I that he twiste
> To make hem love, and that hem liste ay rewe
> On hertes sore, and kepe hem that ben trewe.

The conduct of Troilus during the remainder of Book III (1772–1806) is modeled on that of Troilo (*Filostrato*, III, 90–93), who was always in arms and the most dreaded of any person (save Hector, adds Chaucer); love was responsible for this increase in hardiness and strength. Boccaccio describes Troilo as a servant of love; Chaucer omits this quite unnecessary statement and substitutes for it the much more important courtly love fact that it was love that altered his spirits so within. In time of truce Troilus, like Troilo (III, 91), went hawking or hunting. Bears, boars, or lions were always his prey; the small animals he passed by. There is excellent courtly love doctrine implicit in these lines, for the hero shows his bravery in attacking the larger animals, while his mercy and tenderness become manifest in his letting the small ones escape. In lines closely translated from the *Filostrato* (III, 92) we are told further that Troilus' speech was ever of love and virtue and that he held every mean act in contempt. He delighted in honoring and in easing those in distress (a Chaucerian addition and good courtly love doctrine); the English poet omits Boccaccio's statement that Troilo also delighted in driving away cowards. Troilus rejoiced whenever he knew or heard of any lover who was successful; this statement is also added by Chaucer. So likewise are lines 1793–99, a stanza expanded from the simple statement in the Italian (III, 92) that Troilo considered everyone of whatsoever station lost who lived without love; we may note, though, that this colorless expression ("senza amore") becomes in English the line, "but if he were in loves heigh servise"; this clearly implies a conception of love quite different from that of the *Filostrato*. The words, "loves heigh servise," do more to secure and explain this elevated tone than pages of exegesis and criticism. Added to all this, Chaucer remarks (III, 1796–99):

> so wel koude he devyse
> Of sentement, and in so unkouth wise
> Al his array, that every lovere thoughte,
> That al was wel what so he seyde or wroughte.

Stanza 258, the last in Book III devoted to Troilus, is taken over from the Italian. Though of royal blood, he never cared to harass people because of his pride but was gracious to everyone generally; for this he was thanked everywhere. Boccaccio states that it was Love, who is all powerful, who wished that he should act so as to please others; pride, envy, and avarice he hates, and he yields to everyone. Chaucer incorporates this thought in these words (III, 1804–6):

> Thus wolde Love, yheried be his grace!
> That pride, envye, ire, and avarice
> He gan to fle, and everich other vice.

By adding the words "every other vice" Chaucer puts added emphasis on the virtue of his hero; the typical courtly lover avoids all wickedness and, through love, becomes a paragon of virtue and true nobility.

Coming to Book IV, we find that Chaucer omits entirely the account of Troilo's swooning on hearing of the decision to exchange Criseida (IV, 18–21) and picks up the *Filostrato* account with the following stanza (22), which relates that Troilo returned to his chamber, on the pretense of wishing to sleep, dismissed those accompanying him, and laid himself on his bed. The lines following, 225–59, describe the lover's madness in true courtly fashion and follow the *Filostrato* almost literally. Pale and wan like a dead image, Troilus sat down on the bed while his pent-up sorrow burst forth; then like a wild bull he stormed around his chamber, pounding his breast with his fists and dashing his head to the wall, his body to the ground, in order to destroy himself. His tears and sobs deprived him of his speech and he could scarcely utter this imprecation (IV, 250–52):

> O deth, allas, why nyltow do me deye?
> Acorsed be that day which that nature
> Shoop me to ben a lyves creature!

Chaucer substitutes direct discourse for Boccaccio's statement that Troilo often burst out in strange words, demanding nothing but death, scorning and blaspheming both the gods and himself. After this madness was over and likewise the tears which followed, Troilus spoke (260–336). In the first part of this monologue (260–87) he addresses Fortune in lines which follow only generally the corresponding passages in the *Filostrato* (IV, 30–32). Troilo begs Fortune to tell him what he has done, what he is guilty of, why she deceives him. Chaucer adds the lines (IV, 263–66):

> Is ther no grace, and shal I thus be spilt?
> Shal thus Criseyde awey, for that thow wilt?
> Allas, how maistow in thyn herte fynde
> To ben to me thus cruel and unkynde?

Then follow lines 267–69, in which Troilus asks Fortune why she deprives him of joy, him who has honored her all his life above all the other gods. These lines are taken over from

the Italian (IV, 30), but those which complete the stanza
(270–73) are added by Chaucer; here Troilus views himself as a tragic character (strongly reminiscent of the definition of tragedy in the *Monk's Prologue*):

> O Troilus, what may men now the calle
> But wrecche ot wrecches, out of honour falle
> Into miserie, in which I wol bewaille
> Criseyde, allas, til that the breth me faille?

In words taken from the *Filostrato* (IV, 31) he goes on to
ask Fortune why, if she was envious of his joy, she did not
deprive his father, the King, of his life, or kill his brothers,
or slay him. This query as to why Fortune did not slay him is
suggested by the succeeding stanza (32) but is transformed
with exquisite Chaucerian grace. The remaining lines addressed to Fortune (281–87) are taken over from the *Filostrato* (32): Had you left me Criseyde, I should not care
whither you would steer me; but you have deprived me of
her; that is your way, to rob a person of what is most dear
to him in order to prove your own changeable violence:
"Thus am I lost, ther helpeth no defence" (IV, 287). Troilus
now addresses himself to the God of Love in words suggested only in part by the Italian poem (IV, 33). Each
lover prays to the god as one who best knows his heart and
all his thought, but while Troilo asks how his doleful life
shall be occupied if he loses this peace, this happiness, Troilus
wants to know what will happen if he forgoes what he has
bought so dearly. Troilo continues in a very general way:
Love, who once comforted me, what shall I do if she is
snatched from me, she to whom I gave myself entirely through
your will? Troilus asks more specifically: Since you have
brought Criseyde and me into your favor and sealed our
hearts, how can you refuse to be kind to us? In the next
stanza (43) Troilus expresses the determination to lament
his misfortune alone, so long as he continues alive in torment
and cruel pain; this (295–98) is taken over from the *Filostrato* (IV, 34), though the statement that he will live alone

is due to Chaucer, as are also the remaining lines (299–301) in which Troilus says that he will never see it rain or shine but, like Oedipus, will end his sorrowful life in darkness and die in distress. The rest of the Italian stanza (34) is converted into lines 302–8, in which Troilus asks his soul why it does not flee from the most doleful body that ever lived; he commands it to leave his heart and follow Criseyde, "thi lady dere," for its right place is no longer in him. Lines 309–15 adapt *Filostrato*, IV, 35, quite faithfully: What are you going to do now, "woful eyen two," since your pleasure was all in seeing Criseyde, except stand for nothing and weep out your sight? Since she is gone who was wont to make you happy, in vain have I two eyes, your virtue being away. The lover now addresses himself to his mistress: Criseyde, sovereign lady, who shall now give comfort to the pain of the sorrowing soul that now cries out? Chaucer takes these lines (316–18) from the *Filostrato*, IV, 36, but substitutes for "dolce bene" the words "sovereign lady," thus giving the passage an added courtly love significance. Troilus begs her (in words not found in the Italian) to receive his spirit when he dies, for that will always serve her; it is no matter though the body die. The next stanza likewise is independent of the *Filostrato;* here Troilus wishes steadfast love ("love of stiel") and a long life of joy to lovers who are set high on the wheel of Fortune; furthermore he begs them (IV, 327–29),

> But whan ye comen by my sepulture,
> Remembreth that youre felawe resteth there;
> For I loved ek, though ich unworthi were.

This is a definite courtly love addition, for the courtly lover was always expected to be humble and to regard himself as unworthy of his lady's love. The final stanza of this monologue (330–36) expresses Troilus' hatred of Calkas and is condensed from the three stanzas (38–40) in the *Filostrato* in which Troilo couches his malediction in considerably more virulent terms. Before the entry of Pandarus, a scene which has already been discussed,[8] the poet tells us (337-43) that a thousand sighs, hotter than a burning coal, burst from his breast to feed his woe, for which reason his tears never stopped. Troilo behaves in much the same fashion (IV, 41); but whereas he falls asleep for a short time, Troilus, we are told, as the result of his torments sinks into a trance (IV, 341-43):

> so his peynes hym to-rente,
> And wex so maat, that joie nor penaunce
> He feleth non, but lith forth in a traunce.

We may now take up Troilus' monologue on predestination (958-1078), a passage not even so much as suggested in the *Filostrato* but transcribed with great fidelity from the *Consolation of Philosophy* (5 pr. 3. 7-71), Boethius' discussion of free will as related to the foreknowledge of God. I shall not attempt to give a detailed account of this philosophizing, for the complexities and contradictions of Troilus' reasoning, as well as his thoroughness and the appropriateness of the passage at this point, would only suffer by such paraphrase. Briefly summarized, however, the sense of the passage is that whatever happens, happens of necessity; many great clerks have held conflicting opinions on this matter of free will and destiny; so artful are they, I do not know whose opinion I may hold. After a brief consideration of these contradictory views (974-1008), Troilus offers his own solution of the problem (1009-85): whether the prescience of God is the certain cause of the necessity of things that are to come or whether the necessity of the things to come is the certain cause of the "purveyinge" (IV, 1048-50),

> men may wel yse,
> That thilke thynges that in erthe falle,
> That by necessite they comen alle.

He therefore concludes that man has no free will.

Discussion of this passage has been as varied as it has been lengthy. The earlier critics tended to view it as an artistic blemish and united in condemning it. Later criticism, however, leans to the opposite extreme and regards it as an integral part of the poem. Professor Patch is on the right track when he says, "The speech is not intended as a sample of dialectic fireworks but as an outburst of human emotion." [9] Yet the old view still persists and even so recent a critic as Lewis writes that this discussion of free will would have seemed to Boccaccio "as much an excrescence as it does to the modern reader; to the unjaded appetites of Chaucer's audience mere thickness in a wad of manuscript was a merit. . . . This passage is only one of many in which Chaucer departs from his original for the sake of giving his readers interesting general knowledge or philosophical doctrine." [10] Kittredge insists that the passage is not a digression, yet states that it is doubtless "inartistic and maladjusted." [11] This last remark is scarcely warranted; such might easily be the impression from a rapid reading of the passage, but the more I study the monologue, the more convinced I become that it is fully in character. As Patch remarks,

Nothing . . . could be more beautifully adapted to the scene than this speech by Troilus. It is his way of saying "I've never had a chance," and he sets out bravely to prove his case. It is involved and confusing, but the boy gets bravely through with it. He is extraordinarily conscientious at every step, and develops his argument with the most elaborate, the most scrupulous care. *Of course* he would be verbose and repetitious and longwinded. Pandarus does not take the speech (so far as he hears it) as instructive, but comments, "Ey! who seigh ever a wys man faren so!" Troilus has certainly been "going on"; and nothing could be more delightful, and, I feel, nothing under the circumstances could be more like a young man—like Troilus.[12]

In words that reëcho the views expressed by Kittredge,[13] Root expresses the opinion that the soliloquy may be

prolonged beyond its due proportion . . . but it is no more a digression than are the soliloquies of Hamlet. It is thoroughly in accord with the character of Troilus as Chaucer conceived him. For Troilus in his love for Criseyde there is no such thing as free choice. It was his destiny that he should love Criseyde; and from the moment that he confides in Pandarus, his destiny is in the hands of his friend.[14]

And now, it may very properly be asked, what has all this to do with courtly love? A very great deal; for, granting the correctness and penetration of these distinguished critics, nevertheless I do not feel that they have said the final word on this passage—nor do I pretend that my remarks partake of finality. However, I do feel that if the monologue is studied from the point of view of courtly love, a new avenue of approach will be opened which will throw additional light on the problem and make possible a more satisfactory conclusion than has heretofore been suggested. My point is that the whole concept of courtly love was something entirely foreign to the idea of free will.[15] The classical idea of a god whose arrows cause love to spring up, together with the troubadour conceit of love originating through the eyes, implies that men must love "by necessitee"; for no one is able to protect himself against a god who may at any time attack without warning nor can a man be held responsible if he sees a lady and then suddenly finds himself in love with her. So likewise is the lover's conduct entirely foreign to the idea of free will; as the slave of his lady, he is absolutely powerless and is able to do nothing of his own choice. Examples to substantiate the correctness of this view of courtly love as something quite opposed to freedom of the will could be supplied in abundance but since the *Troilus* is the object of this study, it will be much more to the point to note the views which our hero expresses about destiny and love. In the first book he speaks of himself as one that must "loven thorugh . . . destine" (520). In Book III Troilus' appeal to the gods is that of a mere child of fate; he ends (III, 733–35),

> O fatal sustren, which or any cloth
> Me shapen was, my destine me sponne,
> So helpeth to this werk that is bygonne.

The whole theme of the predestination passage, as has been pointed out above, is that freedom of the will does not exist (IV, 958–59):

> For al that comth, comth by necessitee;
> Thus to be lorn, it is my destinee.

Troilus' death is regarded as caused by fate: "Fate wolde his soule sholde unbodye" (V, 1550) and "Ayeyns which fate hym helpeth nat to stryve" (1552). There are several occasions on which Troilus holds Fortune responsible for his troubles. Thus in Book I he tells Pandarus that it is difficult to help him (I, 837–40):

> For wel fynde I that Fortune is my fo;
> Ne alle the men that riden konne or go
> May of hire cruel whiel the harm withstonde;
> For, as hire list, she pleyeth with free and bonde.

The four stanzas of reproach addressed to Fortune (IV, 38–41, i. e., ll. 260–87, discussed in an earlier part of this chapter) all go to show that Troilus regarded himself as one of Fortune's toys. The apostrophe to Fortune in Book III is probably the best summary of Troilus' attitude (III, 617–20):

> But O, Fortune, executrice of wyerdes,
> O influences of thise hevenes hye,
> Soth is that, under god, ye ben oure hierdes,
> Though to us bestes ben the causes wrie.

This point of view is well summed up again in the conclusion to the predestination passage (IV, 1072–78):

> And overe al this, yit seye I more therto,
> That right as whan I wot ther is a thyng,
> Iwys, that thyng moot nedfully be so;
> Ek right so, whan I woot a thyng comyng,
> So mot it come; and thus the bifallyng
> Of thynges that ben wist bifore the tyde,
> They mowe nat ben eschued on no syde.

The reader may with some justice claim that there is an unnecessary mingling of the terms fate, destiny, and fortune in these pages. My only defense is that "so saith myn auctour"; and, like him, I am not concerning myself with shades of philosophic distinction but rather with such statements as seem to reveal Troilus' convictions on this topic. The conclusion is inevitable that, so far as he is concerned, there is no such thing as freedom of the will. Bearing this in mind along with the brief remarks I have made on the concept of courtly love as something opposed to free will, I conclude this discussion of the predestination passage with the suggestion that it is fully in keeping with Troilus as a courtly lover and that, furthermore, since it perfectly represents the courtly love attitude, its presence in the poem is fully justified.[16]

The account of Troilus' behavior during the day on which Criseyde leaves for the Greek camp (V, 22–91) is modeled closely after the corresponding passage in the *Filostrato* (V, 1–6, 10–13). Boccaccio relates that when Antenor was exchanged for Criseida, her lover stood there in sorrow the like of which no one had ever seen. Chaucer expands these three lines into the stanza (22–28) in which we are told that Troilus, helpless and inexperienced, like a man suddenly bereft of all joy, was attending his lady "evere more," as if she were the topmost branch and root of all his pleasures "here before." The English poet concludes with this couplet, which rather definitely foreshadows the future turn of events (V, 27–28):

> But, Troilus, now farewel al thi joie,
> For shaltow nevere sen hire eft in Troie!

While Troilus waited, he concealed his sorrow so manfully that it was scarcely seen in his expression; this is taken over from the *Filostrato* (V, 2) and is good courtly love doctrine in that it continues the policy of secrecy and dissimulation; but Chaucer omits the equally courtly lines which relate that Troilo wished to be alone, to weep in solitude, and give vent to his sorrow. He tells us instead that Troilus waited with certain people at the gate where Criseyde should ride out, so downcast that, though he would not complain, he could scarcely sit on his horse because of his distress. Both poets relate that Troilus shook with anger and asked himself why he allowed the exchange, why he did not take revenge, and if it were not better to die at once than to live on thus languishing (cf. V, 36–49, and *Filostrato*, V, 3–4). Both poets agree in their explanation of their hero's inactivity: he feared that in the pursuit of such a course Criseyde might be slain (V, 54–56):

> lo, this was al his care.
> And ellis, certeyn, as I seyde yore,
> He hadde it don, withouten wordes more.

The two accounts unite in their description of what happens during the rest of the scene (64–91; *Filostrato*, V, 10–13). Accompanied by many knights Troilus rides out a great distance with Criseyde and would have gone farther but had to turn back; Antenor was exchanged and Troilus, in spite of his sorrow, kissed and welcomed him joyfully. In taking leave he rode up and took her by the hand and she began to weep tenderly; then come his final words to her: "Now hold youre day, and do me nat to deye." Without speaking to Diomede or his followers Troilus turns back toward Troy. Such is the departure of the lovers; one need scarcely remark that in this scene Chaucer holds so close to his source that he has introduced hardly any change in the character of his hero.

When Troilus returns to Troy, he goes to his palace and is in such sorrow that he retires immediately to his room, not mindful of anything, nor did anyone dare say a word to him. This is substantially what Boccaccio tells us (*Filostrato*, V, 15), though Chaucer seems to emphasize the sorrow of his hero by referring to him as "this woful Troilus" suffering "in sorwe aboven alle sorwes" and "with a swollen herte." This helps to supply the proper atmosphere for the account of his anguish which follows (204 ff.). However, the English poem offers a far more poignant description of Troilus' suffering; by so doing, of course, Chaucer greatly adds to the courtly love element. Troilo, we are told, cursed the day he was born, the gods and goddesses, nature, and those who consented to Criseida's surrender; Troilus is considerably more definite in his imprecations, however, for he curses Jove, Apollo, Cupid, Ceres, Bacchus, Venus, his birth, himself, his fate, nature, and "save his lady, every creature" (210). Boccaccio's statement that Troilo deeply repented not having tried to escape with Criseida is a fact which Chaucer does not mention. He does, however, add a stanza (31, i. e., ll. 211–17) which relates that Troilus goes to bed and suffers torments there, like Ixion in hell, until dawn when the tears begin his "herte a lite unswelle" so that he can give expression to his feelings in the complaint which follows (218–45). Only about half of this plaint is found in the *Filostrato* (V, 19–25); a part of this passage, as Rossetti points out, is addressed to Pandaro, and is apparently spoken on the following morning; [17] but Troilus' lament is unbroken and uttered in solitude. Troilo exclaims: What a night is this! If I figure correctly, it was at just this time that I kissed the white breast, the mouth, the eyes, the beautiful face of my lady, and often embraced her. Chaucer puts all this in the form of questions: Where is my beloved and dear lady? Where is her white breast, her arms, her clear eyes that were with me last night at this time? Now I must weep alone and find nothing to embrace except a pillow. Chaucer takes this from the *Filostrato* (V, 20) but omits Troilo's statement that he feels love becoming greater and hope less because of the sorrow which outstrips it.

The next stanza (V, 225–31) is a composite from stanzas 18, 21, and 24 of the *Filostrato:* How shall I get along? When shall she come again? I know not; why did I let her go? I would rather have been slain. My heart, my sweet foe, my lady, see how I die and you will not rescue me. The line, "to whom for everemo myn herte I dowe" (230), added by Chaucer, is genuine courtly love doctrine, which demands that the lover surrender his heart completely to his lady. The rest of the soliloquy (232–45) is only partly suggested by the queries of Troilo (25): Who sees you now? Who sits with you? Who listens to you? Who speaks to you? To this Chaucer adds: Who now can comfort your heart's strife and who speaks for me now in my absence? No one, alas, and that is all my worry, for I know it goes as badly with you as it does with me. The next stanza opens with Troilus' question of how he is to survive ten days when he has all this trouble the very first night. This recalls IV, 1598–99, in which Troilus tells Criseyde that he will easily get along until the tenth day, since she is going to return; this statement is suggested by the corresponding passage in the *Filostrato* (IV, 155: since I cannot pass one hour without great torment if I do not see you, how shall I manage to pass the ten days until you return?). It is at once evident that these lines are much closer to the passage in Book V which we are discussing. The rest of the stanza is Chaucer's own: Troilus wonders how Criseyde, on her part, will endure such sorrow for him and fears that, before she returns, her womanly face will become "pitous, pale, grene" because of her longing for him.

The account of Troilus' dreams and of his suffering during the night (246–66) is suggested by stanzas 26 and 27 of the *Filostrato*. There, however, the words are spoken by Troilo and addressed to Pandaro; in the English poem they are put into indirect discourse. All the trembling and weeping, though apparently caused by the terrifying dreams, are typical courtly love symptoms and entirely appropriate; but, as Chaucer himself avers, not all the men alive could describe Troilus' sorrow and pain (V, 270–73):

> Thow, redere, maist thi self ful wel devyne
> That swich a wo my wit kan nat defyne.
> On ydel for to write it sholde I swynke,
> Whan that my wit is wery it to thynke.

The morning after the return from the visit with Sarpedoun, Troilus and Pandarus go forth to gaze on Criseyde's
house. Troilo, as becomes his decidedly more sentimental nature, apparently lingers fondly over the happy scene; Troilus,
however, is affected differently and in a fashion more typical
of courtly love. His heart grows cool, his face pales, and without a word he passes by the house and, "as God wolde," begins
to ride fast so that no one can notice his appearance. It is
then that he apostrophizes the palace (540–53); Troilo does
likewise, recalling the brightness of the place when Criseida
was there, Criseida who bore his repose in her eyes; now the
palace is dark and he does not know if it will ever have her
again (V, 53). Troilus' apostrophe is based upon the *Filostrato* account but is greatly elaborated; Chaucer employs
striking figures and makes his lines much more poetic and
impressive. The following lines have no counterpart in the
Italian (V, 547–53):

> O paleis, whilom crowne of houses alle,
> Enlymyned with sonne of alle blisse,
> O ryng, fro which the ruby is out falle,
> O cause of wo, that cause hast ben of lisse,
> Yit, syn I may no bet, fayn wolde I kisse
> Thi colde dores, dorste I for this route;
> And farewel, shryne of which the seynt is oute!

Troilus now tells Pandarus about his "newe sorrow" as
well as his "joies olde," with so "dede an hewe" that everyone might have pity for his woe. The appropriateness of such
"an hewe" to a courtly lover scarcely needs to be noted; this
detail is added by Chaucer. Troilus proceeds to ride up and
down, recalling all the happy sources of his pleasure. This
fills more than two stanzas (565–81) and is developed from
the *Filostrato* (V, 54–55). We need not concern ourselves
with this reminiscing but may note that Chaucer enriches
the passage with two courtly love additions. Thus, in one
place Criseyde said to him: "Goode swete, love me wel, I
preye"; and in another she beheld him so well that, until

death, his heart would be bound to hers (574); this exempli-
fies the unqualified devotion of the courtly lover, as do also
lines 575 ff., in which Troilus remembers a place where Criseyde sang so beautifully and melodiously that he can still
hear the sound of her voice; this is fully in keeping with the
command that a lover keep his lady always in mind. I do not
know why Chaucer saw fit to leave aside most of *Filostrato*,
V, 55, for it is good courtly love material: there Criseida's
beautiful eyes captured me with love; there she was when she
inflamed my heart with a greater passion; there, when her
worthiness condescended to my pleasure; there I saw her
haughty; and there my lady showed herself humble to me.
Possibly the English poet felt that in omitting such details
he was putting Troilus' feelings on a higher plane, and thus
his action may be explained as part of his tendency to introduce a greater refinement into the English poem.

Troilus now addresses his remarks to Cupid (582–602)
in words suggested by *Filostrato*, V, 56–57. Here he begs the
God of Love to return Criseyde to him. Chaucer's words,
though substantially the same as Boccaccio's, breathe an
entirely different spirit. They have a distinctly fatalistic air
about them and with no great stretch of the imagination
might easily be addressed to Fortune or Destiny; this is quite
in keeping with what was said above about the kinship of
the two ideas.[18]

After this Troilus goes to the gates and ponders the scene
of their last meeting together (603–16). To Troilo it sometimes seemed that he had grown pale and that therefore men
sometimes pointed him out and asked why he was so subdued and disheartened; there was really no one who pointed
at him, but he suspected those who he thought knew the
truth. Chaucer converts this into distinctly courtly-love
phraseology, for Troilus imagines himself disfigured, pale,
and "waxen lesse than he was wont," and fancies that men
ask about his "hevynesse." But Chaucer explains that this
was only a part of his melancholy (i. e., his love melan-

choly) that he had such a fantasy. Further Chaucerian lines (624–27) relate that on another occasion he imagined that all who went by pitied him and said they were sorry that Troilus should die. In this manner did he pass the time and (V, 629–30)

> Swich lif right gan he lede,
> As he that stood bitwixen hope and drede.

We may now examine the song which Troilus composed to ease "somwhat his woful herte." This *cantus Troili* fills lines 638–44; the lament for Criseida in the corresponding section of the *Filostrato* fills five stanzas (62–66), but Chaucer utilizes only the opening one, which he converts into lines of high poetic value. He compares Criseyde to a star whose light he has lost; for dark in torment, night by night with wind astern, he sails toward his death (V, 642–44):

> For which the tenthe nyght, if that I faille
> The gydyng of thi bemes bright an houre,
> Mi ship and me Caribdis wol devoure.

After singing this song, he soon fell to sighing again. Every night as he gazed at the moon he told it all his sorrow. These lines (650–58) follow the *Filostrato* (V, 69), but as they do not tell us much about Troilus we may pass them over. The rest of this scene (659–86) follows the *Filostrato* account (V, 68, 70–71) though considerably enriched in the English version; as, for example, when the reference to Phaeton's driving amiss the cart of his father, the sun, is introduced to emphasize Troilus' feeling that the nights are longer than they used to be. While Troilo stood on the walls and gazed toward the Greek camp, fancying Criseida here or there, Troilus is much more realistic (or does this prove him less so?); for the air that is so sweet comes from her and is a relief to his soul, and the wind that hour by hour grows stronger derives from his lady's deep sighs; and the proof of this (V, 676–79)?

in noon othere space
Of al this town, save onliche in this place,
Fele I no wynd that sowneth so lik peyne;
It seyth; "alas, whi twynned be we tweyne?"

Thus did the time go by until the ninth night was past, Pandarus being with him constantly, always seeking to comfort
him and trying to encourage him with the hope that Criseyde
would return and quench his sorrow (680–86; cf. *Filostrato*,
V, 71).

The portrait of Troilus (V, 827–40), inserted along with
that of Criseyde and of Diomede, is taken from the *Frigii
Daretis Ylias* of Joseph of Exeter. As Root points out,
"Chaucer's portrait of Troilus is less dependent on sources
than are the portraits of Diomede and Criseyde." [19] The
passage emphasizes Troilus' qualities as a valiant soldier and
well-developed young man, though it does not fail to mention certain qualities that may properly be associated with
him as a courtly lover. He was (V, 832–33)

Oon of the best entecched creature,
That is, or shal, whil that the world may dure,

and he was in no degree second in the performance of deeds
of daring belonging to a knight (V, 838–40):

Al myghte a geant passen hym of myght,
His herte ay with the firste and with the beste
Stood paregal, to durre don that hym leste.

The activities of Troilus and Pandarus on the morning of
the tenth day and the days immediately following have already been discussed in the chapter on Pandarus and hence
need not be examined here in any greater detail. The one
thing that deserves to be remembered about Troilus during
all this trying time is that he never fails to have complete
confidence in Criseyde and thus in his unfailing devotion
to his lady reveals himself as a courtly lover par excellence.
When he sees, however, that she is not going to keep her
promise (V, 1210–11),

> He kan now sen non other remedie,
> But for to shape hym soone for to dye.

Both Troilo (*Filostrato*, VII, 18–19) and Troilus (1212–25) go into a decline. Jealousy returns to them and because of their melancholy they neither eat nor drink and they avoid all company. Troilus becomes lean, pale, wan, and so feeble that he must use a crutch; yet when anyone inquired what he was suffering from, he said that his trouble was "al aboute his herte." In the Italian poem Priam visits Troilo and begs to be told what the trouble is; so also do Hector, Paris, and his brothers and sisters (VII, 21–22). Chaucer relates practically the same incident (though considerably condensed), but all to no purpose (V, 1230–32):

> But al for naught; he nolde his cause pleyne,
> But seyde he felte a grevous maladie
> About his herte, and fayn he wolde dye.

Now follow his dream about the boar (V, 1233 ff.) and Pandarus' comments on the dream,[20] all of which follow the *Filostrato* (VII 23–33, 37, 40–41, 48–50). At the conclusion of Pandarus' remarks and at his suggestion, Troilus proceeds to write a letter to Criseyde (1317–1421); this is taken over quite freely from the *Filostrato*, VII, 52–75 (192 lines), from which it is considerably condensed (104 lines). These omissions may be explained as an attempt on Chaucer's part to focus attention on the anguish of the courtly lover as opposed to the more florid luxuriating-in-sorrow of Troilo. Thus, while the latter pledges fidelity to Criseida (VII, 52)—for at her departure she left his soul confounded in greater misery than anyone believes—Troilus is much more explicit about his suffering: You left me in "aspre peynes smerte," and I have become ever more wretched from day to day; wherefore with "dredful herte trewe," as one driven by sorrow, I write you of my woe, which increases hourly, complaining as I dare or am able to express myself;

and if this letter is smeared, you know it is because of (V, 1336–37)

> The teris, which that fro myn eyen reyne,
> That wolden speke, if that they koude, and pleyne.

Chaucer omits Troilo's suspicions about Calchas as well as his extended metaphors of the mountains, rivers, the sun, et cetera (whose places he longs for, since they all may look on his beloved lady—cf. *Filostrato*, VII, 56–72), and places the emphasis on the hero's sufferings; no one may describe his sorrow; chest of every care, he was alive at the time of writing the letter but entirely ready to send his suffering soul from the body; and everything which formerly gave him pleasure now produces the opposite effect (V, 1378–79):

> But torned is, for which my lif I warie,
> Everich joie or ese in his contrarie.

Troilus urges Criseyde to return and save his life; if pity will not move her, let her think of the promise. Troilo begs Criseida to write him if she is prevented from coming and if he is to have more hope in her; but Troilus is much more tragic in his request (V, 1387–91):

> And if so be my gilt hath deth deserved,
> Or if yow list no more upon me se,
> In guerdoun yit of that I have yow served,
> Byseche I yow, myn hertes lady free,
> That hereupon ye wolden write me.

Though her absence is "an helle" to him, he will bear his woe if she will only write and thus with hope or death deliver him from pain. Troilo is very definite about his determination to commit suicide, and Chaucer very properly omits his uncourtly sentiments when he says that the shame of so inglorious a death will be hers. Troilo remarks that his sorrows have so changed him that Criseida will not recognize him; Troilus is more definite, for he states that his health

and his complexion have so changed that Criseyde will not
be able to know him, Criseyde, his "hertes day," his "lady
free," for whose beauty his heart so thirsts that he can
scarcely hold on to his life. A further courtly love addition
appears in the next stanza (l. 1413), when he bids farewell
to her as one that may command life or death of him; the
same is true of Troilus' concluding words (1419–20):

> In yow my lif, in yow myght for to save
> Me fro disese of alle peynes smerte!

We are already familiar with Criseyde's reply to this
letter (1422–35) and need stop here only to note its effect
on Troilus.[21] As hope diminished, Troilo's sorrow increased
so that from sheer exhaustion he had to retire to his bed
(*Filostrato*, VII, 77). Troilus was affected in much the same
way but behaved in a more typically courtly manner. His
woe increased from day to day and both his hope and
strength grew less. He could neither eat, drink, nor sleep,
nor did he say a word, imagining always that Criseyde was
cruel to him; for which reason he "wel neigh. . .wex out
of his mynde" (1442). Furthermore he could not forget his
dream and its prediction of her unfaithfulness and his misfortune, which Jove in his providence had revealed to him;
on which account he called to him Sibille, his sister, also
known as Cassandra, whom he besought to explain it. These
lines (1450–1519) are a skillful Chaucerian addition; the
English poet "deftly substitutes the divination of Cassandra
for the painful altercation which takes place between that
lady and Troilo in *Fil.* VII, 86–102."[22] Cassandra begins
her interpretation of the dream by telling several stor-
ies showing how Fortune has overthrown "lordes olde"; it
is an imposing array of names that she musters: Tideus,
Meleagre, Polymytes, Ethiocles, Hemonydes, Archymoris,
Amphiorax, Ypomedon, Parthenope, Cappaneus, and so on
(1457–1519).[23] Cassandra's conclusion is (V, 1517–19):

> This Diomede hire herte hath, and she his,
> Wepe if thow wolt, or lef; for, out of doute,
> This Diomede is inne, and thow art oute.

It might be observed that this passage is only hinted at in the *Filostrato* (VII, 26) and in an entirely different context; for there the words are addressed by Troilo to Pandaro, and all we are told is that he told him about the dream and its significance. Immediately following Cassandra's words come two stanzas in which Troilus berates his sister for having interpreted the dream correctly. This is quite different from the *Filostrato* account, for there (VII, 87) Cassandra jeers at his loving a lady of low birth; whereupon Troilo reproves her and through thirteen stanzas defends his love of Criseida (89–101). This may seem to the modern reader somewhat inappropriate at this point, but it may easily be justified if we will but remember that Boccaccio had a personal motive in writing his poem. As Rossetti puts it,

There is a considerable amount of *animus* in the whole harangue of Troilus to Chryseis [*sic*], apparently somewhat beyond its importance in the scheme of the poem, but easily accounted for if we suppose a personal motive concerned in it. The reader will observe how chivalrously Troilus here stands up for his beloved, more than half convinced though he is that she has already deserted and betrayed him. Certainly he does justice to his nationality by "lying like a Trojan" in the assertion of her immaculate purity; but this only makes his singlehearted devotion to her shine the brighter.[24]

The immediate effect on Troilus was that he forgot his woe "for angre of hire speche," and jumped from his bed, as though a doctor had completely cured him; the whole object of his thoughts now was to get at the truth of this; thus he endures his fate (1534–40). But though Troilus participated in the universal sorrow experienced on the death of Hector (V, 1567–68),

> what for sorwe and love, and for unreste,
> Ful ofte a day he bad his herte breste,

nevertheless his thoughts returned to Criseyde, even though he began to despair and to fear that she was unfaithful to him. This is suggested by *Filostrato*, VIII, 2, while the lines immediately following (1576–82) come from stanza 4. Here we learn that Troilo contemplated disguising himself as a pilgrim in order to visit Criseida but gave up the idea not only because of the difficulty of deceiving clever people but also because no excuse would suffice if he were discovered by the Greeks; for which reason he wept often and copiously. Troilus wrote to her frequently, urging that since he was loyal, she should come and keep her promise; Chaucer saw fit to leave out the statement that Pandaro visited her during the truces and courteously reprimanded her for her long sojourn (VIII, 3). The English poet reproduces for us one of the letters (1590–1631) written by Criseyde; this, only hinted at in the *Filostrato* (VIII, 5), has already been considered in chapter VIII.[25]

When Troilus saw this letter, he thought it strange, sighed sorrowfully, and felt that it was the beginning of a change; finally he realized that he might not longer trust that she would hold to what she had promised; for he that loves well is unwilling to believe, in such a case, though he be sorely vexed. Before long, an event happened which proved that Criseyde was "nat so kynde as that hire oughte be," and at last he knew without doubt that all was lost. These lines (1632–45) are developed from suggestions in the corresponding section of the *Filostrato* (VIII, 5–7), where it is related that Troilo, from Criseida's empty promises, became suspicious and, carefully going over all the evidence, concluded that new love and not fatherly affection was the cause of her deception and the reason for her failure to return; soon an event took place which proved the truth of his suspicions about Diomede.

Lines 1646–66 follow *Filostrato*, VIII, 8–10, rather closely; but though Troilo, timid and irresolute, remained not without torment of his love, Troilus is described as

standing one day absorbed in his melancholy and in suspicion of her for whom he would go so far as to die; "in sus-
pecioun" is doubtless a misunderstanding of the Italian
"sospeso." It is interesting to note what different figures are
presented in these few words: Troilo timid, hesitant, tor-
mented by his love; Troilus melancholy, brooding, suspicious
of her to whom he was so devoted. Both poets concur in the
account of the brooch which the hero sees on the armor coat
of Diomede (vanquished by Deiphebus); Chaucer states
that he gave her this brooch on the morning of her departure,
but neither the English poet nor Boccaccio actually relates
this incident; the only suggestion of it is the brooch given
by Criseyde to Troilus (cf. III, 1356–58, a scene not paralleled in the *Filostrato*). When Troilo caught sight of it,
he said to himself that his dream, his suspicion, and his
thought were true. Troilus' reaction is much more characteristically that of the courtly lover, for as he gazed on it,
his heart began suddenly to grow cold; when he recognized
the brooch which he had given her in memory of him and his
sorrow and which she had pledged to keep forever, he
realized that his lady was no longer to be trusted.

Following this he returned home, sent for Pandarus, told
him all about his love, loyalty, and torment, and begged
Death to restore his rest to him (1667–73; *Filostrato*, VIII,
11). The poet now relates Troilus' apostrophe to Criseyde
(1674–1722). These words, the last spoken by Troilus, are
greatly condensed from the corresponding section of the
Filostrato (VIII, 12–21); the Italian poet required eighty
lines, whereas Chaucer was satisfied with forty-nine. Each
lover reproaches his false mistress, but it seems to me that
Troilus is less vindictive, more merciful than Troilo. Suggesting this different tone is the statement (1686–87) that
her reputation for fidelity is now ruined, "and that is al my
routhe." Troilo does not temper his reproaches with any such
magnanimity; his chief complaint against Criseida seems to
be that she has broken his heart and made any future pleas-

ure impossible for him. On the other hand, though Troilus apparently regrets that her image still remains with him against his will, he still finds it impossible to "unloven" her; she it is whom he still loves "best of any creature" (1701). Troilus continues his gentle manner even when he prays that he may have the pleasure of killing Diomede (1702–5) and, instead of the reproaches addressed by Troilo to Jove because of the apparent neglect of his heavenly duties, Troilus substitutes the simple question (V, 1706–8):

> O god . . . that oughtest taken heede
> To fortheren trouthe, and wronges to punyce,
> Whi nyltow don a vengeaunce of this vice?

In words addressed to Pandarus (the account in the *Filo-strato*, VIII, 19, is much the same), Troilus points out that his dream proves the correctness of his view that the gods make divine revelations in sleep and he concludes the mono-logue by expressing the hope that he may soon die in battle. Troilo concludes with the prayer that he may soon meet Diomede and kill him on the battlefield; then he will not mind dying if his enemy is dead and if he can find him miserable in the nether regions. Troilus ends on quite a dif-ferent key, gently reproaching his beloved (V, 1720–22):

> But, trewely, Criseyde, swete may,
> Whom I have ay with al my myght yserved,
> That ye thus doon, I have it nat deserved.

Pandarus' words to his friend, which follow immediately (1724–43), have already been discussed.[26] There is no need to follow Troilus through the few remaining lines of the poem; both authors agree in their accounts: his sorrow is great, but Fortune holds to her course, Criseyde loves Dio-mede, and Troilus must weep "in cares colde." Chaucer, however, anticipates the moral expressed in lines 1835 ff. (V, 1748–50):

Swich is this world, whoso it kan byholde;
In ech estat is litel hertes reste;
God leve us for to take it for the beste!

Troilus fights valiantly, ever displaying his knighthood,
strength, and anger, and always seeking Diomede; they
often meet and fight with each other, but Fortune has de-
creed that they should die at the hands of others. Troilus
is finally killed by Achilles (1806).

The death of the hero marks the end of the narrative, and
hence I should like to pause here in order to make a few
observations on Chaucer's handling of Troilus. If this study
of Troilo and Troilus has revealed nothing else, I think it
has shown conclusively the incorrectness of the widespread
belief that Chaucer took over his hero from the Italian poem
and left him practically unchanged.[27] Chaucer did not trans-
mute Troilus as he did Pandarus and Criseyde, but he did
change him very considerably, so much so, in fact, that he
is a character very different from his Italian prototype.
Troilus is something far more than the love-sick boy of the
Filostrato. True it is that he remains about as much of a
sentimentalist as Troilo and, during the first part of the
poem, at least, is as dependent on Pandarus as the Italian
hero; but as a soldier he is far more valiant; as a lover, far
more noble. It is by elaborating these two conceptions of
his hero that I feel that Chaucer has so elevated him that
the resulting character is one quite different from Troilo.
This change is largely to be explained through the development of Troilus as a courtly lover or, rather, through the
enhancement of the courtly qualities with which he was already endowed and by the addition of others.[28] As the preceding pages have shown, Chaucer lost no opportunity to
improve the tone of his poem, and one of the ways in which
he did this was by strengthening the moral fiber of his hero.
The poet was fully cognizant of the courtly conception of
love as a great spiritual, ennobling, and regenerative force,
and it is this understanding of the courtly love code which

seems to me to explain the great transformation of Troilus.

There are other changes which might also be noticed. Exactly what Troilo's views are on the freedom of the will it is difficult to say, but there can be no doubt that Troilus is an out-and-out fatalist. The reasons for viewing him in this light have already been given, and we need only mention again that this in no way belittles his status as a courtly lover; in fact, it enhances it and makes him the more typical. The interpretation of Troilus as a fatalist and Criseyde as an opportunist of fascinatingly complex character, the one in the hands of some great destinal power, the other running things pretty much to suit herself, makes a reading of the poem far richer and more significant. The eternal problem of what the author means is just as perplexing here as anywhere else, possibly more so. Yet I feel that the proper way to interpret the poem is through a study of Chaucer's actual words combined with what the critic feels to be implicitly expressed. This mingling of the subjective and the objective has its drawbacks of course but so has most criticism. I am about to point out how the apparently contradictory epilogue fits in perfectly with the rest of the poem but, if I may be allowed to anticipate, the view which is expressed there certainly cannot be used as evidence for assuming that Troilus is and always has been an advocate of free will. What the reader is concerned with is Troilus' views as lover of Criseyde and dweller on earth, not as a heavenly onlooker.[29]

Chaucer has worked a very distinct change in the mood of his hero through his additions to the courtly love material. Troilo is far more outspoken in the joys of love in which he revels, but that is no reason for believing Troilus did not share equally in its delights. The reason for our doubts about this is our author's own frequently confessed inability "swich joies to descryve." However, he had no misgivings when it came to describing Troilus' misery; there is no denying that the English hero is a far more melancholy figure

than the Italian. The sufferings of Troilo when separated
from his lady are more than counterbalanced by the exu-
berance and vivacity with which he is inspired by love. This
difference is not entirely beyond explanation. While Troilo's
delight is apparently derived, for the most part, from the
physical enjoyment of his love, Troilus' melancholy is due
to something more than the mere absence of this pleasure;
it is, rather, induced by the severity of the cult to which he
belongs. The God of Love is an exacting deity and demands
the utmost of his worshipers. As one of its most ardent
devotees, Troilus is obliged to become, so to speak, an ascetic of love. Then, too, a good deal may be accounted for by
remembering that one is the product of Italian, the other of
English, genius. Looten expresses this distinction as follows:

Troilo est tout expansion, tout exubérance de paroles. Troilus est un
âme méditative, telle que sera Hamlet. Il a le tempérament des hommes
du Nord : moins en dehors que ceux du Midi, moins à la merci des élans
primesautiers de l'instinct, subissant moins la tyrannie du sentiment,
ils cherchent obstinément la cause de leurs états d'âme. Tels sont les
héros shakespeariens, "The cause"! C'est l'idée fixe d'Othello, il la
poursuit même lorsqu'il est au paroxysme de la jalousie, et quand il la
découverte, aussitôt, il se rue dans le crime et la mort.[30]

There now remain to be considered only those final stanzas
which relate the ascent of Troilus to the eighth sphere
(1807–27). These lines are a close imitation of the death
of Arcita as described in the *Teseide*, XI, 1–3, and are, as
Root points out, "of prime importance in enforcing the
philosophical interpretation which Chaucer has given to his
story." [31] These stanzas have been the cause of considerable
adverse criticism, criticism which seems to me quite unjusti-
fied; for the account of Troilus' ascent to heaven provides
precisely the necessary interlude between the account of his
death (1806) and the philosophizing with which the poet
saw fit to conclude his masterpiece (1835 ff.). As Tatlock
puts it, the otherworldly tone of this passage "is meant to
lead into the unworldly ending which follows; piety with a

pagan touch forms a transition from pagan worldliness to Christian devoutness. It was probably to avoid too abrupt a shift from sympathy to detachment that the four stanzas intervene between the last preceding mention of Troilus, and the account of his death and the slurs on courtly love." [32] And yet I feel there is a still more important fact to be pointed out with reference to these lines. Stanza 262 (i. e., ll. 1828–34) is particularly significant in that it reiterates for the last time Chaucer's conception of Troilus as the ideal lover. On his death the hero ascends directly to heaven; he lingers in no limbo, no purgatory; there is no period of purgation of any kind. On the contrary, his love has been so noble, so spiritual, that he passes at once to his eternal reward. Chaucer's reflections on the death of Troilus are quite different from Boccaccio's comments on the fate of Troilo (VIII, 28): such was the end of his ill-conceived love, such the end of his miserable sorrow, such the end of the splendor destined for the royal throne, such the end of Troilo's empty hope in base Criseida. Chaucer is only slightly indebted to the Italian poet for these lines (V, 1828–34):

> Swich fyn hath, lo, this Troilus for love!
> Swich fyn hath al his grete worthynesse!
> Swich fyn hath his estat real above!
> Swich fyn his lust! swich fyn hath his noblesse!
> Swich fyn hath false worldes brotelnesse!
> And thus bigan his lovyng of Criseyde,
> As I have told, and in this wise he deyde.

These words are a complete acquittal of Troilus and constitute Chaucer's final stamp of approval on the conduct of his hero. It is highly significant that this passage comes immediately after the account of Troilus' ascent to heaven. This helps to remove any doubt from the reader's mind about the proper interpretation of "swich fyn," for it clearly refers not to Troilus' death and the end of everything but rather to the event recounted in the immediately preceding lines, the ascent to heaven. Celestial bliss is the hero's reward for his love, his great worthiness, his nobility. This passage is in the very best courtly tradition, for it presents love as a great spiritual force, a power so great that it has transformed one man and now brings him to eternal salvation. It may be objected that the thought expressed in these lines is directly opposed to that incorporated in the immediately following stanzas and that, therefore, they are out of place. On the contrary, I feel that stanza 262 makes the transition all the more easy and sensible. The author has finished with his elaborate experiment and demonstrated conclusively that the love of the hero for his lady was so exalting and ennobling that it finally brought him to heaven as his last reward. But now the poet, mindful of the lover's trials and sorrows as well, suggests to his readers that all this may be avoided by their forgetting the vanity of the world and by dedicating themselves entirely to the worship of God (V, 1847-48):

> And syn he best to love is, and most meke,
> What nedeth feyned loves for to seke?

The moral of Boccaccio's poem is quite different from Chaucer's. The former (VIII, 29-33) commends Troilo as a model lover and then proceeds at length to condemn the fickleness and instability of woman, who has neither reason nor virtue and is as changeable as a leaf in the wind. Chaucer on the other hand exhorts all "yonge fresshe folkes" who are in love to leave behind all worldly "vanyte," to raise their hearts to God, and to remember that the world is but a transitory place that "passeth soone as floures faire" (1835-41); celestial love is all that counts. Many people seem to be perplexed at Chaucer's attitude and find his epilogue strangely out of place; the whole thing seems to me entirely appropriate and the explanation of its presence quite simple. We must remember that Chaucer was a poet and a poet with a mind, a very fertile one; this mind was, as Chesterton writes, "capacious; there was room for

ideas to play about in it. He could see the connexion, and
still more the disconnexion, of different parts of his own
scheme, or of any scheme." [33] There is the whole explanation; he found a poem of courtly love, saw fit greatly to
enhance that element, and succeeded in making the finest
courtly love poem ever written. Then, his work done, he
stopped, looked back, saw the artificiality not only of courtly
love but of all earthly endeavor and consequently urged his
readers to devote their efforts to the things of eternity.[34]
This conclusion is implicit throughout the poem and is, it
seems to me, inevitable. And in all this Chaucer but proves
himself one of the greatest of courtly love poets. In sub-
ordinating earthly to celestial love the English poet shows
himself akin to the greatest of the Italian writers in this
kind; for as we close the *Vita Nuova* and lay aside the
Troilus, we can have but one thought.

APPENDIX, NOTES
BIBLIOGRAPHY, INDEX

APPENDIX:
TRANSLATIONS

THE FOLLOWING pages contain English versions of the quotations given in the text. To a certain extent (chapters I and VI) I have used the translations of acknowledged authorities (for full details see bibliography *s.v.* Griffin, Ovid, Pound, Rossetti), but in many instances (chapters II, III, IV, and V) I have given my own renderings. All are in prose except the Cavalcanti sonnets, two by Ezra Pound and two others by D. G. Rossetti; what these may lack in literal accuracy they more than make up in fidelity of spirit.

CHAPTER I (OVID)

PAGE
6: *Heroides*, IX, 25–26: He whom not a thousand wild beasts, whom not the Stheneleian foe, whom not Juno could overcome, love overcomes.

Metamorphoses, V, 363–70: Then Venus Erycina saw him wandering to and fro, as she was seated on her sacred mountain and embracing her winged son; she exclaimed: "O son, both arms and hands to me, and source of all my power, take now those shafts, Cupid, with which you conquer all, and shoot your swift arrows into the heart of that god to whom the final lot of the triple kingdom fell. You rule the gods, and Jove himself. You conquer and control the deities of the sea, and the very king that rules the deities of the sea."

Amores, I, i, 3–5: But Cupid, they say, with a laugh stole away one foot. "Who gave thee, cruel boy, this right over poesy?"

Ibid., I, i, 25–26: Ah, wretched me! Sure were the arrows that yon boy had. I am on fire, and in my but now vacant heart Love sits his throne.

Ibid., I, ii, 9: Shall I yield? or by resisting kindle still more the inward-stealing flame that has me?

287

Ibid., I, ii, 17–18: More bitterly far and fiercely are the unwilling assailed by Love than those who own their servitude.

Ibid., II, ix, 1–6: O Cupid, never enough roused in my behalf, O boy lodged in my heart, and doing naught for me—why dost harm me, the soldier who have never left thy standards, and why am I wounded in my own camp? Why doth thy torch burn friends and thy bow transfix them? 'Twere greater glory to vanquish them that oppose.

7:     *Ibid.*, II, ix, 14: For love is leaving me bones naked.

Ibid., I, ii, 19–20: Look, I confess! I am new prey of thine, O Cupid; I stretch forth my hands to be bound, submissive to thy laws.

Ibid., I, ix, 1–2: Every lover is a soldier, and Cupid has a camp of his own; Atticus, believe me, every lover is a soldier.

Metamorphoses, VIII, 142–44: Scarce had she spoken when she leaped into the water, swam after the ship, her passion giving strength, and clung, hateful and unwelcome, to the Cretan boat.

8:     *Amores*, I, viii, 104: Wicked poisons have for hiding place sweet honey.

Remedia Amoris, 138: That is the cause and sustenance of the pleasant evil.

Ars Amatoria, I, 729–30: But let every lover be pale; this is the lover's hue. Such looks become him; from such a countenance let them imagine you to be sick.

Heroides, XI, 27: My color had fled from my face.

Metamorphoses, IX, 535–37: You might have had knowledge of my wounded heart from my pale, drawn face, my eyes oft filled with tears. . . .

Ibid., 581–82: When, Byblis, you heard that your love had been repulsed, you grew pale, and your whole body trembled in the grip of an icy chill.

Ibid., X, 458–59: Color and blood flee from her face, and her senses desert her as she goes.

Ars Amatoria, III, 721–22: When she saw the mark of a body on the flattened grass, her leaping heart beat within her fearful bosom.

Heroides, III, 82: This is the fear, ah woe is wretched me, that shakes my very bones!

Metamorphoses, IX, 521: And she proceeds to set down with a trembling hand the words she has thought out.

Ibid., X, 457–58: But her knees tremble and sink beneath her.

9:     *Ars Amatoria*, I, 607–8: Now is the time for talk with her; away with you, rustic shame! Chance and Venus help the brave.

Metamorphoses, VII, 47: Why do you fear when all is safe?

Ibid., XIII, 858: I fear you alone, O Nereid; your anger is more deadly than the lightning-flash.

Heroides, XI, 28: I scarce took food, and with unwilling mouth.

Metamorphoses, III, 437–38: No thought of food or rest can draw him from the spot.

Ibid., XIV, 423–25: Six nights and as many returning dawns beheld her wandering, sleepless and fasting, over hills, through valleys, wherever chance directed.

Ars Amatoria, III, 675–76: Let the woman regard the youth with more loving looks, and deeply sigh, and ask why he comes so late.

Metamorphoses, X, 402–3: At the name of father Myrrha sighed deeply from the bottom of her heart.

Ibid., XIII, 738–39: There once Galatea, while she let the maiden comb her hair, first sighing deeply, thus addressed her.

Ars Amatoria, I, 735: Nights of vigil make thin the bodies of lovers.

Heroides, XI, 29–30: My sleep was never easy, the night was a year for me, and I groaned, though stricken with no pain.

10: *Metamorphoses*, III, 396–98: Her sleepless cares waste away her wretched form; she becomes gaunt and wrinkled and all moisture fades from her body into the air.

Ibid., VI, 490–93: But although the Thracian king retired, his heart seethed with thoughts of her. Recalling her look, her movement, her hands, he pictures at will what he has not yet seen, and feeds his own fires, his thoughts preventing sleep.

Heroides, VIII, 107–10: But when the dark of night has fallen and sent me to my chamber with wails and lamentation for my bitter lot, and I have stretched myself prostrate on my sorrowful bed, then springing tears, not slumber, is the service of mine eyes, and in every way I can I shrink from my mate as from a foe.

Metamorphoses, III, 474–76: He spoke and, half distraught, turned again to the same image. His tears ruffled the water, and dimly the image came back from the troubled pool.

Ibid., VII, 89–91: But when the stranger began to speak, grasped her right hand, and in low tones asked for her aid and promised marriage in return, she burst into tears and said. . . .

Ibid., IX, 535–37: You might have had knowledge of my wounded heart from my pale, drawn face, my eyes oft filled with tears. . . .

Ibid., IX, 655–56: Byblis lies without a word, clutching the green herbs with her fingers, and watering the grass with her flowing tears.

Ibid., IX, 641–44: And just as, crazed by thy thyrsus, O son

PAGE

of Semele, thy Ismarian worshippers throng thy triennial or-
gies, so the women of Bubassus beheld Byblis go shrieking
through the broad fields.

11 :   *Ibid.*, X, 422–23 : Then she says : 'O mother, blest in your husband !'—only so much, and groans.

Heroides, II, 130 : My senses leave me and I fall, to be caught
up by my handmaid's arms.

Ibid., III, 59–60 : When the monstrous tale fell on my wretched
and terror-stricken ears, the blood went from my breast, and
with it my senses fled.

Metamorphoses, V, 289–91 : He, as if he would follow us,
took his stand on a lofty battlement and cried to us : 'What
way you take, the same will I take also' ; and, quite bereft of
sense, he leaped from the pinnacle of the tower.

Amores, III, ii, 13–14 : Have I caught sight of you as I career,
I will stop, and the reins, let go from my hands, will drop.

Ars Amatoria, III, 713–14 : What were thy feelings, Procris,
when thus frantic thou lurkedst there ? What a fire was in thy
maddened heart !

Metamorphoses, IX, 635–38 : There, they say, the wretched
daughter of Miletus lost all control of reason ; she tore her
garments from her breast, and in mad passion beat her arms.
Now before all the world she rages. . . .

Ibid., XIV, 420–22 : Nor was the nymph content to weep, to
tear her hair and beat her breasts ; (all these she did, indeed)
and, rushing forth, she wandered madly through the Latian
fields.

Ars Amatoria, I, 733–36 : Let leanness also prove your feelings ; nor deem it base to set a hood on your bright locks. Nights
of vigil make thin the bodies of lovers, and anxiety and the
distress that a great passion brings.

12 :   *Heroides*, XI, 27–28 : Wasting had shrunk my frame ; I scarce
took food, and with unwilling mouth.

Metamorphoses, XIV, 431–32 : Finally, worn to a shade by
woe, her very marrow changed to water, she melted away and
gradually vanished into thin air.

CHAPTER II (THE TROUBADOURS)

16 :   Bernart de Ventadorn, XXXIX, 1–8 : When the green grass
and the foliage appear and the blossom on the branch
sprouts and the nightingale raises her voice loud and clear
and begins her song, I have joy from her and I have joy from
the bud and joy from myself and greater from my mistress.
On all sides I am surrounded and begirt with joy, but this is
the joy which conquers all other joys.

17: *Ibid.*, XV, 5–7 : Therefore is my singing superior because I have set and hold my mouth and eyes and heart and mind on the joy of love.

Ibid., XIII, 20–21 : Because of the joy I have, I do not see nor hear nor do I know what I am saying or doing.

Jaufre Rudel, Appel, XV, 22–23 : Sad and happy I shall part from her if ever I see again this far-away love.

Ibid., 43–46 : He speaks truly who calls me desirous and eager for a far-away love, for no other joy pleases me so much as the pleasure of far-away love.

Pons de Capdeuil, MW, I, 338–39 : And it is reasonable and right, in my opinion, that one should love the best with good faith, even if it avails him not ; he is foolish who revolts, but I serve now and never demand anything of her, for one asks enough of a wise lord when he loves and serves him ; then if I love faithfully my lady, whose I am, joy ought truly to come to me from it, for she is the noblest that one can choose in the world.

Guillem de Cabestaing, MW, I, 110 : Love indeed holds me in her command, so that in me begins many a sweet pleasure, and I believe that God made me for her use and for her worth.

18: Girault de Bornelh, MW, I, 184 : Now I have great joy when I remember the love which holds my heart firm in her allegiance : for the other day I went into a garden beautifully covered with flowers and filled with the songs of birds, and when I was in that beautiful garden, there appeared to me the beautiful lily, and she took my eyes and seized my heart, so that, ever since, I have no remembrance or sense except concerning her whom I love.

Peirol, Bartsch, 152, 21 ff. : No man loves well and nobly who complains of Love, however ill she treats him ; as she more grievously binds me and burns and inflames me, I have greater desire.

Bernart de Ventadorn, XXII, 21–24 : For love, when one makes it known everywhere, is not love but vanity ; and it is mean, stupid, and foolish if a man does not attend carefully to whom he confides.

Ibid., VIII, 47–48 : Never through me shall love become known ; of that you may be positive !

19: *Ibid.*, XV, 1–4 : Singing can be of but little worth if the song does not spring from the depth of the heart ; and the song cannot come from the depth of the heart if there is not genuine love-of-the-heart there.

Ibid., XXIV, 17–24 : He who loves and does not become better indeed has a bad and miserable heart. I have improved so much that I look upon no man as richer than I am ; for I know that I love the most beautiful lady and am loved by her, [the most beautiful] whom God created in the world, so far as the earth extends.

Pons de Capdeuil, MW, I, 348: Happy is he whom love keeps joyous; for love is the climax of all blessings, and through love one is gay and courteous, frank and gentle, humble and proud; wherever love is, one carries on a thousand times better wars and courts, whence arise worthy deeds; wherefore I have put all my heart in love; and since I have good expectation that it will enrich me, I do not complain of the distress or the pain that I bear.

20:   Peire Raimon, MW, I, 147: It does not befit a true lover to make much ado; rather ought he to conceal and hide his heart and be thankful for the good and the ill that he sees of love; for one is esteemed on account of courteous qualities and when by knowledge he keeps himself from blundering; for from a good place comes a good recompense; and if there were no love-making and courtship there would be no worth or service or honor.

Arnaut de Marueil, MW, I, 161: She is so worthy that, when I consider well, pride springs from it and humility grows.

Ibid., 183–84: Lady, noble and worthy, courteous and attractive, if I know anything at all, the thought of you which is my heart and my shield, gives and teaches it to me; wherefore, for all my possessions I render you praise and thanks.

Peire Vidal, MW, I, 224: If I know how to say or do anything, she who gave me learning and knowledge should have the thanks; wherefore I am gay and a singer; and all attractive things that I do, I have from her beautiful, pleasing person, even when I only think of her with all my heart.

Raimon de Miraval, MW, II, 121: The most ignorant man in the company, when he sees and gazes at her, ought at parting to be wise and of fine bearing.

21:   Jaufre Rudel, Appel, XV, 36–42: O God, who made everything that comes and goes and who created this distant love, give me the power—for I have the longing—that shortly I may really see my far-away love in a suitable place, so that the room and the garden might ever be to me a palace.

Guillem de Cabestaing, Bartsch, 80, 12–15: For no one wears a ribbon whom I would care to lie with, nor would I be her lover in place of receiving your salute.

Bernart de Ventadorn, XXVIII, 49–54: It should now indeed be the time, beautiful and excellent lady, that, kissing, reward be secretly granted me, if not for another reason, then this: because I am full of desire; for one thing is worth two if the gift is made against the will.

Ibid., XXVII, 41–45: She is not lacking in goodness, unless she has too much boldness, so that one evening she brings me there, where she undresses, in a suitable place and with her arm lays a snare around my neck.

22: *Ibid.*, XXV, 49–50: May she not love me with an illicit love, for that is not fitting.

Ibid., VII, 39–40: I crave so noble a love that my longing is already a gain.

Marcabrun (Berry, p. 78, 19–21): Love is for the most part a bad sort of thing. It has killed a thousand men without a sword. God has not made men so evil minded.

23: Bernart de Ventadorn, XXXIII, 29–35: Lady, I am and shall be yours, ready for your service. I am your sworn and devoted servant and have been yours as a matter of course. You are my first joy and will be my last, so long as my life endures.

Peire Vidal, Bartsch, 117, 27–28: I am her entire property to sell or give away.

Guillem de Cabestaing, MW, I, 115: For even as an infant I was brought up to perform your commands.

Bernart de Ventadorn, XXXI, 49–54: Good lady, I ask for nothing but that you take me as your servant; for I shall serve you like a good lord, whatever may happen as a result of the reward. Behold me at your command, o noble, gentle, gay, and courtly Being! Do not be a lion or bear that you may kill me if I surrender myself to you!

24: *Ibid.*, IV, 1–8: Love, what is your opinion? Do you find any other fool except me? Do you think that I shall love and that I shall never find favor? Whatever you may command me, I shall do, for so it must be; but it is not becoming of you that you always allow me to suffer evil.

25: *Ibid.*, XXV, 59–60: If it should please her, she might kill me, for I should not complain of it at all!

Guillem de Cabestaing, MW, I, 109: The day when I first saw you, lady, when it pleased you to let me see you, my heart left all other thoughts, and all my desires were fixed in you: you placed longing in my heart, lady, with a sweet smile and a simple glance, so that you made me forget everything that exists.

Arnaut de Marueil, MW, I, 161: I turn my eyes, noble, prudent lady, toward the land where you are, and when I cannot bring myself nearer to you, I hold you in my heart, and think here of your sweet courteous person which makes me languish, of the kind looks and the delight and solace, of the worth and the sense and the beauty, of you who have never been absent from my mind since I first saw you.

Peirol, MW, II, 28: When first I saw her, she pleased me so

PAGE

that I could not retain my heart at all; it was entirely with her, and it is still there.

26: Pons de Capdeuil, MW, I, 350: Loyal Love has given me such a fine and firm will that I shall never depart from you, lady, in whom I have my good hope; you are so worthy, courteous in true speaking, frank and gentle, gay with humility, beautiful and pleasing that it is not to be said that you lack any good quality one could wish in a lady; and since your rich worthiness has risen so high, suffer that I love you, for I wish everything that pleases you.

Peire Raimon, MW, I, 146: Wherefore I am devoted and given up to true love and to her whom I desire; for my eyes have made me choose with fine taste the beautiful one who is flower and mirror and light and head and guide of all good breeding: and since so sweetly she wounded my heart with a loving glance, I have thought of nothing else, and no other good has been pleasing to me, and I have no remembrance of anything but her.

Arnaut Daniel, MW, II, 75: For seeing others I am blind; for hearing, deaf; her only do I hear and see and gaze at.

Peire Vidal, MW, I, 241: Now will my song turn to my lady, whom I hold dearer than my eyes or my teeth.

27: Bernart de Ventadorn, XXXI, 9-12: He is indeed dead who does not feel in his heart any sweet feeling of love; and what is life worth without the virtue [of love], except to stir up trouble in people?

Ibid., 29-32: My sorrow is indeed of a beautiful kind, for my sorrow now is worth more than any other joy; and since my sorrow seems so good to me, after my sorrow the good will really be good.

Guilhem IX, Comte de Peitieu (Appel, XI, 25-30): Through its joy it can cure sickness, and through its anger it can kill a healthy man; (it can) make a wise man foolish, and change the beauty of a handsome man, make the most noble man base and ennoble the most lowly.

Cercamon (Appel, XIII, 57-58): Cercamon says: hard it is for the courtier who despairs of love.

Gaucelm Faidit, MW, II, 91: All those who love valor ought to know that from love spring generosity and joyful pleasure, nobility and humility, valor in arms, honorable service, good position, joy, noble way of life.

Aimeric de Pegulhan, MW, II, 165: Yet I find more of good in love: it makes a man of low birth worth something; it makes a simple man speak in a courtly manner; the stingy generous; the traitor faithful; the fool wise; the sinner devout; the proud meek and humble. . . . And many a time it rescues me from

vulgarity whom, without love, one would not know how to
save; and it makes me think and say many good words that
without love I would not know how to utter.

CHAPTER III
(CHRÉTIEN DE TROYES)

Cligés

36 :   3095–96 : Thessala, who was very learned about love and all
        its service. . . .
        3865–68 : You who are wise in love, who maintain faithfully
        the customs and the usage of his court, who never broke his
        law. . . .
38 :   6751–58 : Of his *amie* he has made his wife, but he still calls her
        amie and lady; she can complain of no lack of affection, since
        he loves her as his *amie* and she loves him likewise, as one
        ought to do her lover.

Lancelot

43 :   7133–34 : So much he wrote; he wishes to compose nothing
        more lest he mismetre the story.

Yvain

45 :   1360–63 : His enemy takes his heart, and he loves her who
        hates him most. The lady has well avenged the death of her
        lord, all unwittingly.
48 :   6803–5 : Everything has come to a good end: he is loved and
        held dear by his lady, and she by him.

Lancelot

49 :   3816–19 : He who loves is obedient; he performs quickly and
        willingly whatever his *amie* may wish, since he is her devoted
        friend.
        5928–34 : Lady, never did I see a knight so courteous, one
        who performs so quickly whatsoever you command; should
        you seek the truth from me, he accepts both the good and the
        bad with much the same expression.

CHAPTER IV
(ANDREAS CAPELLANUS)

The shorter passages are sufficiently paraphrased in the text
and are therefore omitted here.

56 :   Accept, Walter, our sound doctrine offered to you by us and
        give up entirely the vanities of the world so that, when the

Heavenly Bridegroom shall come to celebrate the greater nuptials, and a cry shall rise in the night, equipped with lamps you may be prepared to go out to meet Him and with Him go in to the divine marriage, nor need you at the time of the sudden opportunity investigate the late decorations of your lamp and you need not come to the house of the Lord with the door closed and so hear a diffident voice.

Strive therefore, Walter, to have your lamps always ready; that is, keep the ornaments of affection and good works. Also be ever mindful to keep watch, lest the unexpected coming of the Bridegroom should find you sleeping in sin. Take care not to heed the commands of love and its distresses, with continual wakefulness, in order that, when the Bridegroom comes, he may find you vigilant, nor let worldly delight make you trust in the youth of the body to hurl you from the sleep of sin and do not be careless because of the lateness of the Bridegroom, for, as the voice of the same Bridegroom has declared, we know neither the day nor the hour.

60–61 :　The rules of love which follow are the twelve chief laws:

1. Avoid cupidity like the hateful pest and embrace its opposite.
2. Preserve chastity for the sake of the beloved.
3. Do not knowingly attempt to ruin another properly joined in love.
4. Do not seek the love of one with whom natural shame prohibits your contracting matrimony.
5. Remember that lies are harmful under all conditions.
6. Do not have many go-betweens for your love.
7. Being obedient to the commands of ladies you should always strive to add to the service of love.
8. In giving and receiving the comforts of love chastity ought to sustain modesty.
9. Do not be a slanderer.
10. Do not be a revealer of lovers.
11. In all things behave discreetly and politely.
12. In enjoying the solaces of love do not go beyond the desire of your beloved.

63–64 :　The rules are as follows:

1. The fact of marriage is not a suitable excuse from loving.
2. He who is not jealous cannot love.
3. No one can be bound by a double love.
4. It is well known that love increases or diminishes.
5. It is not wise that the lover obtain something against the will of the beloved.

6. A man should not love unless he has reached full maturity.

7. A two-year widowhood in honor of a dead lover is prescribed for the surviving lover.

8. No one ought to be deprived of his love without just reason.

9. No one can love unless he is urged on by the persuasion of love.

10. Love has always been wont to exile itself from the abodes of avarice.

11. It is not fitting for those to love who are ashamed to seek matrimony.

12. A true lover does not desire the embraces of any other except those springing from the affection of his beloved.

13. Love made known is rarely wont to last.

14. Easy granting renders love contemptible; difficult causes it to be held precious.

15. Every lover is wont to turn pale in the sight of his beloved.

16. The heart of the lover trembles at the sudden appearance of his beloved.

17. New love compels the old to go away.

18. Uprightness alone makes everyone worthy of love.

19. If love abates, it disappears quickly and seldom recovers.

20. The lover is always anxious.

21. A lover's affection is always born of true jealousy.

22. A lover's desire and affection grows greater from the lover's suspicion.

23. He sleeps and eats less whom the thought of love molests.

24. Any act of a lover is limited by the thought of his beloved.

25. The true lover believes nothing good save what he thinks pleases his beloved.

26. Love can deny nothing to love.

27. A lover cannot become satisfied with the solaces of his beloved.

28. Ordinary presumption forces the lover to be wrongly suspected by his beloved.

29. He who is harassed by an excessive abundance of voluptuousness is not wont to love.

30. The true lover is constantly, without interruption, occupied with the mental image of his beloved.

31. It is forbidden for one woman to engage in love with two men, and one man with two women.

CHAPTER V
(ITALY AND *IL DOLCE STIL NUOVO*)

75: Love dwells always in the noble heart.

76: Nature did not create love before the noble heart, nor the noble heart before love.

Thus the lady, like a star, causes the enamorment of the heart which is made by nature true, pure, and noble.

77: For do not give that man trust who may not be noble in spirit, not even if of royal descent, if he does not have a heart noble because of its virtue.

I shall be able to say to him: Love had the likeness of an angel, as though from your kingdom; do not hold me to blame if I loved her.

79: Thus the one Guido snatched from the other the glory of the language [i. e., literary fame]; and perchance is born he who will drive both from the nest.

80: A lady begs me, wherefore I wish to say. . . .

Whence comes love and where is it born? What is its own place where it stays? Is it substance, accident, or memory? Is it caused by the eyes or is it desired by the heart?

Love is born in that part of the mind which is called the memory, thus formed (in the same manner that a diaphanous body gives light) by an obscurity which proceeds from Mars; and there has its abode. It is created and felt, from the natural disposition and from the willingness of the mind.

81: It comes from the observed form of the person who is perceived, so that it takes its dwelling and location in the *intellectus possibilis*, as in the subject.

Love is not a virtue, but derives from that perfection which is not rational but feels.

You may go securely, canzone, wherever you please; for I have so embellished you that your content will be very much praised by those who have understanding: to stand with others, you have no desire.

83:     Flowers hast thou in thyself, and foliage,
  And what is good, and what is glad to see;
 The sun is not so bright as thy visage;
  All is stark naught when one hath looked on thee;
 There is not such a beautiful personage
  Anywhere on the green earth verily;
 If one fear love, thy bearing sweet and sage

Comforteth him, and no more fear hath he.
Thy lady friends and maidens ministering
    Are all, for love of thee, much to my taste:
And much I pray them that in everything
    They honour thee even as thou meritest,
And have thee in their gentle harbouring:
    Because among them all thou art the best.
                                —D. G. Rossetti.

Beauty in woman; the high will's decree;
    Fair knighthood armed for manly exercise;
    The pleasant song of birds; love's soft replies;
The strength of rapid ships upon the sea;
The serene air when light begins to be;
    The white snow, without wind that falls and lies;
    Fields of all flower; the place where waters rise;
Silver and gold; azure in jewellery:—
Weighed against these, the sweet and quiet worth
    Which my dear lady cherishes at heart
        Might seem a little matter to be shown;
    Being truly, over these, as much apart
As the whole heaven is greater than this earth.
    All good to kindred natures cleaveth soon.
                                —D. G. Rossetti.

84 : And you know well that I am Love, I who allow you my likeness and bear your every thought.

Subtle the spirit striking through the eyes
Which rouseth up a spirit in the mind
Whence moves a spirit unto love inclined
Which breeds, in other sprites, nobilities.
No turbid spirit hath the sense which sees
How greatly empowered a spirit he appeareth;
He is the little breath which that breath feareth,
Which breedeth virginal humilities.
Yet from this spirit doth another move
Wherein such tempered sweetness rightly dwells
That Mercy's spirit followeth his ways,
And Mercy's spirit as it moves above
Rains down those spirits that ope all things else,
Perforce of One who seeth all of these.
                                —Ezra Pound.

85–86 : Who is she coming, drawing all men's gaze,
Who makes the air one trembling clarity
Till none can speak but each sighs piteously
Where she leads Love adown her trodden ways?

Ah God! The thing she's like when her glance strays,
Let Amor tell. 'Tis no fit speech for me.
Mistress she seems of such great modesty
That every other woman were called "Wrath."

No one could ever tell the charm she hath
For all the noble powers bend toward her,
She being beauty's godhead manifest.

Our daring ne'er before held such high quest;
But ye! There is not in you so much grace
That we can understand her rightfully.
                                        —Ezra Pound.

CHAPTER VI
(COURTLY LOVE IN *IL FILOSTRATO*)
Il Filostrato

93 : Proem: A young man fervently loveth a lady as touching whom nothing else is granted him by Fortune except sometimes to see her, or sometimes to talk of her, or sweetly to meditate upon her in his thoughts. Which now of these three things giveth the greatest delight?
Proem: And this hath saddened my soul so far beyond any proper limit that I can clearly appreciate how great was the happiness, though little realized by me at the time, that came to me from the gracious and beautiful sight of you.
I, 5: Thou art imaged in my sad breast with such strength that thou hast more power there than I.

94 : I, 29: Nor did he . . . perceive that Love with his darts dwelt within the rays of those lovely eyes.
I, 33: And he began to go over again in his mind the pleasure he had felt that morning at the sight of Cressida.
I, 39: Thou takest thy station in her eyes, true lord, as in a place worthy of thy power. Therefore if my service at all pleaseth thee, I beseech thee obtain from them the healing of my soul.
I, 41: And imagined he would draw from her fair eyes water soothing to his intense ardor. Therefore he made cunning attempt to see them often, nor did he perceive that by them the fire was kindled the more.
II, 58: Whilst it calleth ever for that sweet peace which the fair and lovely eyes of this lady, dear lord, can alone give it.

95 : II, 86: Cressida hath with her fair eyes so taken away my life. . . .

II, 98: The splendor of thy lovely eyes.

III, 36: You thrust into my heart darts of love so fiery that I am all inflamed by them. . . . You hold me and ever will hold me in Love's net, bright eyes of mine.

V, 63: There is no comfort, Love, to my griefs save only death, when I find myself parted from those fair eyes in which I have once seen thee.

I, 31: Keeping his desire well hidden.

I, 36: First proposing to hide the ardor conceived in his amorous mind from every friend and attendant, unless it were necessary. . . .

96: II, 8: And I pray thee by the gods, if thou hast any fidelity to our love, that thou discover not this desire to anyone else, because much trouble might follow me on that account.

II, 26: But as long as desire hath been checked in its action and everything like unto it held secret, it seemeth to me reasonable to maintain that each lover may follow his high desires, provided only he be discreet in deed and in semblance. . . .

II, 28: And give you each equal comfort, provided you undertake to keep it secret. . . . Be thou discreet then in keeping such doings concealed from others.

97: II, 74: So the joy of love, when hidden, ever surpasseth that of the husband held perpetually in arms.

II, 69: If perchance regard for my reputation forbid it me, I shall be prudent and keep my desire so hidden that it will not be known that I have ever entertained love in my heart.

II, 77: If it be discovered openly, thou canst regard thy reputation, which heretofore hath been excellent, as lost for ever.

II, 140: But if any request have value in thy sight, I pray thee, sweet and dear my brother, that all that each of us hath said and done, be kept secret.

II, 141: Guard thy lips, for neither he, on his part, nor I will ever tell it.

II, 143: See only that he be prudent and know well how to conceal his desires.

98: III, 15: Nevertheless I swear to thee by the gods . . . thou canst rest assured that in so far as in me lieth, this secret will repose within my breast and that in every act will be safeguarded the honor of that lady who hath wounded my heart.

III, 43: Now is it time to arise, if we wish to conceal our desire.

IV, 153: For if, as now, we wish our love to last, it must ever lie concealed.

I, 48: But this is sufficiently clear and manifest, that in no respect did she seem to care for Troilus and for the love that he bore her, but remained unmoved as one not loved.

I, 53: But she for whom thou weepest feeleth naught any more than a stone, and remaineth as cold as ice which hardens beneath a clear sky, and I waste away like snow before the fire.

99: II, 74: Receive the sweet lover, who hath come to thee at the certain behest of the gods, and give satisfaction to his burning desire.

II, 129: If I understand her, Love constraineth her, but as a guilty person she still goeth skulking behind the shield. But if Love give me strength to suffer, she cannot delay long before coming to quite different speech.

II, 82: Not harsh nor forbidding did she show herself toward Troilus as he looked at her, but at all times cast toward him modest glances over her right shoulder.

100: I, 47: Already had love taken from him his sleep, and diminished his food, and so increased his anxiety that now in his face pallor bore witness thereof. . . .

VII, 19: He ate but little and naught did he drink, so full of anguish was his sad heart. And beside this he could not sleep, except his sleep were broken by sighs, and his life and himself he held utterly in contempt, and pleasure he shunned as fire, and likewise he avoided as much as he might every festivity and every company.

II, 57: My Lord, already in my visage and in my sighs appeareth that which I feel in my heart by reason of the gentle longing which hath seized me because of her beauty.

101: II, 116: For if I let it multiply into too great heat, my hidden desire might appear in my colorless face, which would be no small disgrace to me.

VI, 1: In bitter tears were spent her nights, for by day it was more fitting for her to use precaution, for the fresh and delicate cheeks had grown wan and thin. She was far from her sweet well-being.

102: III, 1: O shining light, whose rays have thus far guided me, as through the halls of Love I took my winged way, now is it fitting that thy redoubled radiance guide my invocation and make it such that the benefits of the sweet reign of Love may in every particular appear set forth by me.

II, 80: Praised be thy supreme power, fair Venus, and that of thy son Love.

I, 34: And thought it would be a great good fortune to love such a lady, and a better still if by long attention he might bring it to pass that nearly as much as he loved her he might by her be loved, or at least not be rejected as suitor.

I, 43: None beside thee can make me joyful; thou alone art she who canst help me.

103: I, 46: And for Love's sake, if the tale speaketh truth, he became so fierce and strong in arms that the Greeks feared him as death.

III, 90: And Love, of whom he was faithful servant, granted him this courage, so much more dauntless than usual.

III, 92: All his talk was of love or of gentle behavior, and full of courtesy. He delighted much to honor the valiant and likewise to cast forth the cowards. It ever pleased him to behold honors bestowed upon youths of modest grace. And he considered lost every one without love, of whatsoever station he might be.

104: III, 93: And though he was of royal blood and could, had he wished, have enjoyed much power, he made himself agreeable to all equally, although many a time a man did not deserve it. So wished Love, which is all-powerful, that he should act so as to please others. Pride, envy, and avarice he held in hatred and deferreth to everyone.

We declare that it could scarcely happen that rustics might be found enrolled in the court of love; like the horse and the mule they are moved to the works of Venus as the impulse of nature dictates. Therefore steady labor is enough for the peasant, and the solace of the ploughshare and the hoe, uninterrupted and without respite, [suffices].

105: IV, 48: Therefore if we lose this lady, many others shall we find.

IV, 51: From her eyes darted the sparks that inflamed me with the fire of love. Passing by the thousands through mine eyes, they brought love with them gently into my heart, where it felt them to its pleasure. Here they first enkindled the fire the exceeding heat of which hath been the cause of every excellent thing in me.

107: *Ars Amatoria*, 367-72: Let her maid incite her, as she combs her tresses in the morning, and add the help of an oarsman to the sail, and let her say, sighing softly to herself, "But, methinks, you will not be able to pay him back yourself." Then let her speak of you, then add persuasive words, and swear that you are dying of frantic love.

109: V, 32: Drive away dreams and fears. Let them go into the winds that they are. They proceed from melancholy and cause thee to see what thou fearest. God alone knoweth the truth of what will be. Dreams and auguries, to which stupid people pay heed, amount to nothing nor have they little or much to do with the future.

VII, 40: No one there was nor is nor ever will be who can with certainty well interpret what fancy can show forth with varied forms in the sleep of another, and many indeed have believed one thing while another opposite and contrary thereto came to pass.

III, 31 : Mirror mine, the newly wed are bashful the first night.

113 : *Inferno*, V, 127–38: For pastime's sake we one day read about Lancelot, how love constrained him; we were alone and without any fear of discovery. . . . When we read how the loving smile was kissed by such a lover, he who will never be separated from me kissed my mouth all trembling. Galehault was the book and he who wrote it [the book and he who wrote it were to us as Galehault was to Lancelot and Guenevere] ; that day we read no more.

308 : *Tristia*, IV, ix, 21–24: Whatever I say shall pass to the
(n. 9) setting sun from its rising and the East shall bear witness to the voice of the West. Across the land, across deep waters I shall be heard, and mighty shall be the cry of my lament.

ABBREVIATIONS EMPLOYED IN THE NOTES AND BIBLIOGRAPHY

Arch	Archiv für das Studium der neueren Sprachen und Literaturen
JEGP	Journal of English and Germanic Philology
LitBl	Literaturblatt für germanische und romanische Philologie
MLN	Modern Language Notes
MLR	Modern Language Review
MP	Modern Philology
NSM	Nuova studi medievali
PMLA	Publications of the Modern Language Association of America
PQ	Philological Quarterly
RR	Romanic Review
SP	Studies in Philology
ZsfRPh	Zeitschrift für romanische Philologie
ZsfFSpruL	Zeitschrift für französische Sprache und Literatur

NOTES

CHAPTER I (OVID)

[1] *Epic and Romance: Essays on Medieval Literature* (London, 1897), p. 395.

[2] *Ibid.*, p. 396.

[3] Stephen Gaselee, *The Transition from the Late Latin Lyric to the Medieval Love Poem* (Cambridge, 1931), p. 33.

[4] Philip S. Allen, *Medieval Latin Lyrics* (Chicago, 1931), p. 325.

[5] Ovid's position in the later Middle Ages is thus described by Edgar Martini in his *Einleitung zu Ovid* (Brünn, 1933), p. 82: "Naturgemäss erregten seine erotischen Dichtungen am meisten Teilnahme und Bewunderung. Seine Ars galt geradezu als eine Art Regel—und Sittenbuch für die höfische Gesellschaft. In dem 'Liebeskonzil von Remiremont,' einer Dichtung des 12. Jhs., wird sie von einer der anwesenden Damen verlesen. Er selbst aber wurde als der hohe Meister weltmännischer Lebenskunst und als unvergleichlicher *Praeceptor amoris* in fast abgöttischer Weise verehrt."

[6] Cf. C. B. West, *Courtoisie in Anglo-Norman Literature* (Oxford, 1938), pp. 6-7: "While the troubadours' acquaintance with Ovid appears to be superficial, his influence on courtois writers, such as the author of the *Eneas* and Chrétien de Troyes, is undoubted. The idea of writing about an 'art of love' at all may be traced to some extent to the author of the *Ars amatoria*, whom the Middle Ages treated on the whole with reverence, as a fount of wisdom and solid principles. Fundamentally, however, the attitude of the courtly lover is probably more in harmony with contemporary religious feeling than with the spirit of Ovid. The cynical advice of the *Ars amatoria* reveals a conception of love so far removed from the seriousness of amour courtois, which both requires and confers nobility of heart and mind, that it is difficult to believe that the actual doctrine of courtly love owes much to Ovid. His influence may no doubt be traced to some extent in the analysis, characteristic of courtly literature, of mental and emotional states, as well as in the conventional descriptions of lovers' symptoms, but the habit of analysis and introspection, though much older than Christianity and independent of it, is in accordance with the Church's teaching as to the duty of self-examination and with the mode of thought of the twelfth and thirteenth centuries, that is to say, with scholasticism."

[7] E. K. Rand, *Ovid and His Influence* (Boston, 1925), p. 121.

⁸ For most of these passages I am indebted to the illuminating article by F. E. Guyer, "The Influence of Ovid on Crestien de Troyes," *RR*, XII (1921), 97 ff.

⁹ Cf. *Ars Amatoria*, I, 17 : "ego sum praeceptor amoris." It is perhaps worth noting that Ovid felt his work would endure ; cf. *Tristia*, IV, ix, 21–24 :

> ibit ad occasum quicquid dicemus ab ortu,
> testis et Hesperiae vocus Eous erit.
> trans ego tellurem, trans altas audiar undas,
> et gemitus vox est magna futura mei.

¹⁰ The editions used are those in the Loeb Classical Library ; cf. bibliography. The appendix (pp. 287–304) contains translations of all literary quotations to be found in this chapter as well as for those which appear in succeeding chapters.

¹¹ W. A. Neilson, *The Origins and Sources of the Court of Love* (Boston, 1899), p. 171.

¹² *Ibid.*, p. 172.

¹³ F. A. Wright, *The Mirror of Venus* (London, 1925), pp. 7–8.

CHAPTER II (THE TROUBADOURS)

¹ *Eros: the Development of the Sex Relation through the Ages* (New York, 1915), p. 130.

² *Ibid.*, pp. 131–32.

³ *The Dark Ages* (Edinburgh, 1904), p. 6.

⁴ *Italian Social Customs of the Sixteenth Century and Their Influence on the Literatures of Europe* (New Haven, 1920), pp. 6–7.

⁵ *Medieval Culture: an Introduction to Dante and His Times* (New York, 1929), I, 299–300.

⁶ Though I have used many separate editions of the individual poets, I have tried in the following pages to restrict my references to the better-known and more generally available collections, such as Appel's *Provenzalische Chrestomathie*, Bartsch's *Chrestomathie provençale*, and Mahn's *Die Werke der Troubadours*. In the case of Bernart de Ventadorn all references are to the monumental edition by Appel ; Roman numerals indicate the number of the poem, Arabic the lines. Quotations from Appel's *Chrestomathie* are also indicated by poem and line. In using Mahn's collection (abbreviated here to MW) it has seemed less confusing to give the references to volume and page. Reference to Bartsch is by page and line. For complete titles, editions used, et cetera, consult bibliography.

⁷ Cf. Hennig Brinkmann, *Entstehungsgeschichte des Minnesangs* (Halle, 1926), p. 56: "Kennwort für sinnlichen Genuss ist *joi*. Wilhelm IX. schon zeigt es in ausgeprägtem Sinn, bei Bernart von Ventadorn ist es geradezu Symbol seiner weltfrohen Einstellung zum Diesseits. Immer wieder wird *joi* als Genuss—und Liebesfreude gepriesen

und verkündet. Der Bergriff 'sinnliche Freude' steht auch im Mittel-
punkt der Vagantenlyrik, nur nicht um ein bestimmtes Wort konzen-
triert."
[8] For further instances cf. XXI, 25–32; XXXIII, 8–11; I, 9–12;
XVII, 41–48. Yet love may also induce the opposite feeling: XXXIX,
9–12; XXXI, 17–20; for the two combined (the sorrow of love itself
a joy) see XLIV, 69–72.
[9] The older criticism (cf., e. g., Diez, *passim*) tended, on the whole,
to accept the poetry on its face value—obviously a dangerous assumption. More recent critics are inclined to err in the opposite direction;
representative is this observation by Stanislas Stronski in his edition
of Elias de Barjols, p. xlix: "Des 'chansons d'amour,' dit-on. Il serait
plus exact de dire des 'chansons sur l'amour.' On est d'accord pour
regarder presque toutes les poésies des troubadours comme des pro-
duits de la tête et non pas de la coeur." Obviously neither position is
entirely correct. We know so little about the private lives of the
troubadours (in spite of the biographies) that it is folly to say cate-
gorically that a given poem is or is not the result of a poet's own
experience; it may be; but could it not also be the result of observation or of the imagination or even of an experience related by someone else? The ways of poetic composition are so varied and intricate
that any unqualified general statement is dangerous. Personally I feel
that Provençal poetry, like any other, presents the greatest variety;
it is both possible and desirable to distinguish the lyrics which are the
expression of genuine feeling from those which are the result of purely
artificial emotion. Bernart de Ventadorn, Arnaut Daniel, and Bertran
de Born are just as genuine and personal, for the most part, as many
of their successors are not; cf. L. F. Mott, *The System of Courtly
Love Studied as an Introduction to the Vita Nuova of Dante* (Boston,
1896), pp. 16 ff. A wise discussion of this matter is that by Eduard
Wechssler in his *Das Kulturproblem des Minnesangs*, I, 213–14; see
also his article, "Frauendienst und Vassallität," *ZsfFSpruL*, XXIV,
159–90, esp. pp. 186–90.
[10] *Euphorion: Being Studies of the Antique and the Medieval in
the Renaissance* (London, 1894), II, 147.
[11] Bernart de Ventadorn was the poet par excellence of this doctrine; more than that of any other troubadour, his was a life of unwavering devotion to Amor. One of his editors eulogizes him quite
correctly in these words (*vide* Appel's edition, p. lxxi): "Bernart ist
der Typus des Trobadors mit all seinen schönen Zügen schwärmer-
ischen Empfindens, blühenden und zarten Ausdrucks, begeisterter
Huldigung des Weibes, völliger Hingabe an die Minne, aber auch
mit der ganzen Einseitigkeit dieses Charakters. Keiner der hervor-
ragenden Trobadors ist so einzig und allein Minnedichter, ohne
einen Gedanken an die Händel dieser oder an die Ansprüche einer
anderen Welt, ohne ein Wort der Politik oder der Sittenlehre oder der
Frömmigkeit in seinem ganzen Werk."

[12] Cf. the excellent article by Wechssler, "Frauendienst und Vassallität," referred to above.

[13] Cf. Wechssler, *Das Kulturproblem des Minnesangs*, I, 270: "Es ist eine alte und täglich neue Erfahrung, dass religiöse und erotische Gefühle in der Seele des Menschen sich eng verbinden und die einen für die andern eintreten können. . . . Indem der Frauensänger der Herrin eine mystische Liebe widmete, setzte er voraus, dass die Geliebte, als wäre sie ein Wesen göttlicher Art, göttliche Verehrung verdiene. Ausdrücklich erwies er der Herrin eine Anbetung, *azorar*, die ihren Ursprung und Sinn im religiösen Leben hatte: Anbetung empfingen vom glaübigen Christen nur Gott, Christus, der hl. Geist, Maria, die Engel und die Heiligen. Viele Minnelieder erscheinen in Stimmung und Haltung wie Gebete frommer Andacht an eine Heilige. Darum wurde es nachher auch möglich, Minnelieder ohne wesentliche Abänderungen oder ganz unverändert auf die Jungfrau Maria zu beziehen. Das ist ein überzeugender Beweis dafür, wie stark das religiöse Element in einem grossen Teil besonders des späteren Minnesangs entwickelt war."

Wechssler's thorough discussion of this phase of the subject is stimulating; see especially chapters XI, XII, and XIII ("Minne und christlicher Spiritualismus," "Minne und christliche Mystik," and "Frauenverehrung und Heiligenkult" respectively).

[14] As a corrective to Schrötter's study see the lengthy article by D. Scheludko, "Ovid und die Trobadors," *ZsfRPh*, LIV (1934), 129–74; cf. esp. p. 172: "Es kann keinem Zweifel unterliegen, dass auch viele andere Trobadors die antike Dichtung im allgemeinen und Ovid im besonderen gekannt haben. Aber unmittelbare Beeinflussung lässt sich kaum nachweisen."

[15] *LitBl*, XXX (1909), 63–65.

[16] *Op. cit.*, p. 48.

[17] Mott, *The Provençal Lyric* (New York, n.d.), pp. 2–3: "What was the source of this efflorescence? Where did it first bud? In what popular element did it strike its roots? These are still matters of learned speculation. What seems practically certain is the fact that no external impulse generated this poetry or influenced its early growth. It stands absolutely by itself. Classic literature, which had continued more or less to occupy the attention of the learned few, had no part in its origin or development. It was the spontaneous product of the conditions surrounding its birth."

[18] *Ibid.*, pp. 56–57: "It was no problem poetry, as so much of our recent verse tends to be. Limited in range, and appealing to the fancy rather than to the heart, it produced no surpassing singer, no Burns, no Heine. But its influence still survives. Like a butterfly among the flowers, it flourished for its brief season, and then perished utterly. And yet, in the artistic impulse which it gave to poetic endeavor, in the civilizing and, with all its faults, elevating influence which it exerted upon European ideals, and in the passionate, tender and brave

romance with which it has gifted succeeding generations, the Provençal lyric remains, and must remain, a precious—in truth, an invalu-
able—contribution to universal literature."

CHAPTER III (CHRÉTIEN DE TROYES)

[1] *Un grand romancier d'amour et d'aventure au XIIe siècle: Chrétien de Troyes et son oeuvre* (Paris, 1931), p. 32.

[2] *Ibid.,* p. 20.

[3] "Des rapports de la poésie des trouvères avec celle des troubadours," *Romania,* XIX (1890), 3.

[4] "Études sur les romans de la Table Ronde. Lancelot du Lac.
II : La Conte de la Charette," *Romania,* XII (1883), 523.

[5] *Ibid.,* p. 523.

[6] Myrrha Borodine, *La femme et l'amour au XIIe siècle d'après les
poèmes de Chrétien de Troyes* (Paris, 1909), p. 280. This conclusion
is further strengthened by the words of Gaston Paris (*op. cit.,* p. 534) :
"Marie, avec sa mère Alienor, avec ses contemporaines Aeliz de France
et Ermenjart de Narbonne, a été l'une des principales instigatrices
d'un mouvement mondain qui se produisit dans la seconde moitié du
XIIe siècle et qui a pour principaux caractères le rapprochement de la
poèsie du Nord et de celle du Midi et la conception d'un amour raffiné,
savant, intimement lié à la courtoisie et à la prouesse, et donnant à la
femme, entant que maîtresse, une importance qu'elle n'avait pas eue
jusque-là. Cet amour est précisément l'inspiration du poème de Chrétien, qui l'a peint, tel que l'avait conçu la théorie de ces cercles élégants,
dans la liaison de Lancelot et de Guenièvre."

[7] "Chrestien de Troyes's Attitude towards Woman," *RR,* XVI
(1925), 236, 238, 241.

[8] Mott, *The System of Courtly Love,* p. 24.

[9] Quotations from Chrétien are from the edition by Wendelin Foers-
ter, *Christian von Troyes sämtliche erhaltene Werke,* Halle, 1884–99
(*Cligés,* 1884; *Der Löwenritter* [*Yvain*], 1887; *Der Karrenritter*
[*Lancelot*] *und das Wilhelmsleben* [*Guillaume d'Angleterre*], 1899).

[10] Mott, *The System of Courtly Love,* p. 28.

[11] *Vide supra,* p. 34.

[12] T. P. Cross and W. A. Nitze, *Lancelot and Guenevere: a Study
on the Origins of Courtly Love* (Chicago, 1930), chap. III, esp. pp.
64–65.

[13] For representative passages cf., e. g., *Cligés:* Beauty as cause of
love: 2730–42; 2761–65; 2813–16. Eyes as the medium of love:
464 ff.; 592–94; 700 ff. Love a sickness: 869–72; 637–39. Love a god
with arrows: 460–61; 692–94. Sighing, trembling, etc.: 541–44;
1590–98. Sleeplessness: 876–84. Love incurable: 646–52. Instances of
this type could be almost indefinitely extended; see, e. g., Mott's *The
System of Courtly Love* or Neilson's *The Origins and Sources of the
Court of Love;* or, better yet, the romances themselves. With regard

to Chrétien's imagery one could not do better than to recall the conclusion of Cross and Nitze, *op. cit.*, p. 97: "Chrétien's imagery comes from other than Provençal sources. . . . In this respect his great master was Ovid."

[14] Since *Erec and Enid* is so far below and *Perceval* so far above the courtly ideal, these romances find no place in this discussion.

[15] *Op. cit.*, pp. 278–79.

[16] Cohen, *op. cit.*, p. 282.

[17] Paris, *op. cit.*, p. 517.

[18] *Vide supra*, p. 23.

[19] *Op. cit.*, pp. 96–97.

[20] Cf. p. 34 *supra* and n. 4.

[21] *Op. cit.*, pp. 518–19.

[22] Indeed, rarely if ever is it possible to take a given poem and state that it does or does not conform to the courtly ideal; practically every poem contains deviations from the courtly system, yet fully deserves to be considered a courtly love document.

[23] *Op. cit.*, p. 4.

[24] "The Influence of Ovid on Crestien de Troyes," *RR*, XII (1921), 225.

[25] Paris, *op. cit.*, p. 520.

[26] *Op. cit.*, pp. 97–98.

CHAPTER IV (ANDREAS CAPELLANUS)

[1] Cross and Nitze, *op. cit.*, p. 68: "It makes little difference how much after 1174 scholars date the *De Amore*, the fact is that Andreas' concept of love and that of Chrétien just about coincide. . . ."

[2] On these points see the generally accepted views of E. Trojel in the *Praefatio* to his edition, *Andreae Capellani regii Francorum de amore libri tres* (Havniae, 1892), esp. pp. i–xii; all references to Andreas in subsequent pages will be to this edition. For a summary of recent scholarly opinion on Andreas cf. Max Manitius, *Geschichte der lateinischen Literatur des Mittelalters* (München, 1931), III, 282–86.

[3] *De Amore*, p. 3: "Est igitur primo videre, quid sit amor, et unde dicatur amor, et quis sit effectus amoris, et inter quos possit esse amor, qualiter acquiratur amor, retineatur, augmentetur, minuatur, finiatur et de notitia amoris mutui, et quid unus amantium agere debeat altero fidem fallente."

[4] For a possible explanation of this fact cf. Martin Grabmann, "Das Werk *De Amore* des Andreas Capellanus und das Verurteilungsdekret des Bischofs Stephan Tempier von Paris vom 7. März 1277," *Speculum*, VII (1932), 79: "Sein Verfahren erinnert hier an die Methode der doppleten Wahrheit bei den Philosophen des lateinischen Averroismus, welche zuerst eine mit den Lehren des christlichen Glaubens in Widerspruch stehende These . . . eingehend begründen

und die dagegen vorgebrachten Einwände entkräften und so daraus, dass sie dieser Lehre zustimmen, kein Hehl machen, dann aber die Glaubenslehre augenscheinlich aus Erwägungen der Vorsicht danebenstellen." Yet it may be equally well explained on the grounds of literary precedent of long standing; cf. the *Ars Amatoria* and the *Remedia Amoris*.

[5] Andreas, *op. cit.*, pp. 360–61.

[6] *Ibid.*, p. 14: "Qualiter amor acquiratur et quot modis."

[7] *Ibid.*, p. 14: "formae venustate, morum probitate, copiosa sermonis facundia, divitiarum abundantia et facili rei petitae concessione."

[8] *Op. cit.*, p. 18: "Sola ergo probitas amoris est digna corona. Sermonis facundia multotiens ad amandum non amantium corda compellit. Ornatum etenim amantis eloquium amoris consvevit concitare aculeos et de loquentis facit probitate praesumi. Quod qualiter fiat, quam brevi potero, curabo tibi sermone narrare."

[9] Cf. pp. 63–64 *infra*.

[10] *Op. cit.*, p. 85: "firmum etenim est et totius meae mentis propositum Veneris me nunquam supponere servituti nec amantium me poenis subiicere."

[11] *Ibid.*, p. 88: "In vanum ergo laboras, quia mundus universus me non posset ab isto proposito revocare."

[12] *Ibid.*, p. 90: ". . . illae mulieres communes, quae neminem reiiciunt, sed omnes indifferenter admittunt et universorum sunt expositae voluptati."

[13] *Ibid.*, p. 91: "Mulier ait: Intra septentrionalem portam me profiteor esse securam, non maledictam."

[14] *Ibid.*, p. 103: "Nam totus amoenitatis locus istarum est voluptatibus assignatus, et cuiuslibet coram eis generis ludebant ioculatores atque psallebant, et omnia instrumentorum ibi musicae genera resonabant."

[15] *Ibid.*, p. 104: ". . . quae tibi praecipiet, studeas diligenter attendere."

[16] *Ibid.*, pp. 105–6.

[17] *Ibid.*, p. 153: "Dicimus enim et stabilito tenore firmamus, amorem non posse suas inter duos iugales extendere vires."

[18] *Ibid.*, p. 154: ". . . vera inter eos zelotypia inveniri non potest, sine qua verus amor esse non valet ipsius amoris norma testante, quae dicit: 'Qui non zelat, amare non potest.'" For this rule cf. *infra*, p. 63, rule II.

[19] *Ibid.*, p. 154: "Hoc igitur nostrum iudicium cum nimia moderatione prolatum et aliarum quam plurimarum dominarum consilio roboratum pro indubitabili vobis sit ac veritate constanti."

[20] Chapter VII, "De amore clericorum"; VIII, "De amore monacharum"; XI, "De amore rusticorum"; XII, "De amore meretricum." IX, "De amore per pecuniam acquisto"; X, "De facili rei petitae concessione."

[21] *Vide supra*, p. 57.

[22] *Op. cit.*, pp. 308–9: "Haec est enim chartula, in qua regulae scribuntur amoris, quas ipse amoris rex ore proprio amaboribus edidit. Hanc te asportare oportet et regulas amantibus indicare, si pacificum volueris accipitrem reportare."

[23] *Ibid.*, pp. 309–12.

[24] *Ibid.*, p. 312: "Singuli etiam, qui ad curiam vocati convenerant, regulas iam dictas in scriptis reportaverunt et eas per diversas mundi partes cunctis amantibus ediderunt."

[25] Cf. pp. 28–29, 68, 69, 86, 98, 118.

[26] Cf. p. 54; and further, pp. 15, 16–17, 18, 58, 135, 170, 198, 311 (XVIII).

[27] Grabmann, *op. cit.*, p. 77.

[28] See also pp. 18, 208, 264.

[29] *Vide supra*, p. 19.

[30] Other instances in Andreas: pp. 141–42, 172, 280, 290.

[31] A number of such parallels are pointed out by Cross and Nitze, *op. cit.*, pp. 6, 7, 8, 13, 67, 68, 70, 72, 73, 74.

[32] Cf. H. Fauriel, *Histoire littéraire de la France* (Paris, 1895), XXI, 323–24: "Ainsi donc, et c'est là un point important à noter d'abord, rien d'essentiel, rien de caractéristique dans toute cette théorie héroïque de l'amour, n'est une pure fiction, encore moins une fiction de l'auteur. Il ne s'y trouve pas un principe, pas un trait significatif qui appartienne en propre au chapelain. Tout ce qu'il y dit, il le dit d'après son temps; il l estrait d'opinions et de doctrine alors répandues parmi les hautes classes de la société féodale. En un mot, l'ouvrage, appelé aussi Fleur d'Amour, n'est guère qu'une amplification, qu'un commentaire de ce qu'il y a, dans la poésie amoureuse du même temps, de plus relevé, de plus original et de plus piquant. C'est la métaphysique sentimentale des troubadours systématiquement délayée en prose dialoguée. Les idées, les maximes que ces poëtes ont jetées et fondues avec plus ou moins de grâce et d'harmonie dans les tableaux de leur vie et de leurs aventures, sont ici présentées sous une forme abstraite."

Discussion of the much debated existence or nonexistence of the courts of love is hardly relevant to this study. But there can be no doubt of their reality; cf. Paris, *op. cit.*, p. 529; Manitius, *op. cit.*, p. 284; Amy Kelly, "Eleanor of Aquitaine and Her Courts of Love," *Speculum*, XII (1937), 3–19.

CHAPTER V (ITALY AND *IL DOLCE STIL NUOVO*)

[1] *Italian Social Customs of the Sixteenth Century*, p. 99.

[2] *Il duecento* (Milano, 1930), p. 114.

[3] *Die sizilianische Dichterschule des dreizehnten Jahrhunderts* (Berlin, 1878), p. 113. Cf. also the quotation on pp. 72–73 *infra*.

[4] *The History of Early Italian Literature to the Death of Dante* (London, 1901), pp. 59–60.

[5] *Euphorion*, II, 80.

[6] Basic for this study have been the works of Azzolina, Savj-Lopez, De Sanctis, Gaspary, Vossler, and Wechssler; cf. bibliography.

[7] *Medieval Culture*, II, 72.

[8] Giorgio Parenti, *La personalità storica di Guido Guinizelli* (Firenze, 1914), pp. 243–45. Subsequent references to the poetry of Guinicelli will be to this volume, where the texts of the *canzone* are to be found on pp. 238–80. See also the text and commentary by Flaminio Pellegrini, "La 'Canzone d'Amore' di Guido Guinizelli," *NSM*, I (1923), 119–37. This text is less conservative but in some respects more satisfactory than Parenti's.

[9] *The History of Early Italian Literature*, p. 101.

[10] *Ibid.*, pp. 101–2.

[11] *Guido Cavalcanti e le sue rime* (Livorno, 1885), p. 105.

[12] Guglielmo Volpi, *Il trecento* (Milano, n.d.), p. 9.

[13] Ercole Rivalta, *Le rime di Guido Cavalcanti* (Bologna, 1902), pp. 123–26. All references are to this edition. Also extremely useful is the earlier edition by Pietro Ercole, *ed. cit.;* the commentary is particularly complete and often illuminating.

[14] Ercole, *ed. cit.*, p. 112: "La Canzone filosofica merita un esame a parte, poichè essa non è veramente una lirica amorosa, nel senso che esprima sentimenti di Guido per una donna, ma è piuttosto l'esposizione di tutta la teoria che Guido dagli studii suoi filosofici e dalle dottrine neo-platoniche s'era formata sulla natura a sull' origine del sentimento dell' amore."

[15] According to one of his editors (Ercole, p. 119) the poem is to be regarded as "un trattato metafisico, non come una poesia."

[16] *The History of Early Italian Literature*, p. 208.

[17] *Medieval Culture*, II, 147.

[18] Cf. the *ballate:* "Posso de gli occhi miei novella dire" (154, ll. 11 ff.), and "Fresca rosa novella" (110, ll. 19 ff.).

[19] *Ed. cit.*, p. 132.

[20] *Vide supra*, p. 83.

[21] *The System of Courtly Love*, pp. 129–53.

[22] Vossler, *Medieval Culture*, II, 163.

[23] Cf., e. g., Konrad Burdach, "Über den Ursprung des mittelalterlichen Minnesangs, Liebesromans und Frauendienstes," *Sitzungsberichten der Berliner Akademie* (1918), pp. 994 ff. and 1072 ff., who favors the Arabian influence, and Hennig Brinkmann, *Entstehungsgeschichte des Minnesangs*, p. 34: "Minnethema und Minnedienst sind in der mittellateinischen Literatur aus christlichen Kulturkreis entwickelt. Erst später wirkt fremder Einfluss ein."

[24] There is no such thing as a history of courtly love; perhaps the most lucid brief account in English is the first chapter of C. S. Lewis's *The Allegory of Love* (Oxford, 1936), pp. 1–43.

[25] An indispensable study of this type is Eduard Wechssler's *Das Kulturproblem des Minnesangs;* cf. *supra,* p. 24 and n. 13. Étienne Gilson in *La théologie mystique de Saint Bernard* (Paris, 1934) supplements and corrects many of Wechssler's views; cf. Appendix IV (pp. 193–215), "St. Bernard et l'amour courtois."

CHAPTER VI (COURTLY LOVE IN
IL FILOSTRATO)

[1] N. E. Griffin and A. B. Myrick, *The Filostrato of Giovanni Boccaccio* (Philadelphia, 1929), p. 24. The admirable introduction is by Mr. Griffin; I am heavily indebted to his excellent discussion of the *Filostrato* as a courtly love document (pp. 70–95). In the following pages all references to the text will be made by canto and stanza number (which numbering, it may be noted, is the same as that of the Moutier edition). Page references will be to Mr. Griffin's introduction.

[2] *Ibid.,* pp. 70–71.

[3] *Ibid.,* p. 72.

[4] Cf. the *donnejaire* in *Arch,* XXXIV (1863), 425, ll. 95–99; Griffin, *op. cit.,* pp. 72 ff.

[5] Cf. *supra,* pp. 91–92.

[6] Edward Hutton, *Giovanni Boccaccio: a Biographical Study* (London, 1910), p. 21.

[7] *La giovanezza di G. Boccaccio* (Città di Castello, 1905), p. 118.

[8] Cf. *supra,* p. 63, rule XIII.

[9] Cf. *supra,* p. 61, rule VI.

[10] Cf. *infra,* pp. 106 ff.

[11] Cf. *supra,* p. 95; also p. 63, rule XIII.

[12] *Ibid.,* rule XIV.

[13] For other examples cf. II, 23, 64, 103, 124, 134. Less interesting but somewhat similar is Criseida's conduct toward Diomede in VI, 13, 29, 34.

[14] Cf. also II, 117, 139; III, 3.

[15] Cf. *supra,* p. 63, rules XV and XXIII.

[16] Cf. *supra,* pp. 8–12.

[17] Cf. *supra,* chap. II, esp. pp. 19–27.

[18] Cf. this description of Boccaccio's treatment of love in *Il Filostrato:* "Les deux amants savourent avec délice leur bonheur, et Boccace le savoure avec eux, dans des descriptions très voluptueuses, qui occupent la plus large place dans la troisième partie de son roman; on sent que son imagination était hantée par certaines visions, dont il ne pouvait se ressasier. Cela ne constitue certes pas une poèsie très saine; mais cette passion sensuelle est exprimée avec une franchise qui est fort eloignée des réticences affectées, des fausses pudeurs, des sous-entendus indélicats ou des ricanements indécents que d'autres con-

teurs ont mis à la mode; ce réalisme est aussi étranger à la grossièreté qu'à la grivoiserie. Pour Boccace, l'amour a un caractère sacré; il n'y trouve pas le moindre sujet de risée, rien à ses yeux n'est plus beau, plus fort, plus vrai; il joue dans sa poésie le même rôle que le nu dans les arts plastiques."—Henri Hauvette, *Boccace: Étude biographique et littéraire* (Paris, 1914), pp. 85–86.

[19] Griffin and Myrick, *ed. cit.*, III, 92; the translation appears on p. 283.

[20] *De Amore*, p. 235.

[21] *Ed. cit.*, pp. 94–95.

[22] *The Medieval Society Romances* (New York, 1924), p. 103.

[23] Hauvette, *op. cit.*, p. 82.

[24] Cf. Karl Young, *The Origin and Development of the Story of Troilus and Criseyde* (London, 1908), p. 45.

[25] However, I shall also differ with him from time to time in order to make what I consider necessary corrections and additions.

[26] *Op. cit.*, p. 46.

[27] *Ibid.*, p. 47.

[28] Cf. the edition by E. G. Parodi, *Il Tristano riccardiano* (Bologna, 1896).

[29] "Il Filostrato di G. Boccaccio," *Romania*, XXVII (1898), 442–79; Young, *op. cit.*, esp. pp. 47–49.

[30] Cf. VII, 32–33, 37–38.

[31] Cf. Parodi, *ed. cit.*, pp. 122–23: "Appressimandosi la notte che lo ree si vuole coricare cola reina Isotta, ed allora sì venne la reina nela camera, e le donne e le donzelle sì la mettono a lletto. E dappoi che le reina fue a lletto, no rimase nela camera se nnoe Governale e Blaguina; e dappoi istante poco, e lo ree sì si ne viene ne la camera e .T. sì gli fae conpangnia. E dappoi che lo ree fue nela camera, incontanente sì s'aparecchia d'andare a letto. E dappoi che fue coricato e .T. sì spense tutti i lumi, e lo ree sì disse: 'Per che cagione ài tue ispengnati tutti i llumi?' E .T. rispuose e disse: 'Questa è una usanza d'Irlanda, che quando una pulciella si corica novella mente allato a ssue sengnore, la prima notte si fanno inspegnare li lumi, perchè la donna non si vergongni; perchè le pulcielle sì sono troppo vergongnose. E questa sì ee una cortesia, la quale sì ee inn Irlanda, e la madre di madonna Isotta sì mi ne pregoe assai, ch'io la dovesse fare.' Allora sì rispuose lo ree Marco e ddisse: 'Ben aggia tale usanza.' "

[32] *Op. cit.*, p. 49.

[33] *Ibid.*, p. 49.

[34] *Op. cit.*, p. 468.

[35] *Op. cit.*, pp. 49 ff.

[36] London, 1902.

[37] Lucy A. Paton, *Sir Lancelot of the Lake: a French Prose Romance of the Thirteenth Century* (New York, 1929). Subsequent references will be to this translation.

[38] P. 187: " 'And wit ye well that ye can have the company of a

more powerful man than I, but ye will never have that of a man that loveth you so well. And since that I would do more than all the world to have your company, well I deserve above all others to have it.' " Lancelot replies: " '. . . Better company than yours could I never have.' " He asks that Galehot grant his request; to which the latter responds: " '. . . Speak boldly, and ye shall have it, if it be in my power.' "

[39] P. 190: "He thought and said that never had he had so good a friend and so true a comrade, and he felt so great pity for him that he sighed from the depths of his heart and wept beneath his helmet, and he said between his teeth, 'Fair Lord God, who can recompense this ?' "

[40] P. 198: " 'Leave the rest to me,' said Galehot, 'for I mean to ponder well thereupon.' "

[41] P. 201: " 'Sir,' said he, 'in God's name, let none know thereof save only we and she, for there are those in the court of my lord the king that would know me well, if they should see me.' "

[42] P. 201: " 'I would fain see him in such wise that none know that it is he save ye and I, for I would that none others have pleasure therein.' "

[43] P. 211: " '. . . Even as he is the most worshipful of men, so is his heart truer than that of any other.' "

[44] P. 212: " 'Certes,' said she, 'thus I grant him that he be all mine and I all his.' "

[45] P. 215.

[46] P. 48.

[47] Cf. the brief reference in Young, op. cit., p. 49, n. 5.

[48] Cf. "Il comento sopra la Commedia di Dante Alighieri" in Opere volgari di Giovanni Boccaccio (Firenze, 1831), Vol. XI. The quotations which follow are from this edition.

[49] P. 60: ". . . Lancelotto, del quale molte belle e laudevoli cose raccontano i romanzi franceschi, cose, per qual ch'io creda, più composte a beneplacito, che secondo la verità."

[50] Ibid., p. 60: ". . . Come amor lo strinse; perciocchè ne detti romanzi si scrive, Lancelotto essere stato ferventissimamente innamorato della reina Ginevra, moglie del re Artù."

[51] "Galeotto fu il libro, e chi lo scrisse: Scrivesi ne' predetti romanzi, che un principe Galeotto, il quale dicono che fu di spezie di gigante, sì era grande e grosso, senti primo che alcuno altro l'occulto amor di Lancelotto e della reina Ginevra: il quale non essendo più avanti proceduto che per soli riguardi, ad istanza di Lancelotto, il quale egli amava, maravigliosamente, tratta un dì in una sala a ragionamenta seco la reina Ginevra, e a quello chiamato Lancelotto, ad aprire questo amore con alcuno effetto fu il mezanno: e quasi occupando con la persona il poter questi due esser veduti da alcuno altro della sala, che da lui, fece che essi si baciarono insieme."

[52] As further indication of Boccaccio's interest in the Arthurian

story, one may note that Book VIII of *De casibus illustrium virorum* is entitled "De Arthuro Rege Britonum."

[53] *Op. cit.*, p. 53.

[54] *Ibid.*, p. 56.

[55] *Ibid.*, pp. 56 ff.

[56] The facts in the following paragraphs are from the biographical study by Edward Hutton; cf. *supra*, n. 6.

[57] *Op. cit.*, p. 57.

[58] *Op. cit.*, pp. 61–62.

[59] *University of Wisconsin Studies in Language and Literature*, No. 2 (1918), 367–94.

[60] *Op. cit.*, p. 6.

[61] Cf. *supra*, p. 61, rule VI.

[62] *Op. cit.*, p. 267: "Nam permittitur amatori sui amoris secretarium invenire idoneum, cum quo secrete valeat de suo solatiari amore, et qui ei, si contigerit, in amoris compatiatur adversis. Sed et amatrici similem conceditur secretariam postulare. Praeter istos internuntium fidelem de communi possunt habere consensu, per quem amor occulte et recte semper valeat gubernari."

[63] *Chaucer and His Poetry* (Cambridge, 1915), p. 140.

CHAPTER VII (PANDARUS)

[1] *Ed. cit.*, p. 107.

[2] *The Indebtedness of Chaucer's Works to the Italian Works of Boccaccio* (Cincinnati, 1916), p. 111.

[3] All references to the *Filostrato* are to the edition and translation by Griffin and Myrick; see chap. VI, n. 1. The text of the *Troilus* is that by Robert K. Root, *The Book of Troilus and Criseyde* (Princeton, 1926); unless otherwise stated, reference to it will be by book and line. My spelling of the proper names follows the texts of these editors.

[4] *Ed. cit.*, p. 422 (n. on 638–44).

[5] Cf. B. J. Whiting, *Chaucer's Use of Proverbs* (Cambridge, 1934), pp. 74–75: "To recapitulate, Chaucer uses proverbs in *Troilus and Criseyde* largely for purposes of characterization. There are some in the narrative, but less than half as many as occur in the dialogue. The greatest number of proverbs are put in the mouths of the most sophisticated and self-possessed characters, Pandarus and Cressida."

[6] *Ed. cit.*, p. 424 (n. on 730).

[7] *Ibid.*, p. 428 (nn. on 946–49 and 950).

[8] *Ibid.*, p. 429 (n. on 969).

[9] C. S. Lewis, "What Chaucer Really Did to *Il Filostrato*," in *Essays and Studies by Members of the English Association* (Oxford, 1932), XVII, 59.

[10] *Ed. cit.*, p. 443 (n. on 522–39).

[11] Cf. T. A. Kirby, "A Note on *Troilus*, II, 1298," *MLR*, XXIX

(1934), 67–68; "*Troilus*, II, 1298, Again," *ibid.*, XXXIII (1938), 405.

[12] *Ed. cit.*, p. 454 (n. on 1347).

[13] *Ibid.*, p. xxix; also p. 455 (n. on 1398).

[14] *Ed. cit.*, p. 100, n. 1.

[15] I regard this scene as Chaucer's own. Young (*Origin and Development*, pp. 139 ff.) maintains that it is modeled on the meeting between Filocolo and Biancofiore in the *Filocolo*, II, 165–83. Cf. Root, *ed. cit.*, p. xxix: "But in the present instance Chaucer's debt to the *Filocolo*, if there be any debt at all, is but a slight one, and confined to minor details of the episode"; *ibid.*, p. xxx, n. 48: "These resemblances may easily be explained as the inevitable coincidences growing out of the general similarity of the two situations, each a clandestine meeting of lovers." Cummings, *op. cit.*, pp. 3–12, also rejects the indebtedness to the *Filocolo*. Cf. also Griffin, *ed. cit.*, p. 101, who regards the parallelism between the two accounts as "no more than what might naturally be expected when two authors of the same epoch are dealing with the same situation, viz., a nocturnal meeting between lovers. Furthermore it is certain from the large number of earlier literary treatments of the nocturnal visit which Young himself has listed (p. 151), that the situation must by Chaucer's time have become a fairly stereotyped one."

[16] Cf. *Filostrato*, III, 24: "oscura e nebulosa"; III, 64: "la notte bruna . . . senza nel ciel . . . stella alcuna."

[17] Cf. *supra*, p. 61, XII; 63, XIII; 64, XXIX.

[18] Cf. *Canterbury Tales*, I, 1165–66 (Robinson's edition).

[19] Root, *ed. cit.*, p. 263.

[20] *Ibid.*, p. 520 (n. on 1086).

[21] Cf. *infra*, pp. 176 f.

[22] *Chaucer and the Medieval Sciences* (New York, 1926), pp. 217–18.

[23] *Ed. cit.*, p. 551 (n. on 1275–78).

[24] Cf. *supra*, pp. 106 ff.

[25] *Chaucer's Troylus and Cryseyde Compared with Boccaccio's Filostrato* (London, 1875–83), p. v.

[26] *History of English Literature* (New York, 1876), I, 134–35.

[27] *History of English Literature* (New York, 1893), II, i, 93–94.

[28] *English Writers* (London, 1890), V, 208–9.

[29] *A Literary History of the English People* (London, 1895), I, 302–3.

[30] *Geoffrey Chaucer* (London, 1928), pp. 127 ff.

[31] *Op. cit.*, pp. 114–15.

[32] *Chaucer: ses modèles, ses sources, sa religion* (Lille, 1931), p. 42: "Nous regardons comme définitives les pages pénétrantes que M. Legouis a consacrées à Pandarus."

[33] *Op. cit.*, pp. 139–41; cf. also *supra*, p. 117.

[34] *The Poetry of Chaucer* (Boston, 1922), p. 120.

[35] *Shakespeare's Problem Comedies* (New York, 1931), pp. 147–48.

[36] *Chaucer* (New York, 1932), p. 146.

[37] *The Complete Works of Geoffrey Chaucer* (Boston, 1933), p. 451.

[38] *Geoffrey Chaucer and the Development of His Genius* (Boston, 1934), p. 177.

[39] *Oxford Lectures on Poetry* (Oxford, 1934), p. 55.

[40] *Ibid.*, pp. 55–57.

[41] *The Allegory of Love*, pp. 190–91.

[42] *Ibid.*, pp. 191–93.

[43] *Ibid.*, p. 194.

[44] "Chaucer's 'Troilus and Criseyde' as Romance," *PMLA*, LIII (1938), p. 60.

[45] *Ibid.*, p. 61.

[46] *Op. cit.*, p. 179.

[47] *Op. cit.*, p. 56.

[48] Cf. *supra*, pp. 106 ff.

[49] "What Chaucer Really Did to *Il Filostrato*," *loc. cit.*, p. 64.

[50] Cf. *supra*, pp. 156–57.

CHAPTER VIII (CRISEYDE)

[1] "The Date of Chaucer's *Troilus and Criseyde*," *PMLA*, XXIII (1908), 285–306.

[2] *The Poetry of Chaucer*, p. 106.

[3] Cf. *supra*, pp. 135 ff.

[4] *Courtly Love in Chaucer and Gower* (Boston, 1913), pp. 162–63.

[5] *Ibid.*, p. 167.

[6] *Op. cit.*, p. 133.

[7] *The Poetry of Chaucer*, p. 108.

[8] *Op. cit.*, p. 56.

[9] Cf. *supra*, p. 63, rule XIV.

[10] *Canterbury Tales*, V, 619 (Robinson's edition).

[11] Cf. Root, *ed. cit.*, p. 448 (n. on 825–77).

[12] Cf. *supra*, p. 64.

[13] Cf. *supra*, p. 63, rules XXI and XXII.

[14] Cf. *Troilus*, III, 1024: "Ye, jalousie is love."

[15] Cf. *supra*, chap. III, pp. 49 ff.

[16] Cf. *supra*, pp. 75 f.

[17] *Op. cit.*, p. 65.

[18] The parallels suggested by Cummings (*ibid.*, p. 65) for lines 456–83 ("account of the growth of Troilus's and Criseyde's mutual infatuation") are not convincing.

[19] Cf. *supra*, p. 63, rule II.

[20] Cf. Root, *ed. cit.*, p. 198.

[21] *Op. cit.*, p. 171.

[22] Root, *ed. cit.*, p. 484 (n. on 1262–67).

[23] *Ibid.*, p. 485 (n. on 1282, citing *Knight's Tale*, A, 3089, and *Legend*, Prol. B, 161–62).

[24] Cf. Lewis, *The Allegory of Love*, p. 196: "Chaucer has lavished more than half his work, if we regard mere number of lines, upon the happy phase of his story, the first wooing and winning of Cryseide: he has spent almost the whole of the third book upon fruition. But the question is not one of arithmetic. It is the quality of the first three books, and above all of the third, that counts; that book which is in effect a long epithalamium, and which contains, between its soaring invocation to the 'blisful light' of the third heaven and its concluding picture of Troilus at the hunt (sparing the 'smale bestes'), some of the greatest erotic poetry of the world. It is a lesson worth learning, how Chaucer can so triumphantly celebrate the flesh without becoming either delirious like Rossetti or pornographic like Ovid."

[25] *Op. cit.*, p. 79.

[26] Cf. Root, "Chaucer's Dares," *MP*, XV (1917), 1–22, and *ed. cit.*, pp. 543 f. L. A. Haselmayer has pointed out ("The Portraits in *Troilus and Criseyde*," *PQ*, XVII [1938], 220–23) that many of the adaptations of the Troy legend make use of catalogues of portraits and that the three portraits which appear at this point in Book V may be regarded as Chaucer's recognition of this traditional feature. This particular device was known to the medieval rhetorician as the *effictio*. It should be noted that Chaucer's three portraits—in place of the long series which was customary—constitute further evidence of our poet's ability to observe a tradition and at the same time to depart from it for artistic reasons.

[27] *Op. cit.*, p. 284.

[28] "Aspects of the Story of Troilus and Criseyde"; cf. chap. VI *supra*, n. 59. (Wilkins, "The Enamorment of Boccaccio," *MP*, XI [1913], 39–55.)

[29] *Ibid.*, p. 382.

[30] *Ibid.*, p. 384.

[31] Criseida (*Filostrato*, II, 73–74) discusses the relative merits of widowhood and matrimony and decides on the former for the very practical reasons that she can thereby retain her liberty, extramarital love is more pleasing to lovers, married men soon lose their ardor, and "water acquired by stealth is sweeter far than wine held in abundance."

[32] *Op. cit.*, p. 103.

[33] *Op. cit.*, p. 146.

[34] J. S. Graydon, for example, takes an extreme view and argues that the traditional attitude toward Criseyde is a mistaken one and that Troilus is really the cause of her desertion; cf. "Defense of Criseyde," *PMLA*, XLIV (1929), 141–77. This position is entirely untenable. Cf. J. M. Beatty's refutation, "Mr. Graydon's 'Defense of

Criseyde,'" *SP*, XXVI (1929), 470–81 ; and J. M. French, "Defense of Troilus," *PMLA*, XLIV (1929), 1246–51.

³⁵ *Op. cit.*, p. 73.
³⁶ *Op. cit.*, p. 185.
³⁷ *Ed. cit.*, p. 451.

CHAPTER IX (DIOMEDE)

[1] Cf. Root, *ed. cit.*, pp. 532–33 (n. on 92–189).
[2] Root, *ibid.*, pp. 532–33 ; Young, *Origin and Development*, pp. 131 ff. ; Cummings, *op. cit.*, pp. 76 ff.
[3] *Vide supra*, p. 228.
[4] Cf. n. 26 *supra* and Root, *ed. cit.*, pp. 541–42 (nn. on 799–805).
[5] *The Poetry of Chaucer*, p. 114.

CHAPTER X (TROILUS)

[1] Cf. *supra*, p. 63, rule XXIII.
[2] On the autobiographical element in the *Filostrato*, cf. *supra*, pp. 91 ff.
[3] Cf. *supra*, p. 194.
[4] Cf. *ed. cit.*, pp. 416–17 (n. on 306–7).
[5] Cf. *supra*, pp. 126 ff.
[6] Cf. *supra*, pp. 149 ff.
[7] Root, *ed. cit.*, pp. 493–94 (n. on 1744–71).
[8] Cf. *supra*, pp. 163 ff.
[9] "Troilus on Predestination," *JEGP*, XVII (1918), p. 405.
[10] "What Chaucer Really Did to *Il Filostrato*," *loc. cit.*, p. 63.
[11] *Op. cit.*, p. 115.
[12] "Troilus on Predestination," pp. 420–21.
[13] *Op. cit.*, pp. 114 ff.
[14] *The Poetry of Chaucer*, pp. 117–18.
[15] Cf. Patch, *The Goddess Fortuna in Medieval Literature* (Cambridge, 1927), p. 96 : "We may remember that in many ways her [i. e., Fortuna's] traits . . . resemble those of the love deity. Fortune is blind, and slings arrows or darts at her victims. These divinities, Fortune and Love, become sufficiently identified for Venus to take over the characteristics of her sister goddess, and by the time of *Les Échecs Amoureux* we find Venus turning a wheel and exalting and debasing mankind. . . ."
Ibid., p. 98 : "This identification of the two figures of Fortune and Love only means that they had very much in common, and that in one aspect Fortune was certainly regarded as concerned with the affairs of love."
Cf. also B. L. Jefferson, *Chaucer and the Consolation of Philosophy of Boethius* (Princeton, 1917), p. 122 : "The most remarkable de-

parture from classical mythology, perhaps, is in the case of the god of love. This god in *Troilus*, not at all the mischievous young archer of conventional love poetry, is given all the qualities of the celestial love described so at length by Boethius ; and to the description of the might of this god throughout all the universe Chaucer devotes almost one hundred lines."

[16] Cf. Young, "Chaucer's 'Troilus and Criseyde' as Romance," p. 50: "Troilus's long meditation and touching prayer in the temple, therefore, give salience to one aspect of his courtliness. It may be that Chaucer's own interest in the scene lay chiefly in its *sentence*, and in its exhibition of Troilus's helplessness in the hands of fate ; but, through intention or by chance, the innovation here brought the young lover into association with the courteous, church-going heroes of romance, such as Chrétien's Lancelot, Guillaume of the *Flamenca*, Durmart of *Durmart le Galois*, and Amadas of *Amadas et Ydoine*."

[17] *Op. cit.*, p. 240.

[18] Cf. *supra*, pp. 262 ff.

[19] *Ed. cit.*, p. 544 (n. on 827–40). On Joseph of Exeter, cf. *supra*, p. 226 and n. 26.

[20] Cf. *supra*, p. 175.

[21] Cf. *supra*, p. 232.

[22] Cummings, *op. cit.*, p. 81. On Sibille, Root notes (*ed. cit.*, pp. 552–53): "The term sibyl is used generically for a female prophet. . . . Chaucer . . . clearly regards the names *Sibille* and *Cassandra* as alternative names of the same person."

[23] The *Thebais* of Statius is the general source for this passage.

[24] *Op. cit.*, p. 288. For "Chryseis" in this quotation, one should doubtless read "Cassandra."

[25] Cf. *supra*, pp. 232 f.

[26] Cf. *supra*, pp. 176 f.

[27] Cf. N. E. Griffin, *ed. cit.*, p. 104: "Chaucer's Troilus remains the languishing, sentimental lover—seemingly a characteristically Italian type—that we find in the Filostrato." F. N. Robinson, *ed. cit.*, p. 451 : "Troilus, the simplest character of the three protagonists, remains much the same as in Boccaccio." De Sélincourt, *op. cit.*, p. 58: "In Troilus, indeed, he makes no radical change." C. S. Lewis, *The Allegory of Love*, p. 195: ". . . The drawing of Troilus' character is no principal part of Chaucer's purpose." Among recent critics, only J. L. Lowes (*op. cit.*, pp. 179–80) concedes that he is different; of Troilus he remarks that his character "as the conventional lover Chaucer has both ennobled and enriched. . . ."

[28] In this connection it may be pointed out that Chaucer is meticulous in his handling of the pronoun of address ; e. g., with only four exceptions (IV, 1209, 1641, V, 734–35, and 1258) neither Troilus nor Criseyde uses the familiar form in addressing the other. Cf. C. C. Walcutt, "The Pronoun of Address in *Troilus and Criseyde*," *PQ*, XIV (1935), 286: "In Chaucer's use of the pronoun of address there

appears to be another element of courtly love which has not been noted before. In a poem of such dramatic power and truly deep understanding of human nature, Chaucer would surely have allowed his lovers to employ familiar pronouns of address—especially in their passionate interviews in Books III and IV—unless he had been constantly aware of a convention which demanded that he do otherwise. The attitude of abject, patient adoration demanded of the courtly lover explains why Troilus consistently addresses Criseyde as *ye* and *yow;* and there does not appear to be any other explanation, for familiar address is invariably connected with the language of passion in the love poetry of other periods and countries."

[29] For a different point of view, cf. Patch's brilliant article, "Troilus on Determinism," *Speculum*, VI (1931), 241: "Troilus on earth may expound determinism with all the determination of his desperate nature; but from the heights of heaven, looking back with more humor, he abandons the idea and admits his folly."

[30] *Op. cit.*, p. 53; cf. chap. VII *supra*, n. 32.

[31] *Ed. cit.*, p. xlv.

[32] "The Epilogue of Chaucer's *Troilus*," *MP*, XVIII (1921), 626.

[33] *Op. cit.*, p. 17.

[34] W. W. Lawrence (*op. cit.*, pp. 148–49) grasps this fact and elaborates it lucidly: "The code of what was right and proper socially was . . . essentially the same for Chaucer as for Boccaccio. But their personal attitude towards this code was not the same; Boccaccio accepted it, Chaucer tested it. There is no repudiation of the system of courtly love at the end of the *Filostrato;* young people are exhorted to pray that Troilo may rest in peace, and to take care that they do not fall victims to fickle women, but rather choose ladies who are noble and constant. To Chaucer, on the other hand, the tale reveals ultimately only the hollowness of the service of Love. Troilus dies in profound disillusion; Criseyde lets passion lead her into breaking both the natural and the conventional laws of true love. What is the answer? Well, Love is not the deity for men to serve; they should put their trust in God, who will treat no man falsely.

> —sin he best to love is, and most meke,
> What nedeth feyned loves for to seke?

In short, the story is, in the hands of Chaucer, an attempt to analyze the validity of the conventions of love by a minute examination of a specific instance, which leads to the decision that those conventions break down as a rule of life."

SELECT BIBLIOGRAPHY

Allen, Philip Schuyler, *Medieval Latin Lyrics*, Chicago, 1931.

Andreas Capellanus: *see* Trojel.

Appel, Carl, *Bernart von Ventadorn, Seine Lieder mit Einleitung und Glossar*, Halle a. S., 1915.

——, *Provenzalische Chrestomathie mit Abriss der Formenlehre und Glossar*, 6te verbesserte Auflage, Leipzig, 1930.

Azzolina, Liborio, *Il "dolce stil nuovo,"* Palermo, 1903.

Barrow, Sarah F., *The Medieval Society Romances*, New York, 1924.

Bartsch, Karl, *Chrestomathie provençale (Xᵉ—XVᵉ siècles)*, sixième édition entièrement refondue par Eduard Koschwitz, Marburg, 1904.

Beatty, Joseph M., "Mr. Graydon's 'Defense of Criseyde,'" *SP*, XXVI (1929), 470–81.

Bernart de Ventadorn: *see* Appel.

Berry, André, *Florilége des troubadours*, Paris, 1930.

Bertoni, Giulio, *Il duecento*, seconda edizione, Milano, 1930. (Storia letteraria d'Italia, Vol. II.)

Boccaccio, Giovanni: *see* Griffin and Myrick; Moutier.

Borodine, Myrrha, *La femme et l'amour au XIIᵉ siècle d'après les poèmes de Chrétien de Troyes*, Paris, 1909.

Brink, Bernhard ten, *History of English Literature*, translated by Wm. Clarke Robinson, New York, 1893. Vol. II, part 1.

Brinkmann, Hennig, *Entstehungsgeschichte des Minnesangs*, Halle (Saale), 1926. (Deutsche Vierteljahrschrift für Literaturwissenschaft und Geistesgeschichte. Buchreihe. 8. Band.)

Burdach, Konrad, "Über den Ursprung des mittelalterlichen Minnesangs, Liebesromans und Frauendienstes," *Sitzungsberichten der Berliner Akademie*, Berlin, 1918.

Cavalcanti, Guido: *see* Ercole; Rivalta.

Chaucer, Geoffrey: *see* Root; Robinson.

Chesterton, G. K., *Chaucer*, New York, 1932.

Chrétien de Troyes: *see* Foerster; Comfort.

Cohen, Gustave, *Un grand romancier d'amour et d'aventure au XIIᵉ siècle: Chrétien de Troyes et son oeuvre*, Paris, 1931.

Comfort, W. Wistar, *Arthurian Romances by Chrétien de Troyes*, New York, 1928. (Everyman's Library.)

Crane, Thomas Frederick, *Italian Social Customs of the Sixteenth Century and Their Influence on the Literatures of Europe*, New Haven, 1920. (Cornell Studies in English, Vol. V.)

Cross, Tom Peete and Nitze, William Albert, *Lancelot and Guenevere: a Study on the Origins of Courtly Love*, Chicago, 1930.

Cummings, Hubertis M., *The Indebtedness of Chaucer's Works to the Italian Works of Boccaccio* (*A Review and Summary*), Cincinnati, 1916.

Curry, Walter Clyde, *Chaucer and the Medieval Sciences*, New York, 1926.

Dante Alighieri: see Moore.

De Sélincourt, E., *Oxford Lectures on Poetry*, Oxford, 1934.

Diez, Friedrich, *Die Poesie der Troubadours*, zweite vermehrte Auflage von Karl Bartsch, Leipzig, 1883.

Dodd, William George, *Courtly Love in Chaucer and Gower*, Boston, 1913.

Ercole, Pietro, *Guido Cavalcanti e le sue rime. Studio storicoletterario seguito dal testo critico delle rime con commento*, Livorno, 1885.

Fauriel, H., *Histoire littéraire de la France*, Paris, 1895. Vol. XXI.

Foerster, Wendelin, *Christian von Troyes sämtliche erhaltene Werke nach allen bekannten Handschriften herausgegeben*, Halle, 1884–99. Vols. I, II, and IV.

French, J. Milton, "Defense of Troilus," *PMLA*, XLIV (1929), 1246–51.

Gaselee, Stephen, *The Transition from the Late Latin Lyric to the Medieval Love Poem*, Cambridge, 1931.

Gaspary, Adolf, *Die sizilianische Dichterschule des dreizehnten Jahrhunderts*, Berlin, 1878.

———, *The History of Early Italian Literature to the Death of Dante*, translated . . . with additions . . . and with supplementary bibliographical notes by Herman Oelsner, London, 1901.

Gilson, Étienne, *La théologie mystique de Saint Bernard*, Paris, 1934. (Études de philosophie médiévale, Vol. XX.)

Grabmann, Martin, "Das Werk *De Amore* des Andreas Capellanus und das Verurteilungsdekret des Bischofs Stephan Tempier von Paris vom 7. März 1277," *Speculum*, VII (1932), 75–79.

Graydon, Joseph S., "Defense of Criseyde," *PMLA*, XLIV (1929), 141–77.

Griffin, Nathaniel Edward and Myrick, Arthur Beckwith, *The Filostrato of Giovanni Boccaccio: a Translation with Parallel Text*, Philadelphia, 1929.

Grimm, Charles, "Chrestien de Troyes's Attitude towards Woman," *RR*, XVI (1925), 236–43.

Guinicelli, Guido: see Parenti.

Guyer, F. E., "The Influence of Ovid on Crestien de Troyes," *RR*, XII (1921), 97–134; 216–47.

Haselmayer, Louis A., "The Portraits in *Troilus and Criseyde*," *PQ*, XVII (1938), 220–23.

Hauvette, Henri, *Boccace: Étude biographique et littéraire*, Paris, 1914.

Hutton, Edward, *Giovanni Boccaccio: a Biographical Study*, London, 1910.

Jefferson, Bernard L., *Chaucer and the Consolation of Philosophy of Boethius*, Princeton, 1917.

Jusserand, J. J., *A Literary History of the English People*, London, 1895. Vol. I.

Kelly, Amy, "Eleanor of Aquitaine and Her Courts of Love," *Speculum*, XII (1937), 3–19.

Ker, W. P., *The Dark Ages*, Edinburgh, 1904.

——, *Epic and Romance: Essays on Medieval Literature*, London, 1897.

Kirby, Thomas A., "A Note on *Troilus*, II, 1298," *MLR*, XXIX (1934), 67–68.

——, "*Troilus*, II, 1298, Again," *ibid.*, XXXIII (1938), 405.

Kittredge, George Lyman, *Chaucer and His Poetry*, Cambridge, 1915.

Lawrence, William Witherle, *Shakespeare's Problem Comedies*, New York, 1931.

Lee, Vernon, *Euphorion: Being Studies of the Antique and the Medieval in the Renaissance*, London, 1894. Vol. II.

Legouis, Émile Hyacinthe, *Geoffrey Chaucer*, translated by L. Lailavoix, London and New York, 1928.

Lewis, C. S., *The Allegory of Love: a Study in Medieval Tradition*, Oxford, 1936.

——, "What Chaucer Really Did to *Il Filostrato*," *Essays and Studies by Members of the English Association* (Oxford, 1932), XVII, 55–76.

Looten, Le Chanoine, *Chaucer: ses modèles, ses sources, sa religion*, Lille, 1931. (Mémoires et travaux publiés par des professeurs des facultés catholiques de Lille, fascicule XXXVIII.)

Lot-Borodine: *see* Borodine.

Lowes, John Livingston, *Geoffrey Chaucer and the Development of His Genius*, Boston, 1934.

Lucka, Emil, *Eros: the Development of the Sex Relation through the Ages*, New York, 1915.

Mahn, C. A. F., *Die Werke der Troubadours, in provenzalischer Sprache*, Berlin, 1846–53. 4 vols.

Manitius, Max, *Geschichte der lateinischen Literatur des Mittelalters*, München, 1931. (Handbuch der Altertumswissenschaft . . . neunte Abteilung, zweiter Teil, dritter Band.)

Martini, Edgar, *Einleitung zu Ovid*, Brünn, 1933. (Schriften der philosophischen Fakultät der deutschen Universität in Prag, 12. Band.)

Meyer, Paul, "Des rapports de la poésie des trouvères avec celle des troubadours," *Romania*, XIX (1890), 1–62.

Moore, E., *Le opere di Dante Alighieri . . . nuovamente rivedute nel testo dal Dr. Paget Toynbee* . . . , quarta edizione, Oxford, 1924.

Morley, Henry, *English Writers*, London, 1890. Vol. V.

Mott, Lewis Freeman, *The Provençal Lyric*, New York, n.d.

——, *The System of Courtly Love Studied as an Introduction to the Vita Nuova of Dante*, Boston, 1896.

Moutier, I., *Il comento sopra la Commedia di Dante Alighieri*, Firenze, 1831. (Opere volgari di Giovanni Boccaccio, Vol. XI.)

Neilson, William Allan, *The Origins and Sources of the Court of Love*, Boston, 1899. (Harvard Studies and Notes in Philology and Literature, Vol. VI.)

Ovid, *The Art of Love, and Other Poems*, with an English Translation by J. H. Mozley, London and New York, 1929. (Loeb Classical Library.)

——, *Heroides and Amores*, with an English Translation by Grant Showerman, London and New York, 1925. (Loeb Classical Library.)

——, *Metamorphoses*, with an English Translation by Frank Justus Miller, London and New York, 1928–29. 2 vols. (Loeb Classical Library.)

——, *Tristia. Ex Ponto*, translated by Arthur Leslie Wheeler, London and New York, 1924. (Loeb Classical Library.)

Parenti, Giorgio, *La personalità storica di Guido Guinizelli. Studi e richerche*, Firenze, 1914.

Paris, Gaston, "Études sur les romans de la Table Ronde. Lancelot du Lac. II: La Conte de la Charette," *Romania*, XII (1883), 459–534.

Parodi, E. G., *Il Tristano riccardiano*, Bologna, 1896. (Collezione di opere inedite o rare dei primi tre secoli della lingua.)

Patch, Howard, *The Goddess Fortuna in Medieval Literature*, Cambridge, 1927.

——, "Troilus on Determinism," *Speculum*, VI (1931), 225–43.

——, "Troilus on Predestination," *JEGP*, XVII (1918), 397–422.

Paton, Lucy Allen, *Sir Lancelot of the Lake: a French Prose Romance of the Thirteenth Century*, New York, 1929. (Broadway Medieval Library.)

Pellegrini, Flaminio, "La 'Canzone d'Amore' di Guido Guinizelli," *NSM*, I (1923), 119–37.

Pound, Ezra, *Sonnets and Ballate of Guido Cavalcanti*, London, 1912.

Rand, Edward Kennard, *Ovid and His Influence*, Boston, 1925. (Our Debt to Greece and Rome.)

Rivalta, Ercole, *Le rime di Guido Cavalcanti*, Bologna, 1902.

Robinson, F. N., *The Complete Works of Geoffrey Chaucer*, Boston, 1933.

Root, Robert Kilburn, *The Book of Troilus and Criseyde by Geoffrey Chaucer*, Princeton, 1926.

Root, Robert Kilburn, "Chaucer's Dares," *MP*, XV (1917), 1–22.

———, *The Poetry of Chaucer: a Guide to Its Study and Appreciation*, revised edition, Boston, 1922.

Rossetti, Dante Gabriel : *see* Rossetti, W. M.

Rossetti, William Michael, *Chaucer's Troylus and Cryseyde Compared with Boccaccio's Filostrato*, London, 1875–83. (Chaucer Society, first series, XLIV and LXV.)

———, *The Works of Dante Gabriel Rossetti*, edited with preface and notes, revised edition, London, 1911.

Sanctis, Francesco de, *History of Italian Literature*, translated by Joan Redfern, New York, 1931. Vol. I.

Savj-Lopez, Paolo, "Il Filostrato di G. Boccaccio," *Romania*, XXVII (1898), 442–79.

———, *Trovatori e poeti. Studi di lirica antica*, Milano, 1906. (Biblioteca "Sandron" di scienze e lettere, n. 30.)

Scheludko, D., "Ovid und die Trobadors," *ZsfRPh*, LIV (1934), 129–74.

Schrötter, Willibald, *Ovid und die Troubadours*, Halle, 1908.

Stronski, Stanislas, *Le troubadour Elias de Barjols*, Toulouse and Paris, 1906. (Bibliothèque meridionale publiée sous les auspices de la faculté des lettres de Toulouse. 1re serie. Tome X.)

Taine, H. A., *History of English Literature*, translated by H. van Laun, New York, 1876. Vol. I.

Tatlock, J. S. P., "The Epilogue of Chaucer's *Troilus*," *MP*, XVIII (1921), 625–59.

Torre, Arnaldo della, *La giovanezza di G. Boccaccio (1313–1341)*, Città di Castello, 1905.

Trojel, E., *Andreae Capellani regii Francorum de amore libri tres*, Havniae, 1892.

Volpi, Guglielmo, *Il trecento*, Milano, n.d. (Storia letteraria d'Italia, Vol. IV.)

Vossler, Karl, *Die philosophischen Gründlagen zum süssen neuen Stil des Guido Guinicelli, Guido Cavalcanti und Dante Alighieri*, Heidelberg, 1904.

———, *Medieval Culture. An Introduction to Dante and His Times*, translated by W. C. Lawton, New York, 1929. 2 vols.

———, Review of Schrötter (*Ovid und die Troubadours*) in *LitBl*, XXX (1909), Heft 2, 63–65.

Walcutt, Charles C., "The Pronoun of Address in *Troilus and Criseyde*," *PQ*, XIV (1935), 282–87.

Wechssler, Eduard, *Das Kulturproblem des Minnesangs*. Band I : *Minnesang und Christentum*, Halle, 1909.

———, "Frauendienst und Vassallität," *ZsfFSpruL*, XXIV (1902), 159–90.

West, C. B., *Courtoisie in Anglo-Norman Literature*. Oxford, 1938. (Medium Aevum Monographs, III.)

Whiting, B. J., *Chaucer's Use of Proverbs*, Cambridge, 1934.

Wilkins, E. H., "The Enamorment of Boccaccio," *MP*, XI (1913),
39–55.

Wright, F. A., *The Mirror of Venus*, London, 1925.

Young, Karl, "Aspects of the Story of Troilus and Criseyde," *University of Wisconsin Studies in Language and Literature*, No.
2 (1918), 367–94.

———, "Chaucer's Renunciation of Love in Troilus," *MLN*, XL
(1925), 270–76.

———, "Chaucer's 'Troilus and Criseyde' as Romance," *PMLA*,
LIII (1938), 38–63.

———, *The Origin and Development of the Story of Troilus and
Criseyde*, London, 1908. (Chaucer Society, second series, XL.)

INDEX

[Pages 287-304 refer to the Appendix (translations); 307-25, to the notes.]

DATE DUE